THE
NVQ
ASSESSOR
VERIFIER &
CANDIDATE
HANDBOOK

THE
NVQ
ASSESSOR
VERIFIER &
CANDIDATE
HANDBOOK

A practical guide to
Units A1, A2 and V1,
and STTTLSS Domain E

4th Edition

Ros Ollin and Jenny Tucker

**KOGAN
PAGE**

London and Philadelphia

First published in Great Britain in 1994 as *The NVQ and GNVQ Assessor Handbook*
Second edition 1997
Third edition 2004 as *The NVQ Assessor and Verifier Handbook*
Reprinted 2005, 2006
Fourth edition 2008 as *The NVQ Assessor, Verifier and Candidate Handbook*
Reprinted 2009 (twice)

Kogan Page Limited
120 Pentonville Road
London N1 9JN
United Kingdom
www.koganpage.com

British Library Cataloguing in Publication Data

A CIP record for this book is available from the British Library.

ISBN 978 0 7494 5110 3

Typeset by JS Typesetting Ltd, Porthcawl, Mid Glamorgan
Printed and bound in India by Replika Press Pvt Ltd

Contents

Preface

The introduction of National Vocational Qualifications (NVQs) in the early 1990s, with their emphasis on the quality and the outcomes of learning rather than the quality of delivery, placed assessment practice under the microscope. National occupational standards for training and development were first produced by the Training and Development Lead Body (TDLB), later replaced by the Employment National Training Organisation (ENTO). A new version of the standards, the Learning and Development standards, was approved in 2002. Like the previous standards, they have been used to create a framework of qualifications comprising both full NVQs and occupational qualifications or small/mini-awards. ENTO envisaged that the assessment standards could be used for any vocational award, but in practice they were used primarily for NVQs.

All those assessing and verifying NVQs (and a limited approved range of other competence-based awards) must demonstrate that they have updated their practice to the new standards in order to continue in the role of assessor or verifier. The assessor and verifier qualifications are each individual units within the Learning and Development NVQ framework, and are commonly known as the 'A&V awards'. As we write, revisions of the assessor and verifier standards are again being undertaken.

Holding an assessor or verifier qualification indicates that you are competent to assess and/or verify NVQs in workplaces in England, Wales and Northern Ireland. Scotland has its own set of qualifications (S/NVQs), though the standards are in line with those sanctioned by the QCA, the regulatory body for England and Northern Ireland. The regulatory body for Wales is the ACCAC (Awdurdod Cymwysterau, Cwricwlwm ac Asesu Cymru). The Republic of Ireland does not operate the NVQ system.

NVQs have been playing a major part in recognizing and raising the skills of existing employees, as experienced workers can use the qualification to be assessed in the workplace against occupational standards, and undertake additional study to fill in any 'gaps' in knowledge, understanding or performance. The current learning and development awards, of which the assessor and verifier awards are a part, have developed alongside these NVQs and have led to more rigour in assessment and quality assurance. Whilst the achievement of an assessor qualification can be, for some, a matter of ticking boxes and jumping through hoops, we remain convinced that those assessors who understand the background to assessment are better able both to work with accuracy and confidence and, more importantly, to encourage their candidates to value learning and continuing professional development. It is quite likely that, in the future, those who assess NVQs in work-based training will take the PPA unit alongside their A1 qualification. Likewise, those who are studying for their certificate or diploma in the lifelong learning sector will often be working alongside NVQ assessment processes, and we hope they will find the references to NVQs helpful.

The focus on assessment has now been extended to include those who assess more general vocational qualifications. Standards for Teaching and Learning in the Lifelong Learning Sector (LLS) were approved by Standards Verification UK (SVUK) in March 2007. For the first time, all awarding bodies offering certificates in initial teacher training will be using the same national standards, and all new entrants to teaching and training in the LLS must take appropriate qualifications from the standards. The certificates and diplomas formed from the new standards are at four levels. Within qualifications at levels 3 and 4 are the units for Principles and Practice of Assessment (PPA). This fourth edition of our book, whilst retaining its NVQ focus, includes a new chapter on the underpinning knowledge for 'Domain E: Assessment in the New Professional Standards for Teachers, Tutors and Trainers in the Lifelong Learning Sector' (PSTTTLLS). The associated unit for the professional standards, 'Principles and Practice of Assessment' (PPA), has much of the same content as the underpinning knowledge for the A1/V1 qualifications and so we feel that it is appropriate to include both sets of assessment standards.

AIMS OF THIS BOOK

This book aims to provide information and advice to anyone wishing to know more about the assessor and verifier qualifications and to those who would

Table 0.1 Roles of those involved in NVQs and vocational education

Person who:	NVQ	Vocational education
Provides the guidance for knowledge and understanding to take place	Trainer	Teacher, tutor, lecturer
Gives additional support, particularly with the specialist subject	Adviser	Mentor, support staff
Is taking the course or qualification	Candidate	Learner, student
Makes judgements on what has been achieved/learnt	Assessor	Teacher, tutor
Monitors the quality of judgements; trains and supports his or her team of assessors/teachers	Internal verifier	Internal moderator
Is appointed by the awarding body to check the quality of the assessment process within a centre	External verifier	External moderator, external examiner

find it useful to know about Domain E assessment. We hope that it will also provide a basis for exploring assessment and verification in general, and give readers a vehicle for examining their current competence and knowledge. It is most relevant to the education system in England and Wales.

The book should be of particular use to:

- candidates working towards becoming accredited assessors or internal verifiers for NVQs, particularly the A&V units;
- those working to becoming teachers in the LLS who wish to get greater understanding of the Domain E assessment standards;
- those wishing to gain a deeper understanding of the principles and processes of NVQ assessment and of current competence-based assessment practice;
- trainers and teachers of NVQ and vocational education assessment practice who require a reference book for themselves or their candidates;
- those who wish to compare the D3 qualifications with the A&V qualifications for the purpose of professional updating.

HOW TO USE THIS BOOK

The book has four parts, each of which is self-contained, as are the chapters. Each chapter has an introductory guide and summary points, for ease of reference.

Part 1 gives an overview of changes in the post-16 sector over the last 30 years, focusing on the developments that have led to improvements in assessment. The context is set both for NVQs and for vocational education in general, setting this in a political and economic framework.

Part 2 is concerned with background knowledge and understanding of assessment, particularly focusing on assessment of competence-based qualifications. There is detailed coverage of the background to assessment and quality assurance processes, the roles of participants, and the specific underpinning skills and knowledge related to assessment practice.

Part 3 is in two sections and is a guide to the standards that assessors and verifiers need to follow in their work practice. Section 1 covers the requirements of the standards relating to A1, A2 and V1 qualifications. The V2 standards are given, but, since it is awarding bodies themselves that train their own external verifiers, moderators and examiners, we do not go into detail on the qualification. Section 2 covers the underpinning knowledge requirements of Domain E: Assessment within the Standards for Teachers, Tutors and Trainers in the Lifelong Learning Sector. This is a completely new chapter and should give readers a good grounding in the processes of assessment as applied to general vocational qualifications. The Principles and Practice of Assessment units at levels 3 and 4 are not covered in this book, but all the relevant background knowledge and understanding information can be found within the chapter.

Part 4 offers practical guidance to candidates, assessors and verifiers on planning and recording processes, as well as suggestions for continuing professional development.

Following the appendices, the book ends with a comprehensive glossary of assessment-related terminology and a listing of supporting materials (further reading and useful websites). We would urge readers to familiarize themselves with the glossary before turning to the substance of the text, as an understanding of the jargon is vitally important for all concerned. One of the major problems encountered by those coming new to NVQs or, indeed, to any occupational area is getting to grips with the language and terminology involved. This is not just understanding what the terms mean; it also means feeling an ownership of the language used. The standards are written in much plainer language than that of their predecessors, but readers will still wish to mentally translate the terms used into language that appears more familiar and appropriate to their own work context.

Broad and thematic suggestions for further reading are given at the end of the book, rather than references for specific chapters. This is a practical text and we consider this layout more appropriate for our readers. Throughout the text, we have given a range of examples, including samples of completed documentation and case studies based on real-life situations, to help illustrate points made.

The majority of this book deals with NVQs, although there is a good deal of crossover to vocational qualifications. In the majority of chapters, we have used terminology that is most common within NVQ qualifications, and hope that readers will be able to 'translate' those terms into the ones commonly used within their own workplaces. The term 'trainer' is used for anyone who is qualified to deliver the relevant knowledge and understanding for assessment. The term 'assessor' is used for those qualified to assess either of the qualifications. The term 'verifier' refers to those qualified to quality-assure qualifications. The term 'candidate' refers to those who are registered for and working towards a qualification with a specific awarding body. In Part 3, Section 2, we look at assessment in non-NVQ contexts, and there we give additional commonly used terminology.

We have provided Table 0.2 as a quick reference.

We hope that the background discussion, explanation and examples we have given will complement and extend the knowledge and understanding of those engaged in both providing and improving the quality of assessment and verification for NVQs and for vocational qualifications in the lifelong learning sector.

Table 0.2 Terminology used in this book

NVQ terms	Terms used in other vocational contexts
Trainer	Teacher, tutor, practitioner, facilitator
Assessor	As above
Verifier	Moderator, examiner (higher education only)
Candidate	Learner, student, person registered to take a qualification

Acknowledgements

This book was first published in 1994. One of us had never used a keyboard, let alone a word processor or computer, neither of us had internet access or a mobile phone, and the government hadn't really got into the swing of the educational change that has since permeated all sections of the sector. At least the internet makes it easier to do the co-authoring for a new edition in 2007, though there is *so* much more to take into account, thanks to the constant new developments in education and training in the UK.

Thanks again to the many centres, colleagues and candidates with whom we have worked in various capacities over the years. The learning and feedback we have gained from them has been invaluable.

We also wish to thank Standards Verification UK, who have given their permission to reproduce the new Professional Standards for Teachers, Tutors and Trainers in the Lifelong Learning Sector.

Finally, as always, thanks to our publishers, especially to Charlotte Atyeo for her support; and, of course, to everyone who has bought or who buys this book.

It should be noted that the views expressed and interpretations of the standards are those of the authors.

Abbreviations

A&V	assessor and verifier
ACCAC	Awdurdod Cymwysterau, Cwricwlwm ac Asesu Cymru (Qualifications, Curriculum and Assessment Authority for Wales)
AMA	Advanced Modern Apprenticeship
APA	accreditation of prior achievement
APEL	accreditation of prior experiential learning
APL	accreditation of prior learning
BTEC	Business and Technology Education Council
CATS	credit accumulation and transfer schemes
CBI	Confederation of British Industry
CCEA	Council for the Curriculum, Examinations and Assessment
CIPD	Chartered Institute of Personnel and Development
CITB	Construction Industry Training Board
C&G	City and Guilds
CPD	continuing professional development
DELLS	Department for Education, Lifelong Learning and Skills
DCSF	Department for Children, Schools and Families
DfEE	Department for Education and Employment
DfES	Department for Education and Skills
DIUS	Department for Innovation, Universities and Skills
ENTO	Employment National Training Organisation
EOSC	Employment Occupational Standards Council
EV	external verifier
FE	further education
FENTO	Further Education National Training Organisation

FMA	Foundation Modern Apprenticeship
HAB	Hospitality Advisory Body
HASAW	Health and Safety at Work (Act)
HEFCE	Higher Education Funding Council for England
ICT	information and communications technology
ILB	Industrial Lead Body
ILPs	individual learning plans
IV	internal verifier
IVC	internal verifier coordinator
JAB	Joint Awarding Body
L1, L2 etc	level 1, level 2 etc. in NQF
LLS	lifelong learning sector
LLUK	Lifelong Learning United Kingdom
LSC	Learning and Skills Council
MSC	Manpower Services Commission
NCVQ	National Council for Vocational Qualifications
NEETS	those not in education, employment or training
NOS	national occupational standards
NQF	National Qualifications Framework
NT	National Traineeship
NTO	National Training Organisation
NVQ	National Vocational Qualification
Ofsted	Office for Standards in Education, Children's Services and Skills
PPA	Principles and Practice of Assessment (unit)
PSLB	Personnel Standards Lead Body
PTLLS	Preparing to Teach in the Lifelong Learning Sector
PSTTTLLS	Professional Standards for Teachers, Tutors and Trainers in the Lifelong Learning Sector
QCA	Qualifications and Curriculum Authority
QIA	Quality Improvement Agency
SCAA	Schools Curriculum and Assessment Authority
SCOTVEC	Scottish Council for Vocational Education Training
SQA	Scottish Qualifications Authority
SSC	Sector Skills Council
SSDA	Sector Skills Development Agency
STTTLLS	Standards for Teachers, Tutors and Trainers in the Lifelong Learning Sector
SVUK	Standards Verification United Kingdom
T&D	Training and Development
TDLB	Training and Development Lead Body
TECs	Training and Enterprise Councils
TEED	Training, Enterprise and Education Directorate
VQ	vocational qualification
VRQ	vocationally related qualification

Part 1

Setting the Scene

Introduction: Skills, Qualifications and Change

The big divide in this country has always been seen to be between those who go on to an academic career, usually resulting in a university degree and then a career, and those who prefer a more practical approach, usually geared to training or the workplace. It is an unfortunate fact that many people in the UK, particularly those who have gone through the academic public school system or the academic school–sixth form–university route, remain ignorant of a huge and important part of the education system, namely that for vocational and skills education and training. Alan Johnson, the then Secretary for Education, was infuriated when not one member of the media turned up to a landmark speech he made in April 2007 regarding the way forward for skills training. It seems that journalists are fixated in supporting the annual debates on school academic success rates. The media steadfastly refuse to recognize the positive difference that the further education system and work-based training make not just to the life chances of millions of people, many of whom are from non-academic backgrounds or who left school with few qualifications, but to the social well-being and economy of the UK. Raising the skill levels of our workforce and school leavers through vocational education and training will be key to the UK operating in the future as a successful competitor in global markets.

In this part, we attempt to describe the current provision for post-16 vocational education and training and explain the drivers for change. We give the background to NVQs and to other common vocational qualifications, finishing with the background to the new qualifications for teachers, tutors and trainers in the lifelong learning sector. There is a useful table listing the relevant changes over the last 25 years or so. Some of what is being proposed in the way of qualifications and structural change is out for consultation as we write. The situation is quite difficult to understand, as there has been such a plethora of change in the last 10 years, with reports, Green and White Papers, not to mention White Papers with green edges, that, in the words of many a young person, 'It done our heads in.' What is clear is that the system is complicated and could do with rationalization. Most people are not interested in the names of qualifications or departments; they have a simpler approach based on whether information is easily accessible and understandable and whether it relates to academic or work-related qualifications. They also want to follow programmes that are relevant and engaging, do not want to repeat material they have studied previously and, wherever possible, prefer to use the technology they have to hand to inform themselves, whether it be mobile phones or the internet.

The urgency of the need to qualify the workforce must surely drive those in positions of influence towards enabling the early creation of a coherent system with minimum bureaucracy and a comprehensive qualifications framework.

Table I1.1 Background to NVQs and national standards

1981   **New Training Initiative (Manpower Services Commission – MSC)**
Identified need to increase skills of workforce to cope with new
patterns of working, developments in new technology and increased
competition from overseas. First mention of need for 'Standards of a
new kind'.

1986   *Review of Vocational Qualifications: A Report by the Working Group*
(MSC and Department of Education and Science)
Concluded that there was a low take-up of vocational qualifications.
Perceived by employers as relying too much on theory as opposed
to practice. Confusion and overlap on the provision available, with
difficulties in access, progression and transfer of credits. Problems with
methods of assessment and little recognition of learning outside formal
programmes.

1986   *Working Together: Education and Training* **(Government White Paper)**
Proposed the development of new qualifications based on national
standards defined by industry and operating within a coherent
qualifications structure.

1986   **National Council for Vocational Qualifications (NCVQ) established**
To carry out proposals from the White Paper, including the accreditation of standards, development of new qualifications framework,

development of NVQs, liaison with awarding bodies and monitoring of quality assurance procedures. NCVQ was set up as an independent body with initial government funding covering England, Wales and Northern Ireland. It has no legal powers but must promote the new vocational initiative through cooperation with relevant bodies. The Scottish Council for Vocational Education Training (SCOTVEC) has the same remit in Scotland.

1986   **New Occupational Standards Branch created at MSC**
Given responsibility for setting up industry lead bodies to develop occupational standards. Where possible, the lead bodies built on existing organizations, eg Industrial Training Boards such as the Construction Industry Training Board (CITB).

1988   *Employment for the 1990s* **(Government White Paper)**
Reaffirmed the need for standards and qualifications based on competence and recognized by employers. Proposed establishment of local Training and Enterprise Councils (TECs) to be responsible at local level for the planning and delivery of vocational training and enterprise programmes.

1990   Training Agency (formerly MSC) becomes absorbed in the Training, Enterprise and Education Directorate (TEED) at the Department of Employment.

1991   *Education and Training for the 21st Century* **(Government White Paper)**
Proposed that General National Vocational Qualifications designed to provide broad-based vocational preparation should be introduced into the national qualification framework.

1992   **National Targets for Education and Training announced**
These set targets for young people, adults and employers.

1994   *Competitiveness: Helping Businesses to Win* **(Government White Paper)**
£300 million to be spent on strengthening education and training. Review of NVQs announced to ensure they 'stayed up to date and continued to observe strict standards'. Five hundred NVQs covering 150 occupations representing 80 per cent of all jobs now approved.

1995   (July) Department for Education and Employment (DfEE) created from merger of Department for Education and the Department of Employment.

1996   **(Jan)** *Review of 100 NVQs and SVQs* **report (Chair: Gordon Beaumont)**
Supported NVQ/SVQ concept. Indicated widespread concern over rigour and consistency of assessment and complexity of language of standards. Eighty per cent of employers considered competence-based standards were right for vocational qualifications.

Table I1.1 *(Continued)*

1996	**(March)** *Review of Qualifications for 16- to 19-Year-Olds* **report (Chair: Sir Ron Dearing)** Made a large number of recommendations for improving current provision. Endorsed Beaumont review. Changed the term 'Core Skills' to 'Key Skills' and suggested Key Skills requirements should be considered when designing NVQs. Recommended the merger of NCVQ and Schools Curriculum and Assessment Authority (SCAA) to support a cohesive academic/vocational qualifications framework.
1996	Education Act: Department for Education and Skills (DfES) created.
1996	*Competitiveness: Creating the Enterprise Centre of Europe* **(Government White Paper)** Emphasized need for providers of training and qualifications to undergo rigorous quality assurance procedures.
1997	Qualifications and Curriculum Authority (QCA) set up.
1997	**Employment National Training Organisation formed from merger of Employment Occupational Standards Council and Occupational Health and Safety Lead Body** The first NTO to represent different groups found throughout all sectors of industry. Publication of *External Verification of NVQs by QCA*.
1998	**(March) QCA publishes** *Internal Verification of NVQs, Assessing NVQs and Revised Common Accord* Responsibility for National Occupational Standards devolved to regulatory bodies.
1999	**QCA publishes** *Developing Assessment Strategies for NVQs*
1999	Further Education National Training Organization (FENTO) Standards for Teaching and Supporting Learning in the FE sector published.
2000	Learning and Skills Act
2000	**QCA publishes** *The NVQ Code of Practice* Clearly sets out ways in which organizations should be accredited to run and assess NVQs. It includes a Tariff of Sanctions to be applied by external verifiers where centres are not in compliance with the Code.
2001	**Special Educational Needs and Disability Act** Result has been to improve access.
2001– 04	**Learning and Skills Council (LSC) publishes the national** *Equality and Diversity Strategy* Addresses widening participation and promotes inclusion.
2002	**Sector Skills Development Agency (SSDA) set up by government to fund and support new Sector Skills Councils** Joint remit for vocational qualification system given to QCA, LSC and SSDA.
2002	*Joint Awarding Body Guidance on Internal Verification of NVQs* Document backed by awarding bodies, which states how internal verification will be approached by them all.

2002   **ENTO publishes the Learning and Development standards to replace the TDLB standards**
Review of National Qualifications Framework.

2002   **(Nov) DfES strategy document** *Success for All: Transforming Post-16 Learning and Skills in England*

2003   **EmpNTO rebadges as ENTO**
Publication by DfES of *21st Century Skills – Realising our Potential: Individuals, Employers, Nation*
Sets out a national skills strategy.

2004   (Feb) First meeting of the Lifelong Learning Executive Group Sector Skills Council.

2004   **DfES Standards Unit produce** *Equipping our Teachers for the Future*
Reforms Initial Teacher Training for the learning and skills sector

2004   (Oct) The DfES-commissioned working group report on 14–19 reform, the Tomlinson Report.

2005   Lifelong Learning UK (LLUK) takes over the role of former NTO's related to education and training, including FENTO.

2005   **Disability Discrimination Act**
Puts a positive duty on the public sector to address disability and equality.

2005   (Feb) DfES 14–19 skills White Paper

2005   **(Nov) Foster review of further education,** *Professionalising the Workforce*

2006   NVQ Code of Practice revised and replaces 2001 version.

2006   **(Mar)** *Further Education: Raising Skills, Improving Life Chances* **(DfES White Paper)**
Skills task force set up. Commitment to produce well-qualified professional teachers for FE and the LLE as a whole.
Train to Gain set up to encourage employers to develop the qualifications and skills of their workforce.

2006   **(Dec) Leitch review,** *Prosperity for All in the Global Economy: World Class Skills*, **sets ambitious targets for 2020**

2007   **(Feb) Secretary of State for Education announces school leaving age will be raised to 18 years by 2013 in England**
Training for Apprenticeships and work-based training will be included.

2007   **LLUK New Professional Standards for Teachers, Tutors and Trainers in the Lifelong Learning Sector are approved.**
SVUK responsible for endorsement.

2007   Change of Prime Minister from Tony Blair to Gordon Brown. DfES replaced by Department for Children, Schools and Families (DCSF) and the Department for Innovation, Universities and Skills (DIUS).

1

The Background to the Vocational Education System and the Drive for Qualifications and Improvements in Assessment

VOCATIONAL EDUCATION AND TRAINING

Preparing for work

Schools have many functions, one of them being to prepare children for the world of work. The Balfour Education Act of 1902 made state education free for all children. At this time, the school leaving age had just been raised to 13, although elementary schools did provide for education up to the age of 15 years. In 1918, the compulsory school leaving age was raised to 14 years, and in 1972 the Raising of the School Leaving Age (ROSLA) Act extended this to 16 years. At 16, most young people choose to enter school or sixth form college, further education and work-based training, or work. There is a group of 16- to 19-year-olds who are not in education, employment or training (known as NEETS).

In January 2007, it was proposed that the school leaving age would rise to 18 years by 2013. It is hoped that this will motivate all young people to keep learning until at least this age, whether that is in school, in further education or at work. Changes to the age at which a child or young person is deemed ready for work are a reflection of the economic and social life of a country. The change of the UK's economic base from agricultural and manufacturing to a predominately technology-based financial and service economy with currently high employment and economic growth means fewer unskilled and low-skilled workers are needed, and more workers need to be qualified at higher levels. State education is funded by the Department for Education and Skills (DfES) and is structured in the following way:

- *3–5:* pre-school education in playgroups and nurseries;
- *5–11:* primary education – infant (5–7), junior (7–11) or primary (5–11) (NB some authorities have middle schools, which cover the ages between 8 and 13/14 years);
- *11–16:* secondary school education, in comprehensive or grammar schools, city academies, or schools that have retitled themselves as colleges, leading to GCSE qualifications, and a range of vocational qualifications from the DfES list of approved courses;
- *16–19:* post-16 education in sixth forms belonging to the school system, separate sixth form colleges or further education college sixth forms, leading to A level qualifications.

There is also a private fee-paying school system. Note that Wales and Northern Ireland have similar systems to that of England. The Scottish system has more differences, with breadth as opposed to depth of learning being emphasized.

Post-16 vocational education and training

Vocational education in this country started in the Middle Ages with the craft guilds and apprenticeships. It is concerned with teaching skills and knowledge related to the world of work. Some readers may remember or have been to technical secondary schools in the 1960s that taught a greater range of work-related skills than did their counterparts.

There is some crossover between schools and providers of vocational education and training. Vocational education and training in England is currently funded through the Learning and Skills Council (LSC). The structure is as follows:

- *14–19:* in the school system as described above, leading to vocational GCSE (formerly GNVQ), BTEC certificates and NVQ precursor programmes;
- *16–19:* in further education colleges, leading to vocational GCSE and vocational A levels (formerly intermediate and advanced GNVQ), BTEC certificates and diplomas, NVQ and other vocational qualifications;

- *19-plus:* in further education colleges, often part time (still referred to by many as 'night school or 'day release'), leading to a wide range of vocational qualifications from entry level to degrees (see below);
- *16–25:* in work-based training but attending college to complete the knowledge base of Apprenticeships alongside units of NVQ qualifications assessed in the workplace;
- *19-plus:* Train to Gain, on employers' premises, offering full NVQs at levels 2 and 3, delivered to an assess–train–assess model.

Vocational education and training is also provided for those in offender institutions, and for people with specific learning difficulties and disabilities. Many employers fund vocational education and training for their employees.

Higher education

The government push for 50 per cent to go into higher education is often misinterpreted as 'everyone having to go to university'. Not so. FE has a thriving partnership with higher education, through Aim Higher, where learners progress within the FE system on to L3/4 studies such as BTEC diploma and foundation degrees, usually with a strong vocational emphasis. Higher education is that accredited by universities or institutes of higher education and leads to higher diplomas or degrees. In England, for example, it is funded by the Higher Education Funding Council for England (HEFCE). College partnerships with higher education provide for the first and second years of degree courses, and occasionally the full degree, to be taught at a college, but the degree is awarded by the university. There is consultation taking place regarding allowing further education colleges to award their own degrees.

The lifelong learning sector

This sector currently includes:

- *further education:* in addition to providing the services described earlier, FE provides much specialist education for those with learning disabilities and difficulties;
- *adult and community education:* in areas where this is still funded by the LSC;
- *offender education:* there is a huge push to educate, to at least L1, the 80 per cent of offenders who have no qualifications and extremely poor basic skills;
- *workplace learning in both the public and private sectors:* employer engagement is being encouraged by the government, who want all employers to

provide training at work for employees with no qualifications, and to encourage all employees to gain an L2 qualification;

- *voluntary sector education:* there is a huge voluntary movement in the UK that supports educational and social development. A 1995 study found that 12 million men and women were involved in voluntary activities in 1.3 million organizations. Voluntary activities usually include some form of learning opportunity. The sector includes formal, non-formal and informal vocational and academic education. Some examples are U3A classes (University of the Third Age), speakers who give talks and provide activities for community groups such as those in care homes, and leisure centres that teach sports to adults.

Figure 1.1 shows the range of providers in the lifelong learning sector, and Chapter 10 gives more detail. Note that FE colleges have, for many years, had link arrangements with schools whereby they have offered vocational experiences to some learners from the age of 14 onwards, and this is set to develop further.

Figure 1.1   Vocational qualification providers

THE EFFECT OF GLOBALIZATION ON THE NATIONAL ECONOMY, AND THE 'SKILLS AGENDA'

Labour came to power in 1997 on the back of an election promise based on 'Education, education, education'. Testing, target setting and inspections have become well-known vehicles for measuring the success of our education and training organizations, in both the public and the private sector. Concerns about the level of learner achievement and the need for a better-qualified workforce have been regularly raised and addressed in different ways over the last 30 years. Main concerns are the low levels of achievement of many school leavers and the high proportion of people of working age who remain unqualified. Whilst there have been real achievements, there is still much to do. NVQs and improved assessment and verification practices have played some part in these improvements.

The 1998 *Learning Age* Green Paper reported on a 6.5 per cent decline in work-based learning. The UK was low down the achievement scale compared to virtually every country in Europe, and our staying-on rate was miserable. In 2000, a Department for Education and Employment (DfEE) consultation paper on vocational education and training stated that:

> with the new century come new challenges and new demands. More than ever, this country needs a high quality vocational education and training system to create a highly skilled and socially inclusive workforce, able to compete in the global knowledge economy. A major skills deficiency in the UK is the low numbers of people holding intermediate level qualifications – 14% in the UK as compared for example with 46% in Germany. Productivity shows a corresponding gap, with the UK's level 23% lower than Germany's.

The Tomlinson Report of 2004, *Success for All*, set out a vision and strategy for 'transforming post 16 learning and skills in England'. Tomlinson, who at the time was Chief Inspector for Schools for England and Wales, looked at the educational progress of learners from the age of 14 years and concluded that England and Wales were so far down the international league table for achievements at 16 that there needed to be significant changes. He recommended that A levels be scrapped and proposed a single system of diplomas. He also recommended significant change needed to extend back to the training of teachers in post-16 education.

The Foster Report of 2005 proposed a reform of teacher training education, with a review of standards for delivery as well as for assessment. The subsequent White Paper, *Further Education: Raising Skills, Improving Life Chances*, took a view that professionalizing the workforce was essential if things were to move on. The skills task force set up as a result of this report recommended a review of vocational qualifications. Teachers would need to be able to assess individual needs effectively to support personalization – assisting all individuals to reach their full potential, whatever their background. It was also suggested that, from 2007, all colleges and training providers should have significant annual continuing professional development plans in place for all staff.

The Leitch review of skills, published in December 2006, *Prosperity for All in the Global Economy: World Class Skills*, set out the UK's goals for 2020. The overall conclusion was that, despite low unemployment and good growth for the last 14 years, the UK could not afford to stand still in the face of a rapidly changing global economy. This report built on the findings of earlier reports, which had raised the issue that, whilst the UK might have an enviable university environment, the country was under-skilled across occupations and at different levels. Leitch reported that one-sixth of those leaving school were still unable to read, write or add up to a level that is acceptable for employment, that the UK's skills base would be inferior to that of many other developed nations, and that 17 million adults had difficulty with numbers and 5 million with functional literacy. Those leaving school with no qualifications at all find it much harder to get employment. There are financial incentives to encourage achievement of qualifications at least to Level 2.

The new Professional Standards for Teachers, Trainers and Tutors in the Lifelong Learning Sector were published in March 2007 and should have been fully implemented by the time this book is in print. One of the radical moves within these qualifications is the requirement for teachers, trainers and tutors to develop their own skill levels in literacy, language, numeracy and ICT (the common core) and to understand the difficulties that many face in acquiring these skills. The importance of the delivery as well as the assessment of learning within the lifelong learning sector is brought centre stage, as a key part of the government's desire for a qualified workforce, able to support the UK as a global player in the world economy.

VOCATIONAL QUALIFICATIONS AND REFORM

The purpose of qualification reform is to respond to the needs of both employers and young people. New standards for the content of vocational qualifications including NVQs have been in the process of being developed and revised on a fairly regular basis over the last 20 years or so.

The current wide range of courses and qualifications is being condensed into the National Qualifications Framework. The new structure should make it easier to combine academic and vocational learning through having natural progression routes through the different levels of the proposed vocational diploma, and between GCSEs and A levels, and to avoid young people having to narrow their choices too early. Proposals are far-reaching. The structure is outlined in Figure 1.2, and the notes underneath give further explanation.

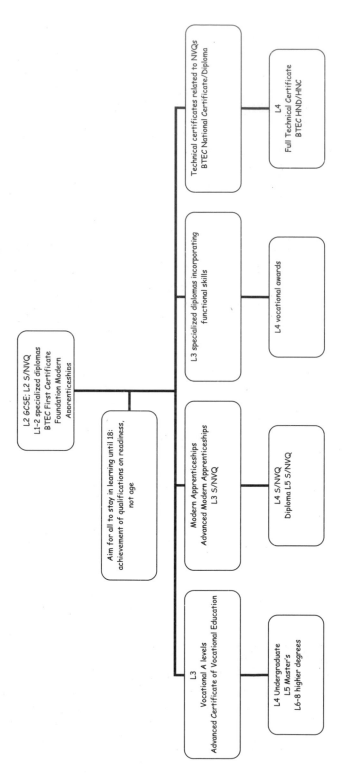

Figure 1.2 Current and planned qualifications and levels

Notes on new qualifications as a response to employability needs (pilot from September 2007):

The purpose of qualification reform is to respond to the needs of both employers and young people. It is hoped that the new structure will motivate young people to keep learning until at least the age of 18, whether that is in school, in further education or at work. The new structure should make it easier to combine academic and vocational learning through having natural progression routes through the different levels of the diploma, and between GCSEs and A levels, and to avoid young people having to narrow their choices too early:

- Candidates achieving five A–C grades at GCSE (the minimum requirement for progressing to A levels) must include English and maths as two of these qualifications.
- Modern Apprenticeships will become Advanced Modern Apprenticeships; National Traineeships will become Foundation Modern Apprenticeships. Apprenticeships will be offered across 80 occupational areas and cover almost 500 qualifications, the majority of which are NVQs. Apprenticeships will be brought within the diploma framework. Employers will be encouraged to improve the quality and number of employment-based training places.
- Specialized diplomas across 14 vocational areas will be available by 2015, with four (ICT, engineering, health and social care, and creative and media) ready by 2008, and 10 available by 2010; it is proposed to merge the existing BTEC diplomas into these, but there is debate suggesting these will operate alongside the new specialized diplomas. These diplomas will include both academic and vocational learning. An L2 diploma can only be achieved if learners also achieve functional English and maths.
- A new range of technical certificates related to NVQ knowledge will be developed. The former BTEC certificates may be subsumed into these, but see above. They will include Key Skills and be benchmarked through external assessment.
- Following their increased take-up, Advanced GNVQs will be renamed Vocational A levels. It is hoped that this will reflect their parity with academic A levels.

National Vocational Qualifications

Prior to the introduction of NVQs, occupational and vocationally related qualifications were linked to training courses, apprenticeships or programmes of study, with students studying for their qualification or certificate either full or part time. Although many courses were well taught, one major criticism was that they concentrated too much on what academic programme designers wanted to include or what had traditionally been expected of an employee, and not enough on what was actually needed at work in the new global economy.

NVQs are intended to be firmly based in the work context and designed for accrediting the skills of working people and providing a system for identifying where skills and knowledge need to be acquired or updated.

National Vocational Qualifications take as their starting point the question 'What skills and knowledge do particular occupational areas need?' They are then concerned with measuring, assessing and accrediting whether someone can actually perform competently within that occupational area. NVQs:

- are based on an analysis of work roles in terms of what functions need to be performed;
- are led by employers and industry-specific professional bodies – not by 'education';
- focus on *the ability to do the job competently* and *not* whether someone is as good as or better than someone else;
- define five different levels of competence (see Figure 1.2);
- concentrate on assessment of outcomes.

The history of standards for assessing NVQs

National Standards for Training and Development were first issued in 1992, and comprehensively revised in 1994, under the direction of the then Training and Development Lead Body (TDLB). In November 1994, three lead bodies that were concerned with generic skills across a range of occupations, the TDLB, the Personnel Standards Lead Body (PSLB) and the Trade Union Sector Development Body, were amalgamated to form the Employment Occupational Standards Council (EOSC). The EOSC took forward the work started by the original three lead bodies to provide a comprehensive range of qualifications. The Employment National Training Organisation (ENTO, formerly EmpNTO) has now replaced the EOSC. ENTO is one of the NTOs that range across the occupational sectors.

ENTO's mission is about 'developing the competence of people who work with people'. ENTO was responsible for standards for learning and development, health and safety, personnel, managing work-related violence, and trade unions, as well as for advice and guidance organizations, the publishing of professional development guides, and the matrix quality standard (an organizational standard). ENTO is still responsible for the Learning Network, a web-based network for assessors and verifiers, where up-to-the-minute information on assessment and verification is available, as are details of updating and training courses, along with an online chat facility for those who are registered members. However, LLUK, the sector skills council responsible for professional development, has taken over from ENTO in the development and endorsement of standards, including PSTTTLLS and NVQ standards for assessment and verification.

The NVQ framework

The NVQ framework consists of 11 occupational areas. Each occupational area has its range of occupational NVQs at a variety of levels. The A&V units are from the range of qualifications and mini-awards from the occupational area designated as 'Developing and extending knowledge and skill'.

Each NVQ has between a three- and five-year 'product life', after which it is subject to revision. New and revised NVQs are therefore constantly coming on-stream. Mini-qualifications are small groups of standards. The A&V units fall into this category as each consists of just one unit. A full NVQ often has 10 or more units. All NVQ qualifications developed from standards need to be approved by the Qualifications and Curriculum Authority (QCA) to ensure that they fit into the overall qualifications framework at the appropriate levels.

This framework is a national system for ordering qualifications according to their complexity of academic content or job role. There are five levels in all, plus an entry level. NVQs in Learning and Development are all at level 3 or above. The assessor awards are at level 3, and the verifier awards are at level 4. This means that candidates for the internal verifier award need to be in a position of managing internal verification procedures, and managing assessors as part of that quality assurance process.

There is no programme of learning or syllabus built into an NVQ qualification. This does not mean that learning programmes are not devised for NVQs. NVQ candidates often attend a further education college or a training centre to gain the background knowledge and to practise their skills. However, in many cases, especially where the candidate has extensive experience in the occupational area, it is the competence of the candidate and the speed at which he or she can prove that competence that is the driving force.

Key Skills

Key Skills were introduced as a result of negotiation between the government and employers, who felt that school and college leavers were ill equipped for the workplace. Six Key Skills qualifications give employees and any student the opportunity to demonstrate the underpinning Key Skills that are needed for effective performance at each of the five qualification levels. Application of number, communication and information technology are perhaps the most crucial, as employees' level of achievement in these Key Skills is often fundamental to their ability to work accurately and efficiently. Team building, problem solving and improvement of own learning and performance are complementary to the core Key Skills and offer candidates the opportunity to show their additional people-based skills that make them effective and valuable employees. Most qualifications are now mapped against the Key Skills specifications, so candidates can demonstrate many of the Key Skills competencies through doing their occupational or vocationally related qualification. Candidates who start an NVQ or any other qualification are likely to be given a Key Skills assessment as part of their induction.

Apprenticeships

Apprenticeships cover more than 80 occupational areas and nearly 500 qualifications and have proved hugely popular. There are two levels, the Foundation Modern Apprenticeship at L2, which lasts a minimum of a year, and Advanced Modern Apprenticeships at L3, which last at least two years. Modern Apprenticeships provide both practical skills and underpinning knowledge and understanding for 16- to 24-year-olds who are already in employment or who have left full-time training. Since 2000, Technical Certificates have been linked specifically to Modern Apprenticeships for the underpinning knowledge element, with the practical skills being assessed via a relevant NVQ. All Modern Apprentices take Key Skills.

Technical Certificates are vocationally related qualifications that are taught off the job and are subject to some external assessment. The certificates often have a broader educational focus within the chosen occupational area. Students learn through programmes that emphasize the development of Key Skills as well as occupational skills.

Both NVQs and Technical or Craft Certificates are based on the same principles of assessment. They are both assessed to national standards, on the basis of evidence demonstrated and presented by the candidate, and are both committed to promoting equality of access to assessment regardless of disability, geographical location, religion, ethnic group or gender. Hence the assessment process and the considerations to be taken into account are very similar in spite of the 'cultural' differences of work and education.

THE BACKGROUND TO PROFESSIONALIZING ASSESSMENT, TEACHING AND TRAINING

When NVQs were introduced in 1993, their assessment was approached by the devising of new competence-based qualifications to be taken by all assessors and verifiers involved. These were derived from the Training and Development (T&D) standards, and known as the D units. In 2004 the T&D standards were revised and replaced by the much easier-to-understand Learning and Development standards. The D units were replaced by the assessor and verifier (A&V) units. All those qualified with the D units should by now have updated to, and be practising according to, the A&V qualifications. The use of NVQs and their assessment and quality assurance in colleges and in the workplace have gained credence with employers and the public over this time. At the time of writing the L&D standards and consequently the A&V units are being revised.

Success for All, the report published in 2004 whose writing was spear-headed by the then Chief Inspector for Schools for England and Wales, Mike Tomlinson, first suggested that a similarly rigorous overhaul be given to the assessment of other vocational qualifications and that the standards for teachers and trainers, whether full or part time, be revised again, into a comprehensive system. It was clear that the partly voluntary system of qualification for teachers in post-16, and the wide range of qualifications on offer, was lacking in rigour and leading to piecemeal quality that was affecting learners' achievement and progression. The FE White Paper *Preparing our Teachers for the Future* in 2006 gave the framework for the development of overarching qualifications for teachers, tutors and trainers in the lifelong learning sector.

The history of assessment standards for teachers

The Foster Report highlighted the poor achievement of England's school leavers against those abroad. This led to a review of teaching processes and ultimately to a review of the standards for lifelong learning teachers. Whereas teachers in post-16 education have always had routes to qualification via a PGCE or a range of part-time qualifications, such as the well-known City & Guilds (C&G) 7307, the development of the FENTO standards informed a new suite of qualifications for teachers from 2000, including for example C&G 7407, though these were not mandatory. Trainers in work-based training often took NVQs in Learning and Development or just assessor awards. The newly established Sector Skills Council, the LLUK, pushed the reforms forward, driving the development of professional standards in all aspects. The resultant work was submitted for consultation and approval to SVUK, the quality assurance arm of LLUK. These standards were published in the spring of 2007 as 'the new 'Professional Standards for Teachers, Tutors and Trainers in the Lifelong Learning Sector'. They cover a range of domains, and consist of overarching standards for practice underpinned by a set of professional values to be observed by all teachers, tutors and trainers whatever the setting of their practice. Assessment is classed as Domain E. The standards are grouped into different units. Domain E standards cover the unit 'Principles and Practice of Assessment' at L3 and L4.

From 2007, all new entrants will need to take the new qualification. Staff will be of two types – associate teachers, who teach a limited range of a subject or group, and full teachers, who teach the full range of a subject across a range of levels. There will be a threshold licence to practise (PTLLS), then a certificate at L3/4 that is likely to be taken by associate staff, and a diploma at L4/5, which is for full teachers. These may also opt for the Cert Ed, at L4/5/6. There is now a requirement for all staff to show they are competent in the core skills of literacy, language, number and ICT. It is expected that many existing staff will take some units as CPD.

For the first time, teaching qualifications for all those in the government-funded post-16 LLS will be mandatory. Not only that, but the qualifications available have been simplified. Whilst individual awarding bodies will develop programmes in different ways, with different assessment patterns, the underpinning values, essential knowledge and essential practice points will be the same for every candidate. This can only be of benefit to trainees and learners.

SUMMARY

This chapter should have helped you with the following:

- the vocational education and training system;
- globalization and the need for a qualified workforce;
- vocational qualifications;
- moves to professionalize teacher and trainer training through the development of new qualifications.

2

The Organizations Involved in the Development, Delivery and Quality Assurance of National Standards

There have been considerable changes to many of the organizations involved. Table I1.1 gives the dates of changes. Some changes have been to reduce the numbers of organizations; others have resulted from approaches to bring key players, such as employers, more closely into decision making. Reforms are proposed to some of the organizations described below. The chapter contains a number of abbreviations and jargon words. The Glossary towards the end of the book explains these terms, and there is a separate list of Abbreviations at the beginning of the book.

STANDARDS AND QUALIFICATIONS REGULATION AND FUNDING

Funding

The Learning and Skills Council (LSC) plans and funds, on a regional basis, education and training for all post-16 and work-based learning in England and Wales (except university education, which is covered by HEFCE). It is responsible for work-based learning, Train to Gain, sixth forms and further education. It holds the UK register of learning providers and provides funding to them based on a target-driven formula. Approved qualifications on the database of the Qualifications and Curriculum Authority (QCA) receive different levels of funding according to whether they require additional resources for equipment or type of learner. Funding is allocated according to whether delivery organizations have met their negotiated targets from the previous year. Underachievement means less money for delivery the following year. It is in the interests of the organization, from a financial point of view, as well as the learner, from an achievement point of view, to ensure that the learner is matched to a programme where he or she is able to achieve and gain a recognized qualification.

Regulation

There are four regulatory authorities for the United Kingdom: the QCA (England), DELLS (Wales), CCEA (Northern Ireland) and SQA (Scotland). The QCA formed from a merger of regional bodies in 2000. Its mission is to 'ensure that the qualifications market is fit for purpose, that qualifications are fair, standards are secure, public confidence is sustained and that the QCA acts as the public champion of the learner'. QCA regulates awarding bodies, accredits and monitors qualifications, and supports the development of vocational learning and occupational standards (as well as more academic qualifications such as GCSE and 'A' level).

Inspection

Four previously separate inspectorates are now merged into the new Ofsted (Office for Standards in Education, Children's Services and Skills). Ofsted's mission is 'Raising standards, improving lives', using inspection and regulatory visits to support providers to:

- promote service improvement;
- ensure services focus on the interests of their users;
- see that services are efficient and effective and promote value for money.

The findings of the hundreds of weekly visits are published in reports, which can be found on the Ofsted website, along with the inspection toolkit for learning and skills inspection.

STANDARDS AND QUALIFICATIONS DEVELOPMENT

Standards development

Sector Skills Councils (SSCs) were first set up in 2002, having been created from mergers of former National Training Organizations (NTOs). The 25 Sector Skills Councils make up the Skills for Business Network and are licensed by the Secretary of State for Education and Skills, though they are independent of the government. They cover 85 per cent of the UK workforce, with those industries falling outside being covered by the Sector Skills Development Agency, which also funds, supports and monitors the Sector Skills Councils (SSCs). Membership of these bodies is made up of representation from the public sector, industry, professional bodies, employer and trades associations, and practitioners. Their role is to minimize skills gaps, to increase opportunities for improving the skills and productivity of the sectors' workforce and business in general, and to promote learning, for example through Apprenticeships, higher education and national occupational standards.

National Training Organisations provide advice, guidance and support for all those using the occupational standards they have devised. The task of identifying, defining and revising occupational standards is done by SSCs and NTOs, which cover specific occupational sectors across the UK.

The Employment National Training Organisation

ENTO is an all-sector NTO that was responsible for providing the current standards used to assess and quality-assure NVQs. ENTO has developed nine suites of occupational standards covering 11 professional areas. Its commercial arm, the Learning Network, provides online support for those who deliver, assess and verify NVQs.

Lifelong Learning United Kingdom (LLUK)

In January 2005, LLUK took over the work of four related NTOs and became responsible for the professional development of all those working in further education, higher education, community learning and development, libraries, archives and information, and work-based learning. LLUK has overseen the development of the new Professional Standards for Teachers, Tutors and Trainers in the Lifelong Learning Sector and has taken over responsibility from ENTO for the standards for assessment and verification.

Standards Verification United Kingdom (SVUK)

This is the quality arm of LLUK and reviews and approves the standards and subsequent qualifications generated through LLUK's activities. It approves specialist qualifications for teachers of ESOL, literacy and numeracy as well as Initial Teacher Training (formerly undertaken by FENTO). It is expanding to cover other forms of workplace training and development.

THE PROVIDERS AND QUALITY ASSURANCE

Awarding bodies

The role of awarding bodies is:

- to deliver and publish qualifications specifications;
- to provide centres with information about qualifications;
- to improve access arrangements for learners;
- to arrange for the marking of examination papers and the checking of coursework marks from centres;
- to award results and grades to candidates;
- to issue certificates to candidates.

All awarding bodies have to apply for accreditation from QCA and then submit themselves for re-accreditation on a regular basis. If QCA is dissatisfied with the quality assurance procedures of an awarding body, then the accreditation to award qualifications is withdrawn.

Awarding bodies register candidates for qualifications and award certificates for qualifications and so quality assurance is a major part of their work. They recruit, train and appoint external verifiers and external moderators to do much of this work. External verifiers have to operate at the V2 award standard (see Chapter 9), which is offered only by the awarding bodies themselves. There is an external moderator award offered by the Open College. Many awarding bodies also sponsor the development of training and assessment materials, produce publications, arrange training for programme deliverers and assessors, and provide consultancy.

The Dearing review of 1996 suggested a rationalization of awarding bodies, since the monitoring of the large number in existence had become an almost impossible task. Over the past 10 years, there has been an attempt to reduce the number of awarding bodies but this has been only partially successful. The number is still large, at over 100. There have been some major mergers, notably with the large public examination bodies, eg OCR was formed from the merger of Oxford and Cambridge, London and the Royal Society of Arts awarding bodies.

The QCA website gives details of awarding bodies and the qualifications they offer.

Quality assurance

Figure 2.1 NVQ quality assurance chain

The QCA NVQ Code of Practice

Inevitably, as the number of accredited centres offering NVQ qualifications increased, so did differences of opinion and of practice between centres, which was unhelpful to both candidates and to perceived and actual quality.

In August 1993, the NCVQ introduced the Common Accord, which was 'intended to enhance the quality and cost effectiveness of NVQ assessment and verification processes operated by Awarding Bodies' (NCVQ, 1993). QCA brought out a new version, *The Awarding Bodies' Common Accord*, in July 1997. In September 2000, the three regulatory authorities published the *Arrangements for the Statutory Regulation of External Qualifications in England, Wales and Northern Ireland*. This was supplemented in 2002 by *The NVQ Code of Practice* (revised in 2006), which sets out:

- agreed principles and practice for the assessment and quality assurance of NVQs and NVQ units;
- the responsibilities of NVQ awarding bodies and their accredited centres in respect of the administration, assessment and verification of NVQs and NVQ units;
- the basis upon which ACCAC and QCA will systematically monitor the performance of awarding bodies in maintaining the quality and standards across the NVQs they offer;

- the sanctions to be applied to centres that do not comply with the Code of Practice.

See Appendix 2 for an explanation of the sanctions.

All accredited centres should have a copy of the NVQ Code of Practice, which can also be obtained from QCA, and all assessors and internal verifiers should have their own copies. The Code of Practice lays down the *minimum* requirements for each assessment and verification role, and centres must have staff qualified to these minimum standards.

Joint Awarding Body Guidance on Internal Verification of NVQs

This 2002 publication was the result of a steering group of a DfEE national project and supplements the previous QCA *Guide on Internal Verification of NVQs* published in 1998. The guidance aims to increase the reliability of assessment practice across the country, and raised the profile and role of the internal quality assurance processes and staff in terms of ensuring national standards were met and of minimizing risk. Again, all centres and internal verifiers should have a copy of, and use, this document for guidance.

Accredited centres

There are thousands of organizations of all sizes from large colleges to small training centres that are approved by awarding bodies to be accredited centres for offering qualifications. Centres offer advice, guidance and training for particular awards, and to register, assess, internally verify and accredit candidates. They are subject to external verification from the awarding body and to auditing from the QCA. Their main link to the awarding body is through the designated external verifier or moderator. If external moderators find a lack of compliance with quality procedures they recommend sanctions be taken by the awarding body. These can range from an action plan to withdrawal of the right to register and certificate candidates unless there is close monitoring of all qualifications. The ultimate sanction is to stop a centre from operating. A survey of centre satisfaction with awarding bodies that QCA reported in November 2006 found that, 'in general, levels of centre satisfaction are encouragingly high'. Hopefully, the quality assurance systems followed by those who have taken the V1 and V2 verifier awards have gone some way to achieving this positive result. It may well be that potential candidates already work for an organization accredited to offer the required qualifications, in which case they may or may not have a choice of accredited centre. Some organizations wanting their staff to take A&V awards will prefer to choose centres that offer a range of qualifications relevant to the work of their staff.

For example, employers with staff following self-development programmes may want an A&V centre that also offers CIPD awards, whereas others will want to choose a centre that specializes in A&V awards and can deliver these for all their staff on employers' premises, irrespective of their occupational area. Yet others will choose a centre they feel happy with, irrespective of any other factors. There are clear criteria laid down in the Code of Practice for the approval of centres. All centres should be operating to the NVQ Code of Practice. A centre may have several sites all operating under the same systems. Awarding bodies will be pleased to supply lists of accredited centres.

Services provided by approved centres

Centres deal with candidate registrations, allocation of candidates to assessors, assessment and certification paperwork, and usually any associated support needed by candidates. Many offer the facility for accrediting prior learning. The variety and quality of the training, support and assessment offered by the centre with which they register is probably the biggest factor in candidates' ability to profit fully from the process associated with gaining a qualification. Candidates or employers need to satisfy themselves concerning the amount of support offered, the ways in which competence and knowledge will be assessed and verified in the workplace and who will be doing this, and the time that candidates are expected to take to achieve their vocational qualification, mini-award or NVQ. The centre should have a range of supporting resources such as reading materials relating to assessment and to the occupational standards with which candidates will be involved.

Clients or organizations concerned will also need to check before they register that the centre can provide the full range of services they need. For some candidates and employers, it will be important to register with a centre that has well-developed electronic systems for delivery of information and for the submission of work for assessment and that can give assessment and feedback electronically. Centres vary very considerably in their physical and human resources, as well as in their ability to support candidates to achieve within acceptable timescales. The list below gives an idea of the range of services that are likely to be offered by accredited centres:

- *briefing sessions* – such as introducing different qualifications and explaining the NVQ system;
- *initial assessment* – such as key skills tests, checking candidates' preferred learning styles, checking previous attainment and advising on any additional support that candidates may require;
- *planning workshops* – action planning to help candidates prepare for assessments;

- *knowledge and understanding workshops* – training in background information;
- *open learning* – providing background materials in electronic or paper format that can be studied at the candidates' convenience;
- *individual support* – one-to-one advice, review and feedback sessions and supporting workplace mentors;
- *group support* – either tutored sessions or self-support groups;
- *workplace assessment* – assessors visiting the candidates' work environment to assess competence;
- *resource-based learning centres* – computers with internet access, and reading materials;
- *accreditation of prior learning* – staff trained to check this and provide action plans.

The costs of qualification

In terms of potential earnings, job mobility and transfer, and personal satisfaction, there is absolutely no doubt that the effort involved for a candidate to get a qualification is highly likely to outweigh any cost, whether financial or personal. The timescale and financial cost for a qualification are difficult to estimate, because these depend on the individual awarding body's charges, the rates charged by different centres, the amount of support required by individuals, and the ability of the staff providing the support, training and assessment. Some candidates have taken just months to complete a whole NVQ, whereas others have taken years to complete a couple of units.

We estimate that a candidate-assessor who is new to NVQ assessment could need to spend around 15 hours developing his or her underpinning knowledge of competence-based assessment through reading appropriate publications and visiting websites, and talking to relevant people such as his or her workplace supervisor, internal verifier or mentor. Planning the assessment for a complete NVQ unit will probably take around an hour per unit initially, and less time as the process develops (especially so if the candidate tackles any option units first, instead of last). Candidates taking typical year-long vocational awards will probably need to put aside at least six hours a week for assignment work, outside of the guided learning time. The majority of the time, and therefore costs, for an NVQ should ideally be on workplace observations, feedback following these, and professional discussion. Skilled planning is needed to ensure that the observation sessions are efficient and effective. Motivation, being well briefed, an overall grasp of the assessment system in use, and plentiful opportunities for demonstrating competence via observation are the keys to efficient and effective accreditation (see Chapter 11 for more details of preparing and planning for assessment in different work contexts).

Costs incurred will be of both variable and fixed types, depending on whether they relate to 'products', such as registration and certification, or processes, such as assessment time. These will vary according to the procedures of the awarding body and the assessment centre selected. Some of the expenses incurred by centres, such as centre approval fees, are likely to be passed on to candidates in some way. Costs are sometimes kept down by centres running group sessions rather than one-to-one sessions; candidates will have to consider whether the financial saving is worth the loss of individual tuition and support. If candidates find that they are spending time on 'portfolio building' without assessment of competence being recorded by assessors at the same time, it is likely that their centre is not using its assessors effectively to assess competence. Candidates would be advised to renegotiate their assessment plans so that the assessor uses more work-based evidence and professional discussion to make assessment judgements.

Charges related to assessment will include all or some of the following:

- centre approval and registration;
- candidate registration (per unit or award);
- support materials and standards packs;
- support workshops;
- workplace assessment;
- unit summative assessment;
- internal and external verification;
- administration and travel costs.

Many candidates find it difficult to complete their qualifications within negotiated timescales. If achievement is your priority, it may be that a centre that charges more, but is firmly rooted in effective assessor-led workplace assessment, may ultimately be the most efficient choice. 'Shopping around' to find the most appropriate package is recommended both for individuals and for organizations.

SUMMARY

This chapter should have helped you with the following:

- the regulatory, funding and quality assurance bodies;
- the development of national standards and qualifications;
- understanding the purposes and functions of accredited centres.

Part 2

Knowledge Requirements

3

The Processes: Assessing Vocational Education, including NVQs

This chapter looks briefly at the assessment process and its place within the broader context of learning and training. It then focuses on the four stages involved in the assessment process.

ASSESSMENT AS PART OF THE TRAINING CYCLE

There are a number of different models for the training process, but, although the terms may vary from one model to another, the essential stages are similar in nature. They all have the following features:

- *Initial review and assessment.* Diagnosis of what the candidate already knows or can do, compared with what he or she needs to demonstrate and learn.
- *Design of learning.* Decisions are made and agreements are reached on what the outcomes of learning should be, how the learning is to take place, what methods and resources will be used, and what timescale is appropriate; this is done with regard to cost-effectiveness, health and safety and equality and diversity agendas. An added requirement is that the training must be designed to meet the needs of each learner; this is called 'personalization'.

- *Implementation.* The learning programme is put into practice.
- *Assessment.* The results of learning are assessed, usually throughout the programme, as well as at the end.
- *Evaluation and quality assurance.* A variety of techniques is used to gain quantitative and qualitative information on the overall effectiveness of the process, from candidate satisfaction to meeting organizational targets.

This sequence is usually seen as a cycle, as the results of evaluation and quality assurance feed back into the process to affect work with the same or the next candidates as they progress through or start their programme. The sequence is followed by both the Learning and Development and the new Professional Standards.

The Learning and Development standards related to assessment have been used to create units that are known as the assessor and verifier awards. These are explained in greater detail in Part 3 Section 1. The new Professional Standards have been used to create units that are part of new qualifications for those working in the lifelong learning sector. These standards are explained in greater detail in Part 3 Section 2.

If you are working with NVQ qualifications, you will need one or more of the following:

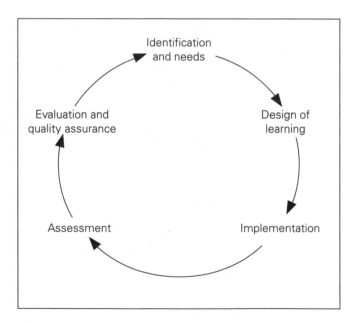

Figure 3.1 The training cycle

- A1 is for those undertaking assessments of workplace performance and knowledge, using a range of methods to carry out the assessment.
- A2 is for those carrying out assessment of skills in the workplace, using observation and questioning.
- V1 is for those verifying the assessment procedures within an organization.
- V2 is for those externally verifying assessment procedures. It is taken by external verifiers, who are appointed to their jobs by awarding bodies. It is not covered in depth in this book, as it is run by the awarding bodies for their own verifiers, though the standards themselves have been included for reference.

Both sets of standards have their associated knowledge and understanding, and both have workplace assessment as a key component. The assessment criteria both of the assessor verifier awards and of the Professional Practice standards for PPA cover the assessment of what a candidate can competently do in the workplace, and this aspect is tested through workplace observation. Knowledge and understanding can be inferred to some extent from performance, but need to be checked through a variety of other means, whether this is by questioning and discussion of the candidate in the workplace or by the writing of a researched assignment.

A true story and cautionary tale

When assessor awards were first introduced in 1994, one of us, having recently gained her own D33 award, visited a very experienced construction tutor in the construction department of a large college. He was taking the D33 unit and I was his assessor. I observed as two construction students inserted window frames into partly built walls, and the candidate for the D33 award, whom we shall call Bill, monitored progress. He ticked off the various tasks that each candidate did and pronounced himself satisfied. I reminded him that he needed to check the knowledge and understanding of each candidate. He flatly refused to do this. There was muttering of 'jumping through hoops for this new award'. I said that was OK by me but unfortunately I couldn't progress him in his award as he'd not asked the candidates any questions relating to their knowledge. He agreed to ask the questions, but warned me it was a complete waste of time since neither candidate could possibly have achieved the task unless he had known what he was doing. So he turned to one candidate, whom I shall call Dean, and asked him a technical point connected with health and safety, about fitting the window. 'I dunno,' said Dean. 'What do you mean?' said Bill. 'You did this in the theory class yesterday.' 'I was off sick,' said Dean. Flummoxed, Bill asked Dean how he'd managed to complete the task if he hadn't known what to do. 'I copied him,' said Dean, pointing at the other candidate.

I've always remembered that instance, particularly since it occurred so early on in my life as an assessor, and have used it many times as an illustration. It's quite true that smart learners can make a good attempt at a job, particularly if they have some previous experience. Whether such learners can be considered safe, and whether they would understand how to do the job in different circumstances, is debatable. Needless to say, Bill was happy to complete the required elements of his qualification and went on to many years of excellent NVQ assessment and, later, verification practice.

THE ASSESSMENT PROCESS

Most people involved in assessment will be covering the assessment process as a natural part of their work, and the four stages involved will be familiar to them, although they may not have identified these stages explicitly.

In this chapter we will be looking in detail at what each stage actually involves.

Stage 1: planning for assessment

All candidates should be fully familiar with the assessment requirements of their qualification long before they are assessed, and no candidate should ever have a 'surprise' assessment. NVQ candidates should always have been involved at the planning stage and will have negotiated, following training and in advance of any assessment activity, the assessment process for each unit being taken. Candidates who are new to qualifications at any level will initially need a lot of help and guidance. However, they can still be given opportunities to make their own suggestions and choices without putting them in a situation where they feel overwhelmed. Skilled assessors and practitioners can give additional written guidance to assignments that enables candidates to understand what is being asked of them but falls

Table 3.1 Stages of the assessment process

Stage 1	Stage 2a	Stage 2b	Stage 3	Stage 4
Planning for assessment with candidate	Reviewing performance and knowledge evidence	Judging all evidence against agreed standards	Recording decisions and giving feedback	Contributing to quality assurance processes

short of 'giving the answers'. Candidates for vocational awards may have a variety of different assessments, including work-based assessments, to complete. Much time can be saved if they draw up plans for how they intend to tackle each assignment and seek approval that they are on the right track *before* starting their work. Many candidates with various learning difficulties successfully complete NVQs and vocational qualifications. Again, with support and guidance, they will be able to contribute ideas towards the way their assessment can be achieved.

The NVQ assessor and the candidate will meet to plan how and when a unit, or units, is going to be assessed and by whom. Once the candidate understands the requirements of each whole unit and the associated assessment process, planning meetings should not be too lengthy. Ideally, candidates will have regular assessment by their assessor through workplace observations, followed by feedback and review of the assessment plan. The assessor who is not in regular face-to-face contact with candidates, perhaps because much of their assessment is being done by a vocational observational assessor (A2), needs to keep in touch by other means, such as telephone or e-mail or via the candidates' e-portfolio if this system is being used, in order to monitor progression of the planned assessment programme.

Although planning for assessment will normally take place on an individual basis, there may be times when the planning takes place with a whole group of candidates. This might be because a specific activity, eg an assignment, has been set up that covers a number of competences. Whatever way the planning meeting takes place, candidate(s) and assessor need to be clear on a number of key areas:

- *What* competences or criteria will be assessed?
- *Who* will be involved in the assessment?
- *When* will they be assessed?
- *Where* will they be assessed?
- *How* will they be assessed?
- *How* will achievement be recorded and confirmed to the candidate?
- *When* will feedback be given?
- *How* will feedback be given?

Examples of planning for assessment

- A candidate working towards an NVQ in motor vehicle repair is assessed at the garage where he works. As the assessor in this case is the owner of the garage, and they see each other every day, assessment takes place on a fairly continuous basis, with the assessment plans for each relevant unit being continuously reviewed and updated. They also take advantage of spontaneous opportunities for assessment, for example the candidate suddenly gets a job that will give him the chance to demonstrate a particular competence and so arranges, more or less on the spot, that he should be observed and assessed. The key to this type of planning is that both need to be clear initially with the competences required for each unit of the NVQ and with the methods and opportunities available for assessment. They also need to establish a procedure for taking advantage of these 'spontaneous' opportunities that may occur.

- An assessor is assessing a candidate working towards an NVQ in Beauty. They have a meeting to review the unit assessment plan, where they discuss what competences still need to be demonstrated and decide that some competences related to nail care have not yet been covered. The candidate gives the assessor a number of dates and times when she will be carrying out a full nail treatment and they arrange a convenient time for the assessor to come and observe her. They then check if any other competences could be covered at the same time and decide that the candidate could also be assessed on some elements related to health and safety and customer care. Assessment plans are drawn up for these units.

- Catering students at a local college working in a training restaurant have a group meeting with their tutor before they go into a lunchtime session where they are serving at table. They agree on a number of competences that they should have the opportunity to demonstrate during that time and that can be observed and assessed. After the session, the assessor works with the students to update their individual unit assessment plans and record their progress.

- A candidate wishing to submit evidence for APL towards an NVQ in Photographic Processing has a first meeting with her primary assessor. During this meeting the assessor acts as adviser and helps the candidate to match her past experience against the requirements of the NVQ and works with her to identify what evidence will be appropriate to support her claim and how to prepare her portfolio of evidence. They agree on an appropriate timescale and possible date for assessment. During this planning meeting the assessor explains his role, making a clear differentiation between the advising process and the assessment process that follows it. The assessor draws up plans for each NVQ unit, which identify what APL evidence will be brought forward and what methods will be used to complete the unit assessment. He agrees to make arrangements for assessing the evidence at their next meeting.

- Students who are candidates on a Key Skills programme are given an assignment by a tutor during a classroom session. The briefing for this assignment gives instructions on what needs to be presented for assessment, when it should be presented and the criteria against which it will be assessed.

In all these cases, the details of what will be assessed, any action that needs to be taken prior to assessment and any changes to the already agreed assessment process should be recorded on the assessment plan. Assessment plans and planning are covered in more detail in Parts 3 and 4.

Identifying relevant evidence

It is common to refer to the activities and products that the candidate will perform or produce to demonstrate competence as 'assessment evidence'. 'Evidence' is usually associated with a legal situation where information, videotape or audio recordings, documents, artefacts or witness testimonies are produced to prove the defendant guilty or not guilty. And just as the police and lawyers work to collect and review the evidence in order to make their case for the prosecution or defence, so assessors need to understand and gather information to be certain about the candidates' competence.

The onus is not necessarily on the candidate to provide everything, just as it is not up to the defendant to prepare his or her own case. It is true that sometimes defendants represent themselves, and confident and experienced candidates are likely to need less support from assessors. Defendants are assumed innocent until proved guilty; similarly, it would be wrong to suggest that candidates for NVQs are guilty of incompetence until they provide the evidence to prove themselves innocent; they have not yet demonstrated competence. NVQ candidates in work have often been performing competently for some time, but not had the opportunity to prove they are working to national standards. However, it is useful to bear in mind the rigorous examination given to legal evidence to assess its worth. For example, legal witnesses have to be credible and consistent in their testimony and able to stand up to cross-examination. Legal documents always need the signatures of reputable persons to confirm that they are truthful and accurate. Circumstantial evidence, along the lines of 'Well, he was there at the time, so he must have done it!', is not sufficient, and there must be other hard evidence to back it up. Similarly, witnesses to a candidate's competence must be credible and link their statements to the required evidence standards.

Just as in a court of law, the evidence produced for assessment must clearly relate to the identified required performance criteria or knowledge and understanding requirements, and be able to stand up to rigorous examination. Hence the candidate and assessor should be clear, not only about what they have to do or produce that will provide evidence, but also what *quality* of evidence is needed. During the planning for assessment, they must discuss or consider:

- what types of evidence are appropriate to meet the specified performance criteria;

- what knowledge can be assessed through performance, questioning or discussion;
- how writing done by the candidate can be checked by the assessor to see whether sources are used appropriately and that ideas are correctly attributed;
- arrangements for the assessments;
- how the evidence will be assessed;
- who needs to be involved;
- what documentation and procedures need to be used.

Candidates for workplace assessment should also have discussed the best way to go about identifying opportunities for proving competence. In many cases they will have been helped to produce an action plan that identifies what they need to do prior to assessment. An example of an action plan can be found in Chapter 11.

Access to assessment

Assessors must be mindful during the planning process that individuals are not excluded from access to assessment. Table 3.2 gives some indications of the kind of barriers that might prevent individuals from gaining access to assessment.

There are many different kinds of problems that people might face, and all assessors will have their own examples. Here are a few from our own experience and the measures taken to combat them:

- A candidate in information technology who developed arthritis. A special keyboard overlay was obtained for the computer that helped her to hit the keys accurately.
- A candidate in residential care who could only work on the night shift. An assessor was found who was prepared to conduct an assessment observation during this time.
- A candidate in an engineering firm whose first language was Somali spoke good enough English to carry out his job. However, he needed help in understanding the details of how he was to be assessed. An interpreter was found who attended the planning interviews to make sure that he was able to understand and discuss anything that was necessary.
- A young girl who had been in care since she was a child was placed on an Apprenticeship programme working with animals. She was given a good deal of encouragement and a very slow and gentle introduction to the process of assessment by giving her feedback on an informal basis. When her supervisor was certain she had a good chance of being successful, she suggested that the girl be assessed against one unit of the qualification.

Table 3.2 Examples of barriers to access to assessment

These are some situations that could affect the candidate's access to assessment	
Physical	If a candidate was in a wheelchair and the practical assessments were to take place on the first floor of a building with no wheelchair access.
Chronological	If assessments always took place after 3.30 pm, parents who had to collect children from school could be disadvantaged.
Linguistic	If a candidate's mother tongue was not English, he or she could have difficulty understanding the assessment requirements.
Social	If candidates were lacking in confidence, they could be too nervous to submit themselves for assessment.
Intellectual	If candidates had learning difficulties, they could need much more support before they were ready for assessment.
Resource-based	If the resources, eg equipment needed for assessment, were not readily available, candidates would not have the opportunity to be assessed.
Cultural	If candidates were asked to perform activities that were unfamiliar to them or were abhorrent to them (eg not being allowed to wear the shawl, if a Muslim woman), they might have to refuse assessment opportunities.
Gender-related	If candidates were prevented from doing tasks that the workplace felt were not appropriate even though they were quite capable of doing them, eg male teaching assistant, female forklift truck driver.

Success in this increased the girl's confidence and she could soon be assessed against other units.

- A candidate wanting to be assessed for commercial harvesting was told by the assessor where he worked that he would have to wait until June to harvest the strawberries. This was because candidates had always been assessed harvesting strawberries. When it was pointed out that it was just as possible to assess the candidate harvesting another type of crop, the assessor realized that the candidate could be assessed almost straight away – harvesting winter broccoli!

Stage 2: reviewing performance and knowledge evidence

In assessing an NVQ unit, the assessor will determine the evidence of competence by using at least four different assessment methods. In other vocational programmes, a variety of methods of assessment is commonly used. Some methods of assessment are shown in bold below:

- *performance evidence*: by **observation** of the candidate carrying out a task or procedure that occurs naturally in a work situation, or carrying out a practical activity such as taking part in a discussion or performing an experiment in a science laboratory;
- *differing sources of product evidence*: by **examination of products**, such as memos or reports, assignments or photographs produced by the candidate, or of items the candidate has made, such as a cake, a painted wall or a repaired tyre;
- *evidence from prior experience*: by **reviewing and checking statements** from credible witnesses for relevant evidence from past activities and situations in which the witness has seen the candidate carrying out work to the required standards, and by the candidate presenting assessed work from prior activities;
- *evidence elicited through professional discussion*: by having a **planned, recorded discussion** where the candidate is prompted to talk through his or her role and activities, and shows supporting evidence (ideally captured on video) to validate the knowledge and performance claims being made;
- *knowledge evidence*: by **questioning or testing** the candidate to confirm that he or she understands the principles underlying his or her actions or plans, the consequences of acting in certain ways, and what he or she might do in different circumstances.

Evidence can be:

- *direct* – it reflects their own work, ie candidates either perform it or produce it themselves;
- *indirect* – other people or other sources provide the information about the candidate's work, ie a third party confirms that the candidate is competent in a particular area. This 'third party' can be a person such as an employer or a customer who produces a statement about the candidate, or it can be a qualification that the candidate has achieved.

Once the evidence is reviewed, the assessor needs to decide whether it proves that the candidate has met the required elements and performance criteria, and the scope and/or range of the unit or assignment. When making these judgements, the assessor needs to take a number of different things into

Table 3.3   Terms used in competence-based assessment judgements

The candidate is: Competent	Not (yet) competent
The evidence is:	
Valid	Not valid
Reliable	Not reliable
Sufficient	Not sufficient
Authentic	Not authentic
Current	Not current
Safe	Unsafe

account. The terms used in Table 3.3 are the most common – and the most important – terms involved in assessment judgements. All these conditions need to be met by the evidence provided.

Let us look more closely at each of these terms in turn.

Validity

- *The assessment process and the evidence required should be appropriate to what is being assessed.*

It would not be valid to assess whether a cook could bake a cake by asking him or her to draw a picture of one. Nor would it be valid to assess whether a gardener could plant bulbs by watching him or her sow seeds. Valid assessment implies that the method or methods used are the ones most likely to give an accurate picture of that individual's competence within a particular area.

Old-fashioned methods of assessing a student's ability in a foreign language often lacked validity. It is amazing to think that a person's ability to communicate in French was tested by completing a series of written grammatical exercises rather than by whether they could actually speak and be understood!

Validity has a particular significance in NVQs because what is being assessed is the evidence presented. If the evidence is not valid, ie it is not an appropriate means of demonstrating competence, then the candidate will have to be reassessed using different, or additional and more relevant, evidence. What it is important to grasp is that no evidence is automatically valid or not valid. It is the candidate's interpretation of that evidence and how he or she justifies its relevance that makes it valid.

For example, a photograph of the candidate and another person could be presented as evidence. By itself that photograph has no meaning. However, if the candidate says 'This is a photograph that appeared in my firm's newsletter showing me receiving a prize for apprentice of the year', the photograph takes on a meaning and becomes valid evidence (as long as the candidate can prove that the statement is true). This is why explanatory statements related to any documentary evidence presented are important, as they can give the reasons why the candidate believes a particular piece of evidence to be valid.

Another possibility for invalidity would be if a candidate provided witness statements from colleagues who were also candidates for the same NVQ award. If these colleagues were very experienced in the area, but had just never converted that experience into a qualification, their evidence might well be valid. If, however, they did not really have the depth of knowledge or experience to warrant acting as a witness, the validity of the evidence could be questioned.

Reliability and fairness

- *The judgement confirms that the candidate's performance will be of a consistent standard in a range of different contexts.*
- *The same assessor would make the same judgement about the candidate on a number of different occasions.*
- *Other assessors would make the same judgement about the candidate.*

Another way that subjective judgements can cloud the objectivity of an assessment is in the 'halo and horns' effect, where a candidate is considered 'good' or 'poor' by the assessor and all evidence is judged on that basis, as opposed to being judged on its own merit. Probably the most effective safeguard that can operate here is the assessor's own awareness of where he or she might be biased or have personal preferences, plus a strict adherence to the requirements of the elements being assessed. Reliability and fairness are closely linked. Candidates must have confidence that they will be treated fairly by assessors, that they are not going to have a harsher assessment from one assessor than from another, and that other candidates are not going to be assessed more leniently than themselves. Candidates are entitled to feel confident that they will be treated fairly when working towards their qualification. This means that the assessment process should be free from bias or discrimination. Candidates need to be sure that they will not be discriminated against because of some personal prejudice of the assessor. Most of us would probably agree that many people interpret guidelines differently or consider some aspects of work more important than others. These can all affect our judgements and make them different from candidate to candidate, and different from those of someone else doing the same assessment; hence measures that ensure consistency are essential if we are to be fair to the candidate. Consistency in assessment is also essential for employers or educational institutions, which will be asked to accept that a qualification gives a clear and accurate picture of how someone can perform in employment or in preparation for a higher education programme. These bodies will need to rely on the quality and consistency of the judgements being made.

Sufficiency

- *The evidence is enough to prove competence.*

In our experience, *insufficient evidence* does not usually mean too little evidence but *too little evidence of a relevant kind*. This can result from a 'shopping trolley' approach to the assessment, where all sorts of documentary items are collected in the vague hope that they will provide something of substance. If being assessed is to be meaningful for candidates, an essential part of the process is the thought required in discussing their own performance, in assessing their own strengths and areas for development and in working out what they need to do, make or explain to demonstrate competence appropriately. Without this disciplined identification and selection, candidates will remain unaware of what it is that they do or know that enables them to perform a particular work role. Here are some examples of evidence that is not sufficient:

- a letter (as a witness statement) from an employer that does not refer to the specific competences performed by the candidate;
- a document without any explanation as to its relevance;
- a practical activity with no questioning to show that the candidate has the underpinning knowledge;
- evidence of competent performance on just one occasion or within a very limited time span;
- an assignment answer that asks for three examples of an application to the candidate's work practice, but the candidate gives three generalized examples;
- an assignment that needs referencing and evidence of a range of sources, but the candidate has not referenced accurately and has referred to just two standard textbooks.

Authenticity

- *The evidence is genuine and has been produced by the candidate.*

Some vocational assessment methods, such as end-of-term examinations, provide safeguards to prevent cheating by candidates. An independent invigilator watches them while they write their answers, and there are rules about what items of equipment can be present and strict rules of secrecy about what they might be required to answer. Most candidates who have to present written work, such as assignments, are given information about their centre's policy on plagiarism.

Plagiarism is a deliberate attempt by candidates to pass off someone else's work as their own. Unfortunately, the widespread use of the internet has increased opportunities for people who are tempted to cheat in this way. Assessors often can spot plagiarism, as they become familiar with the writing styles and abilities of their candidates, but luckily there are also websites to help that can identify unacknowledged or wrongly attributed passages lifted wholesale from other sources.

The knowledge requirements for NVQ units and for other vocational awards can be assessed by a variety of methods such as externally assessed written tests or assignments or, more usually, by written answers to pre-set questions marked by a centre assessor. In all these cases, the assessor should apply the appropriate safeguards against copying or cheating.

Some awarding bodies such as City and Guilds have developed extensive banks of randomly generated online questions that can be accessed via the internet by candidates at any time or place to suit them. The random nature of the questions helps to deter cheating.

NVQs and many vocational qualifications are practically based, so sound assessment is crucial. Inaccurately assessing a candidate as competent say in construction or motor vehicle repair could have potentially fatal consequences. *Independent assessment* has been introduced for many NVQs as a double check on the assessment process. An experienced assessor, independent of the candidate, who may never meet him or her, assesses some of the candidate's evidence. Some awarding bodies stipulate exactly what the independent assessor will assess; others request that 'a significant part' of the candidate's work is independently assessed.

Determining whether performance evidence is genuine will obviously be reasonably straightforward if the assessor is observing the candidate actually doing something at work. However, the assessor has to be sure that any end product presented by the candidate as 'one I made earlier' really has been produced by that candidate. Assessors will also have to decide whether witness statements are genuine, and will need to look at original certificates where candidates are claiming that they have prior qualifications. Documents included by candidates may not be their own work. This may be innocent, in that candidates may not have realized that they need to show their understanding and application of policy, rather than including a copy of a company document. Assessors do need to be on the lookout for documentation that purports to come from a candidate but has differences in spelling, sentence structure and/or grammar from other documentation that you know is the candidate's own work.

Currency

- *The evidence can prove that the candidate is up to date on current methods and equipment required in the appropriate occupational area.*

Some examples of where this issue could occur are the following:

- A candidate for NVQ in Business Administration worked in an office 10 years ago. Would this provide evidence that the candidate could work in an office now?
- A candidate for NVQ in Learning and Development has a teaching qualification obtained in 1992. Would this provide evidence that the candidate could work in a training environment now?
- A candidate for an NVQ in Aircraft Maintenance Engineering has been off work for two years because of an accident. Would the candidate still be up to date with the skills and technology required?

There are no hard-and-fast rules here. Obviously every occupational area is different, and some change far more quickly than others. However, as a general rule, areas that deal primarily with people can use evidence that dates back over a greater number of years than occupational areas where rapid changes in technology are likely to make skills obsolete – even those acquired only a few years before.

Safety

There are two possible meanings here. The first, and the intended meaning, is in the sense of:

- *The assessor can safely say that the candidate is competent or has met the criteria.*

In other words, the assessor considers, after considering all the evidence, that the candidate's practice is sound. Assessors must ensure that their judgements are 'safe' by ensuring that the candidate can maintain the standard consistently over time.

The second interpretation is to do with health and safety. Although this is not the intended meaning of 'safe assessment', it is true that:

- *The activities carried out by candidates must be done in accordance with the Health and Safety at Work Act.*

Under the HASAW Act 1974, employees have a responsibility to report unsafe practice or equipment, and to conform to the workplace health and safety policy. The only time an assessor or internal verifier should interfere with an assessment is if health and safety are compromised in any way. The assessment should be stopped and appropriate action taken with the relevant people.

Stage 3: recording assessment decisions and giving feedback

The majority of assessments contain some subjective judgement, particularly when assessment is of more complex skills or knowledge. There are times when a subjective judgement is appropriate, for example when a candidate asks for a personal opinion of a particular idea, process or product. However, in general, so that assessment is fair, reliable and to national standards, it is important that safeguards are in place to make summative assessments as objective as possible. This can be a problem when working to performance criteria where language such as 'relevant' and 'appropriate' is sometimes used. This may lead to subjective interpretations that reflect the personal bias of the assessor and hence are neither fair to the candidate nor a reliable indicator of a 'national' standard. One major safeguard is for the assessor to check out his or her own interpretation of such woolly terms with other assessors and internal and external verifiers. Some consensus might then arise to curb any subjective excesses. Standardization events should be held on a regular basis by internal verifiers so that assessors can check their interpretations of the standards, and of their candidates' achievement of standards, against the judgements of others using the same materials as a baseline.

Again, standardization events will help assessors become aware of biased judgements, and internal verifier sampling will also help to identify any judgements made without a good basis in fact.

Unfair discrimination

Assessors of qualifications must meet good equal opportunities practice, based on equal access to assessment irrespective of age, gender, religion, ethnic group, disability or geographical location. In our experience, there is still a lack of awareness regarding the circumstances in which discrimination can occur. Knowledge about equal opportunities issues, the policies of their own organizations and the legislation that exists can help those involved in assessment to become more aware of what they need to address. One of the most powerful means of preventing unfair discrimination is by an open-minded examination of one's own beliefs and prejudices and how they may affect one's judgement. The subject of equal opportunities is far too extensive to be covered here in any detail; however, here are some examples of how discrimination might affect judgement:

- an assessor being prejudiced against someone because he or she thinks the person is too young to have the required skills, rather than objectively viewing the evidence;
- an assessor in child care being particularly hard on a male candidate because the assessor does not think that this is 'man's work' so wants to discourage him;
- an assessor undervaluing the practical skills demonstrated by a candidate whose first language is Urdu, because the candidate's command of English is not perfect;
- an assessor being over-generous in his or her assessment of a candidate who is a wheelchair user.

Some of these may strike a chord in the reader. If not, dig deeper. The majority of us have at least one significant prejudice that could affect our ability to assess fairly!

NVQs more than other vocational qualifications have been accused of being a mechanical system of collecting pieces of paper, ticking boxes and recording results and, like any system, they can be treated in a minimalist fashion. However, if the stages of the assessment process are covered sensitively and with integrity, NVQs can provide a good developmental experience for candidates. One stage that is fundamental in any development process is the feedback stage, where candidates are given specific information about what they have achieved or not achieved. Candidates are also given the opportunity to discuss this fully with the assessor. An important word in this context is 'discuss'. This implies a two-way process of identifying strengths and areas for improvement, with the assessor using a considerable amount of skill in involving the candidate in analysing what, if anything, needs to be improved before the next assessment.

The skill of giving constructive and helpful feedback is at the heart of successful assessment. If this skill is used, candidates will not just be clear on what they have achieved, but they will be clear on what they need to do to develop or maintain performance. They will also be motivated by the feedback to try to improve on their performance. Some examples of situations where feedback could be given (and received) are: an assessor giving feedback to a candidate who has just had a workplace observation; an APL adviser discussing a candidate's first attempt at a portfolio of evidence; or an assessor receiving feedback from his or her internal verifier. In every case, badly delivered feedback can destroy confidence and trust. This is particularly

Table 3.4 Points to consider when giving feedback

1. Let the candidate have the first say	Give candidates the chance to say why they think they have been given their particular result. If they are competent, build on their understanding. If they haven't achieved competence it is possible they will know why and this will help them to 'own' the feedback they receive.
2. Give praise before criticism	Most people will find it difficult to try to improve if they feel they are failures. By focusing first on their strengths and then helping them to recognize their weaker areas, you can give candidates enough confidence to deal with anything that needs to be improved.
3. Limit what you cover	Don't try to cover everything. Focus on two or three key areas for development.
4. Be specific, not vague	Try to avoid general comments that don't help candidates to identify the issue. It's not very useful to say to someone 'Your writing isn't very good.' It is much more useful to say 'It was difficult to read what you had written, because your writing is rather small and you crowded all your information together without leaving any spaces between the different sections.'
5. Concentrate on things that can be changed	For feedback to be useful it must allow for the possibility of improvement. If there are intrinsic or extrinsic factors that you know cannot be changed, the feedback relating to this is a waste of time. It is far more useful to concentrate on what can be changed.
6. Give the candidate time to think and respond	Successful feedback involves a 'dialogue' between two individuals committed to improvement. If you have given the candidate a new perspective on some aspect of competence it could take some time for him or her to absorb it. Only when the candidate has absorbed it and then responded can the planning for improvements take place.
7. Keep to the standards	As assessor/adviser you must distinguish between when the candidate has done something differently from how you would do it but has still met the standards and when he or she has not performed to the required level of competence. You might draw the candidate's attention to this difference but be clear as to whether it is acceptable in relation to the standards or not.

8. Make sure the candidate understands	Think of the language you are using and ensure it is the right level and tone.
9. Listen to how the feedback is received	Be aware of how candidates are reacting to your feedback. Look for non-verbal cues that they are confused or that they don't agree.
10. End on a positive note	End the feedback session agreeing some positive action that can be taken to address any areas for development that have been identified. End with some encouragement as well!

important if the candidate has not been able to demonstrate competence or achievement and might be tempted to give up and not try again. It is crucial to be sensitive to how the other person is responding to what is being said.

Recording decisions

The results of any assessment, formative or summative, must be written down so that:

- there is a clear record of what the candidate has already achieved;
- the assessment plan is kept updated, showing what else if anything needs to be done prior to final assessment;
- records can be accessed by internal verifiers at any point during the candidate's progress for quality assurance purposes;
- there is proof that the assessment process is meeting requirements agreed between the centre and the awarding body, and that follow the national standards for assessment and verification.

There is more in Chapter 12 on how assessment decisions should be recorded.

Stage 4: contributing to quality assurance processes

Verification or moderation is the quality assurance process associated with NVQs and vocational qualifications. It is carried out within and between centres by internal verifiers and moderators. Awarding bodies appoint external moderators or verifiers to quality-assure their qualifications. In higher education, external examiners perform a quality assurance role for some vocational qualifications. As stated in the Preface, in this book we will use the terms 'verifier' and 'verification' to cover all these quality assurance processes.

Internal verification is at the heart of good quality assurance practice, as internal verifiers can ensure through their monitoring and support of assessors and their assessment decisions that there is fairness, and therefore trust, in the process. This trust in the way in which decisions are being made should lead to assessors taking the lead in being able to confirm the competence of a candidate without requiring either that the candidate provide unnecessary documentary evidence or that candidates are made to wait for assessment decisions 'until the external verifier has seen your work'. The observation of practice, or the observation of documents and processes and systems *in situ*, should encourage the development of diverse and naturally occurring relevant evidence from candidates, with the minimum of documentation. It is the assessor's job to clearly record what he or she has seen and where, and what performance criteria, standards, range and so on have been met on that occasion. We believe that it is the *assessor's records* that are a crucial part of the quality assurance process. The candidate portfolios may need to be seen as part of an audit trail, but checking assessor activity in making judgements is a prime function of quality assurance.

Assessors will contribute to the internal verification process by recording and submitting data (such as dates of assessment, achievement records for candidates, and assessment plans and feedback records). They will also be required to participate in standardization of assessment exercises and be observed doing workplace observations and professional discussions.

Likewise, the internal verifiers will have to provide information to the external verifiers, who will check that they are sampling assessment practice properly and that the centre is conforming to the NVQ Code of Practice or any other relevant policies.

Most organizations will also have their own quality assurance processes, which may require the identification of yet more data, such as enrolments data, and the recording of the destinations of candidates once they have completed their NVQs.

Quality assurance is a vital part of any national qualifications system. All national assessment systems need to ensure that everyone involved in the assessment of candidates is assessing correctly and working to agreed procedures and to an agreed standard of performance. This cannot just be left on trust to individual assessors but needs to be part of a strict monitoring framework that covers not only the individual assessor but also all the assessment within an organization and, finally, all the assessment nationally. QCA is the organization that ultimately guards candidates' interests and the integrity of qualifications.

SUMMARY

This chapter should have helped you with the following:

- key stages in the NVQ and vocational assessment process;
- key terms in the assessment process;
- planning assessment and identifying evidence;
- reviewing performance and knowledge evidence;
- terms involved in making assessment judgements;
- recording assessment decisions and giving feedback;
- unfair discrimination;
- contributing to quality assurance processes.

4

The People: Key Roles in the NVQ and Vocational Assessment Process

This chapter looks at the roles carried out by those involved in assessment and verification, their responsibilities and the requirements they need to meet in order to assess or verify the qualifications. Any system is only as good as the people who take part in it, and the quality of skills and the knowledge of those involved are key factors in making systems credible and worthwhile.

ASSESSMENT SYSTEMS

Most assessment systems have a number of common aspects, as shown in Table 4.1.

These are followed by those who play key roles within the process of assessment. They specify what areas of knowledge and skill are to be assessed, identify the circumstances in which assessment should take place, decide the parameters for achievement or non-achievement and follow procedures for carrying out and documenting the assessment and reporting the outcomes.

Table 4.1 Components of an assessment system

WHAT?	Skills/knowledge/understanding to be assessed.
WHO?	Candidate/assessor/internal verifier/witness/independent assessor/external verifier.
WHEN?	Appropriate place(s), time(s) and opportunity (opportunities) for assessment.
HOW?	Criteria for achievement/non-achievement (in some systems pass/fail).
	Procedures for informing the candidate of requirements.
	Procedures for assessment.
	Procedures for informing the candidate of the results of assessment.
	Procedures for documenting the results of assessment.
	Procedures for monitoring the assessment is accurate.
	Procedures for reporting outcomes.

KEY ROLES IN ASSESSMENT AND QUALITY ASSURANCE

There are a number of participants within the NVQ and vocational qualification system. These are:

- *The candidate* being assessed for a qualification. The candidate must be in a role that enables him or her to achieve the learning outcomes or criteria required. The candidate needs to take responsibility for his or her registration, improving skill gaps identified at initial assessment, and ensuring that he or she plans and carries out the work as agreed with his or her assessor.
- *The primary assessor (A1)*, who identifies clearly, with a candidate, what needs to be assessed and the assessment requirements, determines the most appropriate range of methods to use in assessment and then negotiates assessment opportunities with the candidate and others who may be involved. For many competence-based programmes, this is likely to be on a one-to-one basis. In many vocational courses, this discussion and negotiation may take place early on in the programme and with the whole group. After reviewing and judging a range of evidence, the primary assessor ensures that the results of assessments are properly fed back to, and recorded for, the candidate. Primary assessors sign off complete units and/or individual assignments for candidates. They ensure that all materials and methods used follow good equal opportunities and health and safety practices. They also contribute to, and participate in,

the organizations' quality assurance systems. Within the NVQ system, primary assessors might be working towards their A1 award themselves, in which case a qualified assessor must countersign all of their decisions. It is quite common for the primary assessor of a candidate also to be the same person who instructs, trains or teaches the candidate.

- *The independent assessor (A1),* who is able to give a second dimension to quality assurance at the assessment stage. *Independent assessment is not the same as 'double marking' or standardization, where two assessors assess the same piece of work. The independent assessment is the only one for the prescribed piece of work.* It has been introduced in some cases to replace previous external testing, where work was sent away to be marked by external assessors. The independent assessor does not necessarily meet the candidate (though many do), but does assess an agreed substantial part of the candidate's work, often a complete unit or a complete assignment. Quality assurance will pick out whether this assessment is at variance with assessments made by the primary assessor and whether there needs to be some further investigation of marking. Not all vocational qualifications or NVQs require an independent assessor. The assessment strategy prescribed by ENTO for Learning and Development NVQs and mini-awards (see Appendix 3) does require independent assessment. In some cases, the 'agreed substantial part' is predetermined by the awarding body. Within the NVQ system, the independent assessor must be a fully qualified assessor, in both the occupational area (eg Manufacturing, Learning and Development) and assessment (ie A1).

- *The observational assessor (A2),* who is solely involved with workplace observation and questioning. This is a narrower role than A1, in that the assessor uses just a couple of assessment methods and may never sign off complete units for candidates. A common example is that of a specialist colleague who carries out one or more of the required teaching practices for a candidate on a teaching qualification, but who is otherwise not involved with the candidate's training or assessment. In the NVQ system, observational assessors can be working towards their A2 awards themselves, in which case a qualified assessor must countersign all of their decisions.

- *The internal verifier (V1),* who ensures that the assessment roles are being carried out correctly within the organization and who manages internal quality assurance for the qualifications. This is done by drawing up sampling plans and internally verifying that the judgements made by assessors are correct and to the national standards. Internal verifiers will also monitor and support assessors, liaise with a number of stakeholders such as the awarding body via the external verifier, and produce reports on the assessment and verification practice for which they are responsible. They may undertake the administrative tasks required (see below) if there are no dedicated administrative staff. The importance of internal verification is reflected in the fact that those undertaking it are expected to be working at level 4, in other words holding managerial rather than supervisory status.

- *The internal moderator (OCN Internal Moderator Award)*, who carries out a role similar to that of the internal verifier but in a non-NVQ context. The role covers both verification and standardization.
- *The external verifier (V2)*, who monitors the internal verification and assessment procedures for and between centres. The awarding body for the qualification appoints occupationally competent external verifiers to centres. External verifiers sample a range of judgements made by verifiers and assessors, recording their findings and distributing them to the centre, the awarding body and the lead verifiers. Lead verifiers monitor the performance of external verifiers both qualitatively and quantitatively, as do the awarding body's administrators, who receive copies of, and analyse, their centre's reports.
- *The external moderator (OCN External Moderator Award)*, who carries out a role similar to that of the external verifier but in a non-NVQ context. The role covers both verification and standardization.
- *Centre administrative staff*, who deal with the processing of registrations and certification for the award. They are likely to be involved in the production and distribution of materials related to the awards. They are sometimes the contact people between the centre and the awarding body, and may, on behalf of the internal verifier/moderator(s), keep the awarding body updated regarding centre changes and ensure that relevant staff receive updates from awarding bodies.
- *The inspectorate*, who spot-check the quality of provision in schools, colleges and adult and work-based training and publish their findings.

ROLES AND RESPONSIBILITIES OF PARTICIPANTS IN THE PROCESS

The candidate role

In traditional programmes candidates have often been people whom assessment is 'done to' without the candidates' previous experience being taken into account and without the opportunity for them to be involved in the process. So, in the past, an examination question for telephone engineers on a day-release course might have been along the lines of 'Write an essay of between 600 and 800 words on the history of the telephone.' In a situation such as this, the activities and products required of the candidate were not dependent on who they were or what they had done; everyone, irrespective of background or experience, had to answer the same questions. Nor was the evidence the most valid means of showing that they were capable of doing the job of telephone engineer. However, over the past 40 years, much has been done by many awarding bodies to introduce methods of assessment that are more closely related to real-life work requirements and also to place more responsibility on candidates to reflect on their performance and identify areas for improvement.

The role that candidates take is one of active involvement in their own assessment, recognizing their responsibilities in working with their teachers, mentors and assessors so that their progress is continuous and they achieve their assessments, whether observed or written, at the agreed times. This starts at the planning stage, where candidates are encouraged by the teacher/assessor to identify current skills and past experience and to negotiate the evidence for competence and knowledge and the methods for their assessment. Most candidates will need advice and sometimes a substantial amount of guidance and support, often from an adviser or mentor. Candidates who are familiar with the procedures and evidence required for each unit could, after the initial assessment planning and agreement of unit assessment plans, proceed without any further input or advice from another source, other than liaising with their assessor(s) for the necessary observations and assessments.

The (primary) assessor role (A1)

The assessor is expected to make judgements by using the relevant assessment criteria to decide whether each candidate has met the prescribed standards or criteria. Assessors record the results and feed back to candidates, both orally and in writing. The types of evidence that assessors may judge could include, among others:

- the candidate's oral or written answers to questions;
- observation of the candidate's practice;
- products from the candidate, such as a log book or an item he or she has made, an endorsed video or photographic evidence;
- a report from the candidate or from the candidate's peers;
- judgements from others, including work-based assessors and witnesses;
- evidence from the candidate's prior experience;
- simulation in a narrow range of instances (but *none* in the assessor and verifier awards).

In general vocational education, and sometimes in work-based training, the following sources of evidence are also commonly used, often in addition to many of those listed above:

- reflective journals;
- essays;
- project work.

The need for this range of evidence is based on the idea that competence often entails more complex skills, particularly at the higher levels. The majority of jobs involve a range of situations that need different skills and abilities. In more complex jobs many different competences are required, not all of which can be assessed through direct observation of performance. Take, for example, a situation where a manager in a local government office is working towards a management NVQ. It would be both expensive and time-consuming to observe the manager undertaking all aspects of the manager's role as determined by the standards. Even if much observation was undertaken, not all aspects of that role might actually be observed in day-to-day activities. However, the primary assessor could use other sources of evidence to ensure that this manager was competent, including testimonies from line managers and colleagues, examples of written communications such as memos and letters, minutes of meetings chaired by the candidate, and talking to work colleagues. This variety of sources of evidence will give a more rounded picture of the candidate's knowledge, ability and skills and enable a sound judgement to be made.

The primary assessor needs to be able to assess all these different sources of evidence with rigour, using the performance criteria as the determining factor for competence.

The observational assessor role (A2)

The observational assessor makes judgements about candidates' workplace competence, and gives feedback to candidates in a way that helps their practice to develop. The most straightforward way of finding out if someone is competent in a particular area of work is to watch him or her actually doing it. A hairdresser might write essays about hair styling, produce testimonials from satisfied clients and previous employers and display photographs of hairstyles he or she has created. This will all be valuable evidence, allowing the assessor to infer that the candidate has knowledge, understanding and certain skill levels. However, the surest way of establishing whether the candidate can perform with competence is for an occupationally qualified assessor to observe him or her in a hairdressing salon, styling and cutting people's hair. The other way an assessor might assess directly is by looking at something the candidate has produced, for example a cupboard made by a joiner or a website produced by a media candidate. The assessor will then, through questioning and discussion, find out how well the candidate understands the consequences and context of that activity.

Table 4.2   Examples of performance evidence

Someone using a piece of equipment	Forester using a chainsaw
	Hairdresser using a hairdryer
Someone performing a service	Kitchen assistant following rules
	Care assistant giving a bed bath
	Waiter serving a drink
Someone making a product	Joiner making a cupboard
	Student producing an action plan
Someone showing a particular skill	Candidate working well as part of a team
	Manager negotiating with staff
Someone carrying out procedures	Gas service engineer observing safety procedures

The independent assessor role

Not all NVQs require independent assessment, but this role is mandatory for the assessment of the A&V units. The independent assessor must be fully qualified as an assessor and be familiar with the candidate's vocational area. His or her role is to bring some internal quality control into the internal assessment process. The independent assessor assesses a substantial component of the candidate's work, which may be predetermined by the awarding body. This could be a complete unit within a full NVQ. For the A1/A2 awards, the independent assessor will usually assess one assessment plan for one candidate for a complete unit, with its reviews and explanation. This will be one of the plans that the candidate-assessor has developed and worked through with his or her own candidate. However, the independent assessor could assess any other part of the unit.

Once the independent assessor is allocated a candidate, he or she should take responsibility for liaising with the primary assessor or internal verifier, so that he or she can plan the independent assessment properly. Independent assessment need not take place right at the end of the course. In fact, this is probably a bad idea. This planning may be done at a distance, eg by e-mail or telephone, or the independent assessor may meet with the candidate, though this is much less common.

The internal verifier role

The role of the internal verifier is *to conduct internal quality assurance of the assessment process (V1)*. This role is crucial to the quality assurance of NVQs and of the centres offering them. Its importance is reflected in the fact that those undertaking it are expected to be working at level 4 – in other words, holding managerial rather than supervisory status. Within all but the smallest organizations there will probably be more than one person acting in the internal verifier role. The internal verifier will need to coordinate the activities of the assessors for whom he or she is responsible, including those who may be independent or peripatetic assessors. Internal verifiers may need to manage across a number of related vocational awards areas. The internal verifier is responsible for implementing an internal verification strategy. This must be in compliance with the appropriate assessment strategy for the qualification being taken by candidates. Internal verifiers take responsibility for ensuring that both candidates and assessors show evidence of consistent occupational competence and that assessments and quality assurance conform to national standards. In addition, they must ensure that the centre keeps to relevant codes of practice, such as the revised NVQ Code of Conduct, the JAB Guidance and other documents produced by QCA. It is the internal verifier's role to see that this happens by ensuring that:

- there is regular contact with the awarding body;
- assessors have sufficient occupational competence and have records of recent occupational and assessment updating;
- assessors are given all the necessary help and information they need to be able to assess effectively and efficiently;
- the quality of assessments is monitored and standardized on a regular basis;
- the internal verifier is available to answer queries if assessors experience difficulties.

Large centres will have an *internal verifier coordinator*, who allocates the workloads of all the internal verifiers and is the point of contact with the awarding body and the organization's quality manager. An internal verifier coordinator will usually act as the team leader for the internal verifiers, ensuring that information and procedures are fully consistent within the internal verification team.

It is important to remember that, when awarding bodies give grades to centres, the grade can never be higher than that awarded to the internal verification process. Even if assessment practice, resources and support for candidates are outstanding or satisfactory, but internal verification practice falls short of awarding body requirements, the overall grade given to the centre will show that the centre is not complying adequately with awarding body requirements. However, if a centre consistently performs well at internal verification, then the awarding body may implement a lighter-touch verification process, such as through remote sampling.

Table 4.3 Examples of poor and improved allocation of internal verifiers and assessors within a centre

Example 1	Two assessors, A & B, and one internal verifier, C. Good, because the IV is able to standardize and is separate from the assessment process.
Example 2	Three assessors, A, B and C. Assessors B and C are both qualified internal verifiers. B internally verifies the work of A and C. C verifies the work of B. Not as good, as B and C could get complacent and are also standardizing with each other. There is no standardization between the results of A, B and C.
Example 3	10 assessors, one IV. Good, because the IV can standardize across the 10 assessors, but problematical if anything happens to the IV. Needs a second IV for security and support with decision making.
Example 4	Eight assessors, all qualified as IVs, who work in pairs, verifying each other's assessments. Poor: too many variables of assessment practice and too little independence. Better to select a couple to run the IV, leaving the rest to assess, and build in regular standardization events between the assessors and the IVs. The role of IVC could rotate each year.

The internal moderator role

Internal moderators perform a similar role to internal verifiers, but in a non-NVQ context.

The external verifier role (V2)

Monitoring of quality and consistency at a national level is done through a network of external verifiers appointed through awarding bodies. External verifiers are experienced senior practitioners in the broad area of the standards they verify. Their role is to approve centres that wish to offer qualifications, approve the schemes that approved centres wish to implement, and be assured of the quality of assessment and internal verification procedures – in other words, that they are being carried out to the national standards both for assessment and verification and for the vocational area. *The vocational area for those assessing A&V units is Learning and Development.* As the external verifier is the main link between the centre and the awarding body, he or she should also be the person who can give answers to queries from centres, for example on the acceptability of certain evidence or on the interpretation of certain performance criteria. This means that external verifiers must keep themselves updated with the frequent changes in systems, structures and practice, so that they can respond accurately and swiftly to centre queries as well as make accurate decisions. Usually, external verifiers are line-managed by their awarding body administrative managers and are supported by their regional lead verifier for their occupational area.

The external moderator role

External moderators perform a similar role to internal verifiers, but in a non-NVQ context.

Different combinations of roles

Within the roles identified there are clearly opportunities for different combinations and variations depending on the nature and size of the organization. For example, an assessor may be a work-based observational assessor for one candidate, a primary assessor for a second and an independent assessor for a third. He or she might also be qualified as, or be working towards being, an internal verifier and have his or her own allocation of assessors to support and mentor. One combination of roles that must *never* occur is that of assessor and internal verifier with the *same* candidate. That does not prevent someone from acting as an assessor with one candidate and then as an internal verifier with a candidate who has been assessed by another assessor. Centres need to ensure they have enough staff to avoid compromising quality through internal verifiers having too little time to carry out their role.

Example 1

A candidate working in a large engineering firm is advised and assessed for her NVQ by her immediate supervisor, acting in the role of primary assessor. The supervisor from another section, a qualified A1 assessor, acts as the independent assessor, assessing one of the candidate's NVQ units. The senior manager of the section is the internal verifier, monitoring the process and procedures of the assessment and arranging for external verification.

Example 2

A candidate who is a student on a trainer training certificate programme put on by his local college is given an assignment by his tutor on learning styles and teaching methods. Before the assignment, he has been given an individual interview with his tutor, who has acted in the informal role of adviser, giving him help on how to approach the assignment. This tutor will act as primary assessor, observing the candidate work as a trainer in his organization. The same tutor will also assess the candidate's work diary and the assignment produced and, using the feedback given by the supervisor and other staff working in the organization, make a final assessment judgement. The programme coordinator will take on the role of the internal verifier and will arrange for a significant activity carried out by the candidate to be assessed by an experienced independent assessor. The work will be selected by the candidate in telephone consultation with the independent assessor and will be sent to the independent assessor in the internal mail.

Example 3

A candidate with considerable management experience, working within a local authority, wishes to claim APL towards an NVQ in Management for what she has achieved in the past. One of the local authority training officers, acting in the role of adviser, discusses with her what evidence would be appropriate. Another training officer acts in the assessor's role and makes an assessment judgement on the evidence. The line manager from another section, who has achieved D34 and has demonstrated to the external verifier that he has upgraded his skills to V1, acts as internal verifier.

Example 4

A candidate is trained by her line manager in assessment practices. The organization is small and has joined with two other small organizations to form a consortium, which has registered as an approved centre. Her primary (A1) and independent assessors are from the other two organizations within the consortium, as is the internal assessor. The primary assessor does one work-based observation, but her line manager acts as the observational assessor for all other work-based assessments. This arrangement allows these small centres to run their own awards in a cost-effective and efficient way, without compromising quality or integrity. The activities of all these four staff are managed by a fifth, who takes on the role of internal verifier coordinator.

SKILLS WITH PEOPLE

Candidates have a variety of different needs, and the centre's assessment systems and staff need to be flexible enough to take account of these. The fairness and reliability of assessment judgements can be affected by not taking into account the characteristics of the candidate and the situation in which he or she is working. Let us look at four different candidates and briefly identify considerations in the approach to the assessment of the individual candidates.

NVQ level 1 – Amenity Horticulture

The candidate has learning difficulties and a tendency to get worked up under pressure. However, he has shown a real aptitude for gardening and could hold down a regular job. The assessor should try to be friendly and natural, making as little of the assessment process as possible in order to give the candidate the best chance of demonstrating his ability.

NVQ level 2 – Sport and Recreation

The candidate is 17 years old and working towards this qualification at college. The primary assessor will probably be a college lecturer and might also be using the assessment to monitor the student's general progress and response to the programme. In this situation, the assessor would probably liaise with assessors based in the candidate's workplace to compare judgements on progress in order that the feedback to the student could be as informed as possible.

NVQ level 3 – Registered Care Manager Award

The candidate has worked for a number of years in voluntary service, where she held a position of some responsibility. She then began work in a hospice, where she is dealing with patients sympathetically and effectively. The assessor would need to be aware of the sensitivity of the situation and might consider it appropriate to take the lead from the candidate about how to carry out the assessment. In particular, the feelings of the patients would need to be a major consideration. Witness statements from qualified staff who work closely with the candidate and understand the demands of the NVQ could form a large part of the evidence along with carefully-planned professional discussion.

NVQ level 5 – Learning and Development

The candidate is a senior manager in a local authority. At this level the assessor would expect that the candidate should be well used to pressure and responsibility. The main consideration would be to help the candidate to utilize all opportunities for work-based assessment, ensure that the assessments do not take more of the candidate's time than is strictly necessary, and use APL and recorded professional development as a way of cutting down paperwork for the candidate.

Anyone assessing or advising will be dealing with a variety of different candidates, all with their own characteristics and particular needs. These candidates should not just have assessment 'done' to them but should be encouraged to take an active part in the assessment process. Some candidates may find this easy and, after the initial briefing or induction, will get the idea of what is required and be quite happy to take a proactive role. Many candidates will not find it so easy and may view their required involvement with suspicion and perhaps trepidation. The adviser or assessor may find this a tricky situation and may be tempted to take one of two extreme approaches. One approach might be to abdicate all responsibility and tell the candidate it is up to him or her to manage the assessments. The other approach might be to take on a highly directive role and tell the candidate exactly what he or she thinks the candidate should do. In some cases, the failure of the first approach might lead the adviser or assessor to fall back on the second. The skill for the adviser or assessor is to do neither, but to weigh up the amount of support and guidance appropriate for each candidate at each stage in working towards the qualification.

Some hints on this include the following:

- Ensure the candidate has a clear overview of the whole qualification and of each unit.
- With inexperienced candidates, help them to make choices by the use of structured alternatives, eg 'Would you prefer… or…?'
- Always give candidates the opportunity to make suggestions.
- Avoid immediately rejecting suggestions made by candidates.
- Explore disagreements rather than impose your own point of view.
- Be clear yourself on what you can negotiate and what you cannot.
- Make it clear to candidates what can or cannot be negotiated.
- If candidates refuse to accept your advice, consider this carefully.
- If you are blocking candidates' right to choose, think again.
- If, by not taking your advice, candidates will not produce appropriate work or evidence to meet assessment requirements, make this clear.
- Avoid giving too much responsibility too soon, as this can inhibit some candidates by making them feel overwhelmed.

- Note down on the assessment plan everything that has been agreed and discussed. If there are activities the candidate needs to do that are pre-assessment (eg training or research), these can go on to an action plan.

OCCUPATIONAL COMPETENCE AND CONTINUING PROFESSIONAL DEVELOPMENT

Using the standards for development

As important as consistency in assessment and quality assurance practice is the need to maintain a developmental rather than a mechanistic approach to competence and qualification. In other words, there is scope for occupational standards to be used in holistic, questioning and creative ways rather than in prescriptive, narrow and fragmented ways of assessing competence outcomes. This often needs addressing by the organizations using standards as much as by individuals. When, in 1992, the Training and Development Lead Body first published the standards for assessors and verifiers, the potential benefits of an imaginative approach to their use were given in the executive summary. These were:

- as a basis for job descriptions;
- to identify training needs;
- to develop training programmes;
- as benchmarks for development;
- as a basis for assessment.

The summary also stated the expectation that the National Standards for Training and Development would 'enable employers to design, promote and support the kinds of personal and professional development cultures they needed to create and sustain amongst their workforces' by:

- providing basic requirement specifications that could be used in the purchase of training services;
- indicating the kinds of criteria that should be used to evaluate the progress and outcomes of training programmes;
- acting as an operational guide to the design, development and delivery of training programmes;
- underpinning the introduction and use of innovative, non-traditional training methods, systems and materials;
- incorporating best practice in human resource development planning and strategy design approaches;
- providing ways of reaping the obvious benefits of workplace assessment to specific standards by qualified assessors and verifiers.

The Learning and Development standards (2002) assist this process in extending the range of mini-awards and linking them into some nationally identified areas for development, such as the management of basic skills in the workplace. The Professional Standards for Teachers, Tutors and Trainers in the Lifelong Learning Sector (2007) will provide units that already qualified staff can use for updating purposes.

One of the biggest problems faced by individual candidates and by organizations that are supporting their staff to acquire relevant qualifications is that of discovering either that job roles are narrower than the standards require or that practices and procedures do not tally with the standards' requirements. The discovery of 'gaps' can lead to resentment towards a competence-based approach to outcomes measurement and create problems with trust and motivation. This can be a particular problem where there are difficulties in agreeing on the interpretation of standards, where staff feel threatened (eg does lack of demonstrated competence equal *in*competence?) and where tried-and-tested procedures are being changed to accommodate the new approaches. Sensitive and informed advice from managers, assessors and advisers can help candidates or qualified staff to select appropriate standards, units and/or full qualifications that will be achievable and useful. Discussion related to implementation of standards can in itself be a powerful tool for staff development, as current job roles, programme content and assessment techniques are compared with those that would be required. It is not uncommon to find that a complete programme of staff development takes place, sometimes deriving from the discovery that assessment practices across departments differ significantly. Standards can also be used successfully to give a fair framework to traditional, process-based programmes.

All currently qualified teachers, assessors and internal and external verifiers have a first-hand opportunity to use the relevant standards for updating. They can show how their practice has moved to incorporate the new requirements. The Learning and Development standards and the new Professional Standards also give the opportunity for practitioners to develop both their vocational (Learning and Development) background and specialist subjects through reviewing their current skills and knowledge, and perhaps take new qualifications themselves as a result.

Continuing professional development (CPD)

Assessors are now expected to show both that they are competent in their vocational area or specialist subject, such as Financial Services or Travel and Tourism, and that they have occupational competence in Learning and Development or from the Professional Standards. This occupational competence needs regular analysis against the requirements of the industry. Practitioners need to show how they are monitoring their competence and how they plan to maintain the currency of their skill and knowledge.

Each NTO or standards-setting body has within its assessment strategy clear requirements for the professional updating of its participating assessors and quality assurance staff. Assessors and internal verifiers of NVQs can also update by utilizing the information provided on the ENTO website.

Example 1

For assessors and verifiers of A&V awards, this is currently a minimum of two updating activities per year. These should be planned and clearly auditable. Examples might be attending training sessions on new qualifications, participating in regional standardization exercises, joining in (auditable) sustained online discussions about aspects of internal verification or assessment, or producing and delivering induction programmes for assessors or internal verifiers.

Example 2

From September 2007, teachers, tutors and trainers from the lifelong learning sector need to undertake 30 hours of updating per year. Examples might include acting as external moderator, writing online materials for their curriculum area or any of the examples given above.

Most awarding bodies and professional organizations run regular updating events for their centres.

SUMMARY

This chapter should have helped you with the following:

- the NVQ assessment system;
- understanding the roles of candidates, assessors, verifiers and administrative staff;
- people skills;
- continuing professional development;
- using the standards for organizational and personal development.

5

Assessment: Procedures, Knowledge and Skills Needed to Perform the Roles

All those involved in assessment and quality assurance need a high level of skill in order to do their jobs competently and effectively. These skills are not purely mechanical: they involve the ability to analyse, to choose appropriately, to transfer across different contexts, to be sensitive to individual needs and to absorb and communicate substantial amounts of information. The ability to carry out such activities can only occur in conjunction with the knowledge and understanding of different methods and practices involved in assessment, of different strategies for working with people and of some awareness of the ethical context in which anyone in a potentially powerful role should operate. Some professionals, such as training managers or lecturers, carry out a whole range of tasks, whilst others specialize, eg in assessing or mentoring. This chapter explains different types and methods of assessment, including consideration of some of the more 'people-based' skills that are needed for assessment and verification.

TYPES OF ASSESSMENT

Criterion-referenced assessment

NVQs are criterion-referenced systems of assessment – that is, the candidate is assessed against a set of pre-established criteria. These criteria represent a consensus of opinion over what forms the basis of an 'acceptable' standard. In a sense, all occupational areas are already based on criterion-referenced systems. For example, if a car were having its brakes mended, the owner would want to feel confident that the mechanic was working to an acceptable set of standards within the motor industry. Similarly, a patient being looked after by a nurse would want to feel that the nurse was performing duties to a standard required by any hospital in the country. The creation of sets of national standards for different occupational areas is a reflection of what has traditionally occurred in practice, although there is always professional controversy over whether the criteria identified in the standards are the right ones.

In assessments made against criteria, there are only two possible outcomes for a candidate. The candidate can be judged either competent against the criteria or not yet competent against the criteria. For example, in vehicle body repair, a candidate fitting replacement body panels either *does* or *does not* position the replacement components according to the vehicle manufacturer's specifications. In the first case he or she *is* competent against that criterion, and in the second case he or she *is not* yet competent against that criterion. However, there are obviously many situations where the judgement of competence is more problematic, particularly where the language appears to allow for subjective judgement, and we will be covering these later in this chapter. In criterion-referenced assessment, there is no limit to the numbers of candidates who can be judged competent, as long as they meet the full requirements of the standards.

Norm-referenced assessment

Traditional academic programmes are based on norm-referenced systems where the achievement of the candidate is judged in comparison to the achievement of other candidates. Hence in programmes such as A levels and GCSEs, candidates who get an A grade are judged to be better than candidates who have obtained a C grade. Norm-referenced systems have their basis in the idea that a few will do well, most will do averagely and some will do poorly. That means there is an expectation that a few people will get A grades, a large number of people will get C grades and some will get E or even F grades (see Figure 5.1). If one year it turned out that an unusually large proportion of candidates obtained A grades, the system would be studied closely and revised. Either the examinations would be made more difficult or the examiners making the assessments would be told to assess more strictly. Hence there is no real notion of 'fixed' standards. Every year, when the A level and GCSE results are published and the numbers passing the examination increase, there is a debate about whether standards are falling. It could be that improved teaching methods and revision support enable

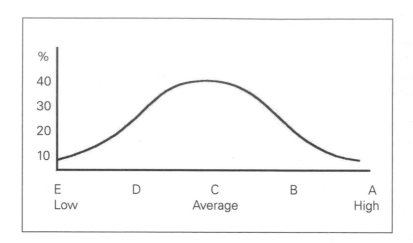

Figure 5.1 Performance distribution curve

more candidates to do better (not forgetting the effectiveness of the AS/A2 system at identifying those who are counselled out of A2 due to the risk of underachievement). However, only a certain number are *expected* to get top grades. More candidates achieving well can skew some dependent processes, for example making it more difficult to get into particular universities because there are more students with good grades available than there are places.

To clarify a major problem in the norm-referenced system, let us consider our previous example of the patient being looked after by the nurse. It would be no consolation to the patient that the nurse was the best in the country if the general standards of nursing care nationally were inadequate and the nurse was merely the best out of a very poorly skilled profession. The problem, then, with norm referencing is that comparisons only suggest that someone is better or worse in a particular group and do not suggest what the minimum standard for performance or achievement actually is.

However, it is true that many employers and higher education establishments do place an emphasis on the achievement of high grades and that norm referencing does provide a means of distinguishing between individual employees or students. The proposed reform of A levels will incorporate additional optional questions to stretch the brightest students and give employers and universities additional guidance when selecting for places.

Formative assessment

Every time candidates receive a judgement on their performance that will cause them to alter certain aspects of it, they are receiving formative assessment, ie assessment that 'forms' their development towards a certain desired goal, just as a metalworker 'forms' a hot piece of metal towards a certain desired shape. This type of assessment takes place on a continuous basis – sometimes formally, but very often informally. Formative assessment that is carried out helpfully and sympathetically can play a large part in motivating candidates, particularly those unsure of their own abilities. The recording of formative assessment outcomes by the assessor will lead to a gradual build-up of positively assessed competencies and/or knowledge and understanding, which will give candidates clear guidance as to what aspects of performance they still need to work on.

Case studies in formative assessment

1. A candidate working in a restaurant is constantly receiving feedback on his performance by the head waiter. From the simple reminder 'You've forgotten the table napkins' to a full debriefing on how the candidate served at table on a busy Saturday night, the head waiter is providing feedback that will shape the candidate's future performance to the desired goal of being the perfect waiter. If the candidate is working towards an NVQ, this formative assessment will also give him an indication of when he will be ready for a formal end assessment.

2. A candidate studying for her L4 Certificate in Teaching and Training in the Lifelong Learning Sector receives feedback on her reflective journal, which she writes up on a weekly basis along with reflections on her teaching sessions. This feedback, given six weeks into the course but before the candidate has done any formal assignments or been assessed in the workplace, enables her to prepare better for the future assessments by alerting her to the fact that she must improve her written English and the writing of session objectives and develop the range of methods she is using with her own learners.

3. A candidate working towards an NVQ in Learning and Development is receiving formative assessments from a number of different people. These are her supervisor, who sits in on some of her training sessions, other trainers in her area of work with whom she discusses various aspects of work on a regular basis, and the clients she is training, who are asked to evaluate each session they attend. These are in addition to the more formal formative assessment that the candidate has received from her assessor, who has made a diagnostic observation visit to one of the candidate's sessions.

4. A candidate for the NVQ in Cleaning and Support Services has regular tutorial times with his assessor following workplace observation and the completion of written tasks. The assessor uses progress review forms to identify how the candidate is doing, how well and what he has achieved, and where and how he needs to improve. This is a formal method of providing formative assessment. As the candidate achieves different

Table 5.1 Formative and summative assessment

	Characteristics	Purpose
Formative assessment	Ongoing continuous feedback for improvement	To diagnose and plan
Summative assessment	Final summing up of achievements at a particular point in time	To describe and accredit

areas of his units, the various performance criteria, scope and knowledge are marked off on his assessment record.

5. A mature candidate in Information Technology, attending an open-learning workshop, is very nervous about the idea of 'being assessed'. She is given regular constructive formative feedback on her progress, with a chance to discuss how she can improve. The candidate is given encouragement to decide when she feels ready for a formal assessment.

Summative assessment

Summative assessment represents a formal summing up of the candidate's achievement on completion of a particular piece of work. In the case of many vocational qualifications, including NVQs or mini-awards, this will be at the completion of each unit. An assessor will make a final judgement on the whole of a unit after making a series of formative assessments. The results of this assessment will be recorded to stand as a statement of the candidate's competence at the time of the summative assessment.

Academic qualifications usually have a series of assignments and/or projects. Summative assessment will occur on the completion of each of these pieces of work. However, the final summative assessment will not be able to be given until all parts of the qualification have been achieved.

Other examples of summative assessment include:

- end-of-year/end-of-course examinations;
- end-of-unit tests for craft certificates;
- the final grade given to completed projects or assignments.

METHODS OF ASSESSMENT

There are a number of assessment methods. This next section considers six of these methods in detail: observation, oral and written testing, simulation, professional discussion and the assessment of prior competence. These are the methods commonly used in NVQs and work-based vocational qualifications, but these methods are also used within other types of qualification.

Observation: assessing practical competence

This is the main method by which competence should be assessed and involves either observation of performance or examination of the end product. Many people in work will have been involved in informal assessment of performance by observing and making judgements about how effectively someone is doing his or her job. Instructors or trainers will be used to watching how an individual trainee learns or behaves, and will make mental notes on areas of strength and areas where the trainee may need help. These observations also need to be recorded in writing, preferably using a checklist derived from the required competencies, with a space for detailing the evidence that has been observed.

The person carrying out an observation may find it useful to follow these key points on the observation process:

- Be clear about what is being assessed and the processes involved.
- Ensure that the candidate has been involved in the planning process and clearly understands what will happen.
- Use a checklist as an aide-mémoire (reminder) if it helps.
- If not familiar with the place of assessment, try to visit it beforehand.
- Try to give the candidate some control over the conditions, eg ask the candidate's opinion on the best place for the assessor to stand or sit and, if feasible, respect his or her wishes.
- Keep out of the eyeline of the person being assessed.
- If the candidate's work involves interacting with clients or colleagues, keep out of their eyeline and workspace.
- Avoid becoming involved in the assessment process.
- When clients are involved, make sure the candidate knows that the needs of the client should take precedence over the needs of the observing assessor (though hopefully, by following occupational standards, both will be accommodated!).
- Make sure that anyone else involved is informed and reassured about the presence of an observer.
- Ensure that, whenever possible, there is time after the observation to give immediate feedback and discuss what has been observed.
- Make sure that all external visitors to the candidate's workplace (eg assessors, verifiers) comply with the requirements of the organization and with relevant legislation, such as the Health and Safety at Work Act.

Example 1: Observation in the workplace

If we look at the floor plan in Figure 5.2, a number of factors would influence where the observer performing the assessment was positioned.

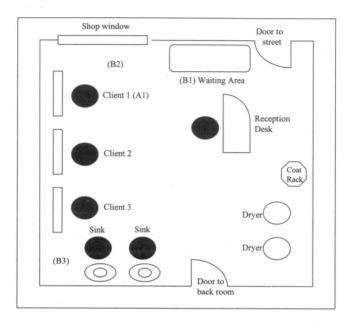

Figure 5.2   Floor plan of a hairdressing salon

If the assessor worked in the salon, both clients and staff would be used to his or her presence and hence the assessor might choose to stand right next to the candidate when he or she was working with the client (A1). If the assessor came from outside the salon, his or her presence would be more noticeable and this would have to be taken into account. If the observation was assessing general client care and service, then the assessor could sit on a seat in the waiting area (B1) and arrange that the candidate always worked in the position nearest to the shop window, ie the position with client number 1. The assessor could then move to have a final look at the finished 'product' once the client's hair had been styled. However, if the observer were assessing competence in perming hair, then close observation of techniques and procedures used would be essential.

In this case, the assessor would need to be next to the candidate and, in that situation, would obviously need to decide where he or she could stand (B2 and B3) to cause the minimum disruption. There, it would probably be a good idea to ensure that the candidate was not working in the client number

2 position. This would be because the assessor would have to stand in the small space between two sets of clients. Possibly position B2 might be the least intrusive for both the candidate and the client. Bear in mind that the assessor can ask questions during an observation, as long as he or she does not distract the candidate at crucial times.

Example 2: Observation of a group working

An assessor for NVQs in Learning and Development or Management might have to conduct an observation of someone conducting a meeting, giving a presentation or running a training session.

The danger here is that the assessor will find him- or herself physically in the middle of the group, and this is bound to affect the 'normality' of the situation.

Apart from the general points already mentioned, it could be useful to:

- arrive before the group meets and place a chair at the back of the room outside the area where the rest will be sitting;
- apart from greeting people briefly and pleasantly if appropriate, minimize conversation with members of the client group, as otherwise the dynamics of the group may be altered;
- avoid too much eye contact;
- use a method of recording the observation that is as unobtrusive as possible – rustling papers can prove disruptive in a quiet environment where people are concentrating on what is being discussed, and the use of video recorders can unnerve those who are not used to them.

In certain circumstances, it may be inappropriate or impossible for the assessor to be present when a candidate is performing a task or carrying out a procedure. In such cases, witness statements, audiotape or videotape (*if accompanied by an explanation and matched to the requisite criteria*) may be used as admissible evidence.

Questioning: assessing knowledge and understanding

The use of questions, either oral or written, is the main method for establishing whether the candidate has knowledge and understanding across a range of contexts and contingencies. This is vital, as, without knowing what exactly he or she is doing, why and what the possible alternatives are, there is little possibility that an individual will be able to transfer any skill from one situation to another. Instead of the desired highly skilled and flexible workforce, we might end up with a nation of robots.

There are limits to what an observation can tell the assessor about how much someone actually understands about what he or she is doing. An observation is at a particular time and place, in a particular environment, under a particular set of circumstances. For example, the assessor could observe someone using a computer. The observation may not enable him or her to tell whether that person could cope if a fault appeared in the program or if he or she were working on a different type of computer, or if he or she were working in a busy environment with a lot of time pressure. Well-constructed and relevant questioning can find out this information from the candidate.

We can often infer a good deal about what people know by what they do or what they produce. For example, if we observe someone involved in child care instructing small children to wash their hands before eating, we can infer that the child care assistant knows at least one basic rule of hygiene. Similarly, if we are shown a completed press article produced by a journalist, we might infer that he or she knows how to structure information and spell words correctly. However, we must be very careful in inferring just how much someone knows from what we see that person do. In the first example, the child care assistant could just be copying what he has seen others do, without any knowledge of the reason why he is doing it, in which case he probably has no concept of the 'idea' of hygiene and hence would not be able to transfer this rule across to another situation. In the case of the journalist, we may be satisfied that she has produced the article herself, but has she used a dictionary to help her spell? Has she used a standard format to structure her article? In both examples, the key to assessing whether someone really knows something needs to be taken from the level of qualification. At lower levels, the definition of knowledge could just involve 'has information about', and the understanding required could be very limited. At higher levels, the definition of knowledge should include a deeper understanding of the knowledge aspects related to the element plus a broader ability to transfer and make connections between ideas and practice.

It is obviously important to choose questioning methods appropriate to the activity being tested. The next sections will consider the different types of oral questions and written tests that can be used.

Open and closed questions

Broadly speaking, questions can be divided into the categories of 'open' and 'closed' types, which have distinctive features and functions. Open questions associated with prompt words such as 'How?' and 'Why?' offer the opportunity for candidates to respond fully and in their own words. Closed questions are associated with phrases such as 'Do you think...?', where the candidate can only respond with 'Yes' or 'No', and with prompt words such as 'What?' and 'Where?', when the candidate is required to respond with specific factual information.

Choosing the right type of question

Assessors need to be clear on why they are asking the question and what answer or answers will be acceptable. At levels 1 or 2, it is likely that questions will be simple and closed because specific factual knowledge is being tested. For example, at NVQ level 2 in Construction, a candidate might be asked to give five examples of construction work that would need to be protected against the weather while other work was being finished. The assessor will know the range of acceptable answers and will accept any five of these answers from the candidate. Some more open questions may also be appropriate, for example asking the candidate why he or she is using a particular process or piece of equipment. It is likely that the answers to these questions will be fairly short and simple.

Table 5.2 Different functions of questions

Function	Example
Set at ease	'Would you like a coffee?'
	'What sort of journey have you had?'
Ask for general information	'What were your responsibilities as…?'
	'What have you been doing in the past year?'
Ask for specific information	'What is your name?'
	'How do you save data on a disk?'
	'Precisely what does that entail?'
Ask for further information	'Could you tell me some more about that?'
	'Can you give me some more details?'
Identify agreement or disagreement	'Do you think he acted correctly?'
	'Did you agree with the way she dealt with that situation?'
Ask the reason or justification	'Can you tell me why you used that particular technique?'
	'Why is ice put in the glass before pouring the drink?'
Ask for opinions, ideas	'What do you think of this product?'
	'Do you believe in positive discrimination?'

At level 5, the question-and-answer process will inevitably become far more complex. For example, a strategic manager (the candidate in this case) may need to show that he or she has an effective management style. The candidate's underpinning knowledge of why he or she has adopted a particular style over others could be assessed by a variety of techniques. These could include questioning and discussion between the assessor, the candidate and the candidate's colleagues, and demonstration by the candidate that his or her chosen style results in positive outcomes from the candidate's staff and the achievement of corporate objectives. This would be far more useful and valid than asking the candidate to write a report or assignment on 'Comparing and contrasting different management styles, with special reference to the work situation.'

Oral questioning

In most work contexts the testing of knowledge and understanding in NVQs will normally be oral rather than written. For example, a supervisor will ask an employee why the employee has increased the speed of a manufacturing process, how the employee intends to use the new floor polisher in a safe manner, or what the ratio of sand and cement is to water for a particular mix of concrete. Every occupation has its underpinning knowledge and understanding requirements, which are used as a basis for assessment. In order to carry out an oral assessment, assessors need a thorough knowledge of the standards, so that they are able to ask appropriate questions. The A&V awards each have their own set of questions that candidates can use for self-assessment.

An assessor could ask questions at appropriate times during an observation or set aside a separate time after the observation to ask *all* the necessary questions together. Alternatively, the assessor may choose to question knowledge and understanding across the range or scope of the element once all performance evidence has been assessed. The assessor and candidate through discussion should make these decisions. The knowledge evidence needs to be judged in the light of all the other evidence the assessor has gained about the candidate's competence.

Questioning skills

- *Putting the candidate at ease.* It goes without saying that candidates are likely to be nervous, and the assessor needs to be sensitive to this. The more confident candidates feel, the more likely it is that they will be able to give a true representation of what they really know. It usually helps if candidates actually know what the procedure will be, know that they can ask for a question to be repeated and know that they can take their time answering.
- *Ensuring the language is at the right level and can be understood.* Be clear as to what is being tested and avoid using over-complex language if this is not necessary. Be aware of what candidates' normal range of vocabulary

is likely to be and take that into account when phrasing questions. Distinguish between essential technical jargon that candidates will need in their vocational area and inessential use of over-sophisticated vocabulary.

- *Not asking leading questions.* Assessors should be careful not to use questions that could lead candidates by giving them a clue to the right answer. Assessors should also be aware of any preferences or opinions they might hold that could affect the way they ask questions. It is just as easy to lead candidates by the tone or inflection of voice or by some facial expression or body movement. One assessor we know would automatically purse her lips and lean forward slightly if the answer she was getting was incorrect. However difficult it may be, a neutral but pleasant expression is the ideal!

Examples of leading questions are:

- 'Your client seemed a bit uncomfortable, didn't she?'
- 'Don't you think you should have cleaned the floor before the wood-work?'
- 'Why would you say uPVC was better than wood?'

Written testing

There are a number of different types of written testing used within vocational qualifications, and the choice of the appropriate test format depends entirely on what level and complexity of knowledge and understanding need to be demonstrated. The main ones are:

- *Yes/No or True/False response.* A statement is followed by either a Yes/No or True/False response to be ticked or circled.
  Example: A larch tree is an evergreen.   True/False
- *Objective tests (multiple choice).* A question is asked followed by several alternatives, out of which one must be selected.
  Example: A chronological filing system is one where files are arranged according to:
  (a) geographical area
  (b) initial letter of surname
  (c) date received
  (d) reference number
- *Gapped statements.* A statement or longer piece of text is given, with a space or spaces left for the candidate to complete.

Example: Foods that are high in fibre include… and…
NB: Sometimes the candidate is free to write any appropriate word and sometimes the word or words can be selected from a given list.

- *Short answer tests.* These give a series of questions that require answers of a few words or a few lines.
  Example: Explain briefly how a colour correction filter works.
- *Essays.* These cover set topics, usually with a defined number of words, often involving research through reading and including the structuring and development of ideas.
- *Example:* Discuss how different learning theories can be used in planning training programmes.
- *Reports.* These cover a set subject with clearly defined objectives based on practical research and laid out with headings, following a conventional report structure.
  Example: Write a report on the procedures for employee appraisal within your organization, with recommendations for improvement.
- *Assignments/projects.* These cover set topics, usually entailing some practical research and written explanation and analysis of what has been discovered.
  Example: Choose one specific client group in the community, eg young mothers, pensioners, etc. Find out what services are provided for them and their opinion of these services. Compare local to national provision. Present your information using both written and visual means.

Difficulties in assessing knowledge and understanding

All of the methods we have set out can test knowledge from a simple to a sophisticated level. However, it is evident that those requiring more complex responses will be far more useful in establishing whether the candidate actually understands and can apply the knowledge he or she is demonstrating.

The more complex the activity the greater possibility there is of showing competence against a number of different elements and the more opportunity there is for demonstration of other skills. The assignment given in the example above would also enable candidates to demonstrate a variety of key skills, including *communication*, *working with others* and *problem solving*. If it involved analysis of data, candidates could also cover *application of number*, and if the results were produced using a computer then *information technology* would also be covered. However, there are a number of difficulties in the assessment of knowledge and understanding:

- In workplace assessment, the assessor primarily has to make a decision on how much knowledge and understanding can be inferred from what a candidate is doing or what he or she has produced. Sometimes this is straightforward, particularly if the assessor is in regular contact with the candidate and has observed the candidate a number of times covering a range of situations and contexts. However, sometimes this could be misleading, for example assuming that a trainer being assessed 'knows' about different learning theories because he or she has used a number of different teaching methods.

- The more complex methods of testing knowledge such as essays also pose difficulties for the assessor. The material produced by the candidate is more individualized and there is far more in the way of information and ideas to disentangle; hence the demands on the assessor to have very clear ideas of what will or will not be acceptable and what is or is not relevant are far greater. Such assessments have obvious advantages, in that candidates have a full opportunity to express themselves if appropriate. However, the potential for subjective and unfair assessments can be considerable. It is important that the assessor has a clear marking scheme *prior* to the assessment being distributed to candidates, and that both assessor and candidates know the marking criteria (spelling, whether references are required, level, number of expected examples, etc). This helps the assessor to mark objectively and the candidates to meet the criteria.
- There is sometimes a problem in being sure about the depth of knowledge to be demonstrated, and it can be difficult to gauge this from reading the standards. There is no easy answer here, and guidance should be obtained by consulting with external and internal verifiers and ensuring consistency of understanding and practice between assessors through standardization and moderation exercises. However, it is possible to form some idea of the depth of knowledge required by referring to the description of the level of qualification. For example, NVQ level 1 refers to 'routine and predictable work activities', whereas level 5 refers to a 'significant range of fundamental principles across a wide and often unpredictable range of contexts'.
- The limitations of testing knowledge in relation to specific elements rather than covering larger, interrelated areas are also seen as problematic by some assessors. This can be an issue if knowledge at all levels is treated in an over-simplistic way. However, it is important to remember here that a substantial piece of evidence could provide proof of knowledge and understanding across a whole group of elements. It is up to those advising and assessing to help candidates to realize this holistic approach where appropriate. Assessors' reports should identify all the relevant criteria covered by such pieces of evidence. Candidates should not be disadvantaged by assessors who ask the *candidate* to do the cross-referencing for them.

Many vocational qualifications, including some NVQs, contain externally marked assignments where the candidates answer a set question in a specific timescale in particular circumstances. There is a variety of ways in which this is done. Often, candidates are given the topic in advance, so they can research and prepare for a given number of days. The assessment may then be done at the centre in supervised conditions, perhaps with the use of the notes candidates have made. Centre-marked assignments are another option. The purpose of this type of assessment is to encourage candidates to be able to show their knowledge, rather than trying to catch them out.

Setting tests and devising marking criteria for projects and assignments

This book cannot go into the depth required on this broad subject, but readers are referred to the texts in the 'Further reading' section (in 'Supporting Materials'). The crucial factors are that test questions need to be designed so candidates cannot guess the answers and that assessors need to share with candidates the basis on which they will be marking assignments *prior* to issuing the project and assignment briefs.

Simulation

The amount and nature of simulation for individual qualifications will be stipulated in the syllabus supplied by the awarding body and will have been laid down by each NTO or SSC. Simulation is a method that enables a very limited set of circumstances to be demonstrated. These are usually connected with particular areas, such as dealing with a fire or a spill of hazardous chemicals, that might never arise in normal work practice but where the candidate must know how to respond. From 2007, it has been decided that some work placements regularly used for NVQ assessment, such as catering kitchens and restaurants within FE colleges, provide only limited workplace experience. At the time of writing this is being disputed by some organizations, for example FE colleges whose kitchens provide for 60 covers twice a day and that hold a centre of excellence rating for their training and premises may feel their premises are no different from, and may be superior to, many high street restaurant environments.

Professional discussion

This method gives the candidate an opportunity to talk through, demonstrate, show and clarify aspects of his or her work that still need evidencing and/ or for which other types of assessment are less appropriate. The assessor should plan carefully for professional discussion following the assessment of substantial evidence towards an element or unit so that it is clear to the assessor what 'gaps' still need to be addressed by the candidate. The formative assessment and subsequent plan need to be agreed with the candidate, who can then prepare properly. Professional discussion should ideally be workplace based and candidate led. This also gives opportunities for the offering and protection of confidentiality and security and the demonstration of complex competencies, knowledge and understanding. The professional discussion must be recorded in some way. An audio recording is unobtrusive and gives proof of the discussion without interfering with the activities of either candidate or assessor. The assessor can take photographic evidence to augment the recorded conversations. There is no necessity to transcribe the conversation. If the camera can record date and time, this is often a more acceptable form of recording 'live' evidence than is video, and sits well alongside an indexed audiotape. A video recording can be used where it would cause no disruption to normal work activity and where the candidate feels it would aid his or her demonstration of competence. The third method of recording, taking down the discussion verbatim, is the most difficult to do, as the assessor is less able to give full attention to the candidate, and the discussion can become stilted owing to the need to write everything down exactly as it is spoken.

Assessment of prior competence and experience

Candidates who have a good grasp of the standards and have been working to them for some time will, particularly at NVQ level 3 and above, benefit from using evidence from prior achievements. They can identify recent and relevant evidence within their workplace and ask for witness statements to back this up. The professional discussion can be used to explore the candidates' background and how this affects their current practice. There will still need to be at least one assessment of current competence by the assessor.

SUMMARY

This chapter should have helped you with the following:

- the terminology used in assessment;
- different types of assessment;
- different methods of assessment;
- skills in observation and questioning;
- problems in assessing knowledge and understanding.

Part 3

The Requirements of the Standards

Section 1

The Learning and Development Standards for Assessment and Verification

Introduction: Using the Step-by-Step Guides to Workplace Assessment and Internal Verification

Section 1 explains the requirements of the performance criteria in A1, A2 and V1. This section is for anyone interested in understanding the good-practice requirements for the assessment of work-based competence, whether via an NVQ or via other competence-based programmes. Assessors and verifiers qualified to D32/33 and D34 will need to familiarize themselves with the requirements of the new standards and demonstrate that they are operating to the requirements of A1, A2 and V1 as appropriate. Those readers who are familiar with the previous D unit awards will recognize the welcome simplification in the language of the standards that had been hoped for by so many. In fact, it was the complicated language of the former standards that led us to write the first edition of this book in 1994. Since the standards and supporting materials published by ENTO are now so much more straightforward, the step-by-step guides in this edition are somewhat different from those in previous editions of this book.

We will refer you to the text elsewhere in the book where necessary and also to relevant materials on ENTO's website. Each awarding body offering the award has developed its own support materials and documentation, usually available at a very small cost, and you will find it helpful to have this material, as well as any additional documentation that is provided by the centre with which you are taking the award.

One of the new pieces of information is the Learning and Development assessment strategy that has been developed by ENTO (see Appendix 3). Each NTO has developed an assessment strategy for its NVQs, and these need to be read in conjunction with the standards for that NVQ. An assessor who was assessing, say, a candidate-assessor for A2 whose candidates were taking NVQs in Engineering, and who was going to cover the work-based assessment as well as the overall unit advice and assessment for A1, would need to meet the requirements of both the Engineering NTO assessment strategy *and* the Learning and Development NTO assessment strategy.

A final point

If you are a candidate-assessor or candidate-verifier, remember that your own primary assessor, workplace assessor, independent assessor and internal verifier should be modelling the competences in the awards. The process you follow with them should be the same as the process they help you to follow with your own candidates or assessors. They should be encouraging you to discuss and ask for clarification on any points that confuse you and be providing you with clear assessment plans that cover each whole unit being taken. *Make sure they do their job!*

THE STANDARDS

The Learning and Development awards are made up of sets of related standards grouped into units. A unit is a definable task or number of related tasks. The task is subdivided into sub-tasks or elements. Each element comprises a number of performance criteria, which specify what is required for competent performance. The scope of the unit is defined, ie the range of circumstances in which it could be carried out, as well as the underpinning knowledge that every candidate should have in order to perform the tasks with understanding. A1, A2 and V1 each consists of a single unit with four elements. Low-unit-number qualifications are known as mini-awards. Most full NVQs have around 10 units. The A1 and A2 awards are part of the NVQ in Learning and Development at level 3. The V1 award is part of the NVQ in Learning and Development at level 4.

A1 and A2

A1 and A2 now include aspects of the former D36 ('Advise and support candidates to identify prior achievement') within them.

Assessors of full units need to take A1, which is the broader of the two awards. It covers the common assessment processes of:

- planning unit assessment, to include a range of methods, with candidates;
- assessing a range of evidence sources covering competent performance, knowledge and understanding;
- giving feedback and recording results;
- providing records that contribute to the quality assurance system.

A1 has developed from the previous D33, in that planning has an increased focus, and there is an explicit link into the standardization and quality assurance processes of the centre. The requirements to have three assessment plans with reviews for *complete* NVQ units for a minimum of two different candidates, three assessments and two assessment records also reflect a desire that candidate-assessors show evidence of supporting candidates over a sustained period of time. The range of methods for assessment that candidate-assessors need to show competence in using has also been increased to cover a minimum of four. The introduction of recorded professional discussion (preferably by video) gives the opportunity for the candidate to offer more evidence orally and for the assessor to be able to check a wider range of the candidate's knowledge. If video or timed and dated photographs are used, there is no necessity to include materials in the portfolio that can be seen on the images. (See Appendix 4 for Evidence Requirements for A1 and A2.)

A2 will be needed by assessors who are involved only in workplace observation and the assessment of knowledge relating to the observed activities.

It should be extremely difficult for candidates who are not bona fide assessors to get the awards, just as it should be impossible for candidates to get the award if their internal verification system is not geared to continuous sampling and standardization, of which they are an integral part.

David Morgan, Director of Marketing and Communications at ENTO, has said:

> Without an effective, robust internal quality assurance process that is underpinned by a clear strategy, assessor-candidates will be unable to achieve the new A1 unit, as this unit requires the assessor-candidate to contribute to the internal quality process or internal standardisation... Therefore for those organisations whose Internal Verification practice is that of end loading portfolios of evidence then their assessor-candidates will not be able to achieve their award.
>
> (*Learning Network for Assessors and Verifiers Newsletter*, issue 2, Spring/Summer 2002)

V1

V1 is now an award at level 4. The internal verifier (IV) is therefore deemed to be operating in a 'managerial' or coordinating role, liaising with internal and external quality assurance staff. There is a greater emphasis on the analysis and evaluation of the findings from verification activities.

IVs who are currently qualified to D34 must provide updating evidence that they themselves understand and meet the new criteria for IVs at level 4. This updating means that IVs need to be fully familiar not only with D32/33 but also with A1 and A2. They themselves need to be operating at A1 in order to carry out V1.2 satisfactorily.

IVs now need to demonstrate explicit monitoring of observation of assessors, and checking of the decisions of assessors across candidates over time. The IV role has always been the key to a centre's quality, and the new V1 awards enhance this.

Table I3.1   Roles and qualifications and experience needed by A1 assessors

A1 assessors who assess only their vocational subject can do any of the following:	A1 assessors who assess A1/2 and/ or V1 in addition to, or as part of, their vocational subject can do any of the following:
– train others in the background to the assessment of their particular vocational award, eg horticulture, care, retail, construction; – assess competence in the workplace related to their specific vocational area; – assess knowledge related to workplace competence related to their specific vocational area; – assess evidence from a variety of other sources, including simulation, professional discussion, evidence from prior achievements or experience; – act as independent assessors.	– train others in the background to the assessment of their particular vocational award, eg horticulture, care, retail, construction, learning and development; – induct others to the requirements of the new assessor awards; – assess competence in the workplace for their own vocational area plus the A&V awards; – assess knowledge related to workplace competence for their own vocational competence and for the A&V awards; – assess evidence from a variety of other sources, including simulation, professional discussion, evidence from prior achievements or experience; – act as independent assessors.

A1 assessors assessing only their subject and *no* A&V awards need:	A1 assessors assessing their vocational subject *plus* the A&V awards need:
– a vocational qualification in their subject area at level 3 *or* experience in their subject area that gives them competence at level 3; – A1; – to meet the assessment strategy requirements of their subject-related NTO.	– a vocational qualification in their subject area at least at level 3 *or* experience in their subject area that gives them competence at level 3; – a vocational qualification in the area of Learning and Development at least at level 3 *or* experience in the Learning and Development area that gives them competence at least at level 3, eg NVQ 3 in Learning and Development, Cert Ed, PGCE, C&G 7306/7 or equivalent; – A1/A2/V1 according to job role; – to meet the assessment strategy requirements of their subject-related NTO; – to meet the assessment strategy requirements of the ENTO.

6

Guide to Unit A1: Assess Candidates Using a Range of Methods

The standards in this unit are followed by those who:

- assess candidates against agreed standards of competence using a range of assessment methods;
- give candidates feedback on their assessment decisions; and
- contribute to the internal quality assurance process of the centre.

This covers all primary assessors and independent assessors, whatever their vocational competence. It is crucial that assessors for A1, A2 and V1 are exemplary in their practice of the standards, as candidate-assessors and candidate-verifiers are likely to use them as role models.

A1 assessors do not necessarily assess performance themselves, as they may use the judgements of others (eg A2 assessors or witnesses). They will, however, assess the whole of the evidence provided by candidates for complete units.

Giving candidates an overview of how they can demonstrate competence and knowledge for a clear set of tasks, as defined in an NVQ unit, helps them to progress clearly and swiftly to achievement.

A1 has four elements:

- A1.1: Develop plans for assessing competence with candidates.

- A1.2: Judge evidence against criteria to make assessment decisions.
- A1.3: Provide feedback and support to candidates on assessment decisions.
- A1.4: Contribute to the internal quality assurance process.

Candidates should have received any necessary induction and training they need in order to complete the unit *prior to planning for the assessment*. If this does not happen, candidates and assessors may find that the process becomes confused and unnecessarily prolonged. It is unfair to start the assessment planning process before candidates are ready to demonstrate competence and knowledge.

Assessors should check that candidates are registered with their awarding body prior to starting assessment. Submissions for certification of NVQs and mini-awards cannot be made within 10 weeks of registration.

A1.1: DEVELOP PLANS FOR ASSESSING COMPETENCE WITH CANDIDATES

(a) Develop and agree an assessment plan with candidates

The assessment process starts with planning between the assessor and the candidate. Each unit needs its own assessment plan. The plan needs to cover the whole unit. This process will be documented and include arrangements for reviewing and updating the plan as circumstances change. The process needs to be agreed, so negotiation may need to take place. Dated signatures of both assessor and candidate are taken as confirmation of agreement.

A good starting point is getting candidates to talk through what they do at present in relation to the unit in question. This should suggest the types of evidence that are most suitable for demonstrating competence, and the methods for assessment. The assessment plan documentation should allow all the details for the assessment for the whole unit to be noted.

The assessment plan should give a clear indication of *what* will be assessed, *how* it will be assessed and *when* it will be assessed. There will need to be reference to others, such as witnesses, workplace and independent assessors and the internal verifiers, who will all need to be involved. The candidate(s) will need to have an input into the plan (particularly in thinking through the other people who will be involved in the assessment), be able to ask any questions and be able to offer any appropriate suggestions or amendments. The assessment plan should indicate what competences or criteria are being assessed and clearly identify the appropriate methods that the assessor will use to make his or her decisions regarding the candidates' competence. It should indicate when and how feedback will be given, what records will be made of achievement, and how and when the plan will be reviewed.

It should be clear to the candidates how they will know when they have achieved competence for the whole unit and how this will be recorded.

(b) Check that all candidates understand the assessment process involved, the support available to them and the complaints and appeals procedure

Your candidates' understanding of the planning process can be checked through the asking of open questions, such as 'So how do you think...?' and 'What will happen next...?' Ask them to identify the support they think is available. Support might include their assessor, a learning centre, work colleagues, awarding body literature and websites. Make sure that candidates have a copy of the complaints and appeals process that will have been agreed by the external verifier with the centre. Question your candidates to check their understanding and their knowledge of how and when it might be used (though, of course, the fact that assessors will follow best practice after using this book and following all available advice should render this unlikely!). Keep notes of the discussion so you can each have a copy of them at the end of the session.

(c) Agree fair, safe, valid and reliable assessment methods

Assessors should plan to use at least four methods of assessment with candidates to assess their competence and underpinning knowledge. These methods can include assessing the prior experience of the candidate, questioning, professional discussion, workplace observation by a qualified assessor, the use of witness statements, simulations in an agreed limited range of contexts for some NVQs (but no simulation is allowed for A1, A2 or V1 candidates), projects and assignments. Chapter 5 gives additional information that should help you to meet these criteria.

(d) Identify appropriate and cost-effective opportunities for assessing performance

Direct observation of performance can take a considerable amount of time and be costly in terms of the assessor's time and the candidates' costs, but several elements of a unit or of several units could be covered in one well-planned observation visit. Opportunities for assessment of competence will generally occur during candidates' normal work time. You, the assessor, need to check with the candidates that time(s) and place(s) arranged for the assessment are as natural and efficient for all parties as possible. Candidates should be involved in identifying these opportunities and selecting those that will be the most convenient and offer the possibility of covering a number of elements.

The cost of assessment materials will also play a part in efficiency of assessment; it is cheaper to work with farmed salmon than cod these days! Assessor and candidate need to decide whether assessment of non-performance evidence and the professional discussion is likely to be more cost-effective if done at the candidate's workplace, close to his or her documentary evidence and possible witnesses, or at the primary assessor's premises. It is important to estimate in advance the time that each assessment is likely to take and the breadth of criteria that will be assessed, so that neither party is disadvantaged by cost or by an unplanned lengthy or, just as bad, too short visit.

(e) Plan for using different types of evidence

See Chapter 3 for a fuller explanation. The use of as wide a variety of relevant types of evidence as possible will give your candidates the opportunity to show depth of understanding, the complexity of what they do, and a range of ways of working over time with their own vocational candidates.

(f) Identify how the past experiences and achievements of candidates will contribute to the assessment process

When candidates wish to use evidence from accreditation of prior learning (APL), an issue to consider is the recency of their evidence of competence. A candidate producing a computing qualification dating from the late 1970s will not be providing evidence of *current* competence in modern computer technology, whereas a qualification that is only one year old may well be acceptable. Currency of competence is obviously particularly important in areas where technology is in use; however, there may be other areas, eg the care sector, where a qualification obtained a number of years ago may still be judged appropriate and sufficient. You and the candidate need to check via the internal verifier for the NVQ in question to determine whether the awarding body has set time limits on past experience and achievements. Witnesses' statements and testimonials referring to past competence need to identify clearly the criteria the candidate has met. Original certificates for qualifications will need to be produced by the candidate. It could be that the professional discussion could be planned to allow the candidate to explain the evidence from prior assessments, experience or learning. Candidate and assessor need to discuss whether this evidence is likely to give proof of performance competence or of knowledge, and how it is likely to correlate with the required performance criteria and knowledge.

(g) Identify and agree any special arrangements needed to make sure the process is fair

Candidates for assessment should have received all necessary training and practice prior to their assessment. A candidate who normally works on a night shift but is asked by his or her assessor to be assessed during the daytime would not have been given access to fair assessment. The candidate would be in an unfamiliar situation and might experience poor concentration and disorientation owing to being on a different shift. Nor would the assessment give a reliable indication of how that person could perform in normal circumstances. Table 3.2 gives some examples of the difficulties that might be experienced by candidates.

(h) Identify how other people will contribute to assessments and what support they may need

The primary assessor will make the majority of assessments, but he or she may be assisted in this process by a number of others, such as:

- other workplace assessors with whom the assessor may need to co-ordinate;
- credible witnesses, who will need to write statements or talk to the primary assessor;
- an independent assessor, to whom the candidate will need to send agreed evidence;
- internal verifiers, who may request to sample the assessments.

In addition, the following will be or could be involved:

- line managers or supervisors, who may wish to be involved with feedback;
- technical staff, to make sure the appropriate facilities are available;
- quality coordinators or managers, who may need reports;
- candidates' colleagues who may be affected;
- administration staff, for processing registrations and certification requests;
- caretakers and car parking and security staff.

Many of these other people will not need support as such, but will be involved as part of the quality and administration process surrounding assessment.

(i) Identify how to protect confidentiality and agree arrangements to deal with sensitive issues

Candidates need to know what arrangements the assessor will make to keep their work safe. The demands of legislation will need to be followed. Both parties will need to comply with the Data Protection Act and the Mental Health Act regarding the disclosure of information about candidates and decide how to assess necessary documentary evidence that cannot be removed from the workplace, while meeting the requirements of the Copyright Act. Candidate and assessor also need to clarify whether there are any sensitivities surrounding the assessment, such as difficulties with staff, premises or other organizations, that need to be addressed prior to the assessment.

(j) Agree how you will handle any difficulties or disputes during the assessment

Discussion during this planning stage should reduce the likelihood of difficulties or disagreement. It is important that the assessor is clear about what is or is not negotiable, and candidates should be made aware of this. For example, if the awarding body requires a written test, candidates must complete this even though they may be unwilling. The option here is basically 'Do it, because if you don't you can't get the qualification.' However, you would obviously take into account whether a candidate is objecting because he or she needs encouragement or more guidance in order to provide this sort of evidence.

It may be that you cannot resolve the difficulties yourself. You may suggest another assessor to the candidate or suggest that he or she talks to the internal verifier. You may feel that it would help if the candidate talked to other candidates who have been through the process.

If assessments have to be cancelled by either party, there need to be clear lines of communication and guidelines to minimize disruption and to facilitate the earliest possible reassessment opportunity.

The most likely problem will be that the candidate disagrees with the assessor's judgement or that the assessor and candidate cannot find common times to carry out assessments. Both parties need to be clear about the options available, for example whether the use of another assessor is possible. The complaints and appeals procedure is there as a last resort.

(k) Agree when assessment will take place with candidates and the other people involved

It is most helpful to everyone involved for dates and times to be set early for the different assessment activities planned, even though some may need to be rescheduled, eg because of bad weather or illness. Negotiating dates with the candidate gives targets for achievement and should be a motivating experience. Any changes will need to be noted on the assessment plan. If you or your candidate find it difficult to set dates during your planning session, it may be worth considering whether the candidate is at the right stage to begin the assessment process. The candidate may need a longer period of training or may need to involve his or her workplace more fully in the process before proceeding. Failure to set dates usually results in an unsatisfactorily long period before candidates complete their award.

(l) Agree arrangements with candidates for reviewing their progress against the assessment plan

Agreeing arrangements for reviewing progress is best done following feedback sessions from each formative assessment. It could be done face to face, by telephone or via e-mail contact.

(m) Review and update assessment plans to take account of what the candidates have achieved

The review will result in the assessment plan being physically updated, with new dates and actions. If the candidate is not physically present at the review, but has verbally agreed, or responded to e-mail, the assessor will need to send an updated copy of the assessment plan to the candidate as soon as possible. Reviews should always be documented in some way and any revision of assessment plans recorded on them, and be signed and dated by both parties at the time, as evidence of agreement.

A1.2: JUDGE EVIDENCE AGAINST CRITERIA TO MAKE ASSESSMENT DECISIONS

(a) Use the agreed assessment methods to assess competence in appropriate situations

The A1.1 plan will state the assessment methods that the assessor and candidate have agreed will be used unless amendments are negotiated and agreed between the candidate and the assessor. To achieve A1, the candidate-assessor will need to use a minimum of four appropriate assessment methods across three assessment plans. Most assessment methods are easily linked to particular situations – for instance, evidence of performance is best assessed through observation or witness testimony, and evidence of knowledge and understanding through questioning, testing or professional discussion.

(b) Use the past experiences and achievements of candidates as part of the assessment of their current competence

Planning will have helped candidates to identify what evidence from their past achievements and experiences is relevant to the assessment of their competence. It is wasteful for candidates to repeat activities or qualifications that they have assimilated into their everyday practice. Their skills and knowledge should become apparent as the foundation of their current practice. If in doubt, the most straightforward way of checking current achievement is to ask candidates to carry out the relevant process or activity. For instance, assessors could ask to see candidates carry out a number of different functions using a modern computer or ask them to explain how their background affects their current practice. Letters of validation or witness testimonies carefully linked to the standards might be sufficient to confirm some of the competences claimed, though assessors should always check the authenticity of witnesses.

(c) Ensure that the evidence comes from the candidate's own work

Where assessment is based on documentary evidence or made products, you will need to ask questions so that you can be assured that the candidate concerned has been the originator of the evidence. Few candidates deliberately cheat. However, misunderstandings can result in candidates including written documents produced by their organizations or their trainers rather than themselves.

Professional discussion allows the assessor the opportunity to check a range of queries he or she might have after assessing the different strands of evidence. The assessor, having made a judgement and given feedback, can prepare the candidate for the discussion by identifying the areas where he or she feels more explanation or evidence is needed. The candidate-assessor can then share his or her ideas, knowledge, understanding and practice with the assessor, through discussion, which would ideally be held at the candidate's workplace and led by the candidate. The discussion could include backing up what is said by reference to documents, products or other persons in the workplace.

(d) Make safe, fair, valid and reliable decisions about the competence of candidates only on the agreed standard

Safety, fairness, validity and reliability are explored in Chapter 3. Once the assessor is presented with evidence, eg an observation report, a witness statement, a set of written answers or evidence of prior achievement, this must be assessed using the agreed methods against the standards. Studies have shown that, in general, the degree of error made by NVQ assessors is about the same as that made by assessors of public written exams and that, overall, assessors' judgements are sound.

Noting down why, as an assessor, you have decided that certain evidence meets or does not meet the standards is good practice and should form part of the written feedback to candidates. It should help with minimizing the risk of subjectivity and/or bias. It is good practice to date each assessment you make and to record the results immediately. In order to be fair and reliable, you must ensure that the knowledge you want the candidate to demonstrate is closely tied in to what is identified in the element and does not wander into the realms of what you think the candidate should know. For example, NVQ Retailing has an element on unpacking stock, and one knowledge requirement relates to the candidate's responsibilities under the Health and Safety at Work Act. The assessor needs to be clear that, in this instance, he or she is only assessing the candidate's knowledge of health and safety in relation to unpacking goods, including lifting, carrying and the correct use of equipment.

(e) Collect evidence from the other people involved in the assessment process

Collecting evidence from other people about your candidates should be done in the most effective and cost-efficient ways, whether by telephone, e-mail, written documents or face-to-face meetings or via your candidate. Keep records of how you obtained the evidence and how you checked the authenticity of witnesses. Your internal verifier should check how assessors approach authentication and validating of witness statements.

(f) Apply any agreed special arrangements to make sure the assessment is fair

Language, ethnicity and gender issues have been studied as areas where fairness might be compromised. Translators or signers may need to be used for some candidates. Examples and situations that are not dependent on being fully familiar with British culture should be used where possible, as long as the integrity of the assessment is not compromised. Assessors should be careful that their judgements are not influenced when assessing women in traditionally male roles and vice versa.

(g) Base all your decisions on all the relevant evidence of candidates' performance and knowledge

It is only by studying the totality of candidates' evidence that the assessor is in a position to decide on whether candidates have met the standards, so it is necessary to base your decisions on *all* the relevant evidence. Take this from as many places as possible (see Table 7.1).

When we look at someone carrying out an activity, we can often see that the individual knows how to do something under a particular set of circumstances. This may be sufficient for the knowledge requirements you are assessing. For example, in NVQ level 2 in Retailing, the element involving recognition of hazardous goods and substances has a knowledge requirement that the candidate should know the location and use of protective clothing and equipment. When assessing, you might observe the candidate go to a storeroom or locker and put on some appropriate protective clothing. It would then be quite reasonable to infer that the candidate had filled that particular knowledge requirement related to the element.

We can often infer a good deal about what people know by what they do or what they produce. For example, if we observe someone involved in child care instructing small children to wash their hands before eating, we can infer that the child care assistant knows at least one basic rule of hygiene. Similarly, if we are shown a completed press article produced by a journalist, we can infer that the journalist knows how to structure information and spell words correctly. However, we must be very careful in inferring how *much* someone knows from what we see him or her do. In the first example given, the child care assistant could just be copying what he has seen others do, without any knowledge of the reason why he is doing it. In this case he probably has no concept of the 'idea' of hygiene and hence would not be able to transfer this rule across to another situation. In the case of the journalist, we may be satisfied that she has produced the article herself, but has she had her spelling and grammar checked by others or used a computer spell- or grammar-check? Has she used a standard format to structure her article? In both examples, the key to assessing whether someone really knows something needs to be taken from the level of qualification. At lower levels, the definition of knowledge could just involve 'has information about', and the understanding required could be very limited. At higher levels, the definition of knowledge will probably include a deeper understanding of the knowledge aspects related to the element plus a broader ability to transfer and make connections between ideas and practice.

There are obviously difficulties in inferring knowledge from performance, particularly at higher levels. A notable exception to this is where the product evidence itself contains evidence of knowledge and understanding, such as a formal in-depth report on organizational training needs produced by a candidate involved in human resource development and presented as evidence for an NVQ in Learning and Development.

You, as the assessor, need to be fully familiar with the standards your candidates must achieve and be confident that your decision is supported by their evidence. If you have any doubt, ask your internal verifier for advice.

(h) Explain and resolve any inconsistencies in the evidence

As you are making a judgement of someone's competence based on a range of evidence, there may be occasions when the level of competence suggested by one piece of evidence is not supported by other evidence. For example, you may have a written testimonial from a previous employer stating that the candidate always followed health and safety procedures, but one observational assessor's report states that there were instances when this had not happened. In this case, you would give the candidate feedback that he or she had not met this requirement consistently and that, during the next observation, this competence would need to be satisfactorily demonstrated. In order to be sure, you would probably question the candidate closely about his or her understanding of health and safety procedures and look for additional third-party evidence as well, eg from the candidate's supervisor at work.

Another example is of an NVQ Business Administration candidate, assessed by a number of observational assessors, who appears to be having little difficulty in achieving elements related to filing but a great deal of difficulty with elements related to stock-keeping. This might raise an issue regarding the candidate's numeracy skills. To check these, you might see how she is doing on her Key Skill 'application of number'. If her numerical ability is adequate, has she understood her stock-keeping training? If she does not have any problems with her assessors, and no particular dislike of this area of work, you might look more closely at the level of consistency among assessors. Are some expecting more than the standards require? Clarification will probably come by talking to the candidate and to other assessors and by asking for advice from the internal verifier.

The most worrying form of inconsistency is that where you suspect cheating, plagiarism or some other form of malpractice. If after checking the evidence with the candidate you still have doubts, contact the internal verifier or the awarding body as soon as possible for advice.

(i) Make a record of the outcomes of assessments by using the agreed recording system

As your candidates' primary assessor, you are likely to make several formative assessments as well as a summative judgement on the different types of agreed evidence for a whole unit. You will use at least four assessment methods in making this overall judgement. Once you are sure of your decision, enter your findings into the system – paper or IT based – used by your centre. There should be a tracking sheet where you record the criteria that the candidate has achieved, with the dates of assessments, and space to record who made the assessment decisions. If a candidate has successfully met the criteria for a complete unit, this will need entering on the record of achievement. You should make written notes to support your decisions that will remind you of the types of evidence you have reviewed, the methods used for assessment and why the evidence met or did not meet the criteria. You may want to record what was particularly good or particularly weak about the evidence. This record will provide the basis of feedback to your candidate and will also assist external and internal verifiers in their auditing processes.

(j) Speak to the appropriate person if you and the candidate cannot agree on the assessment of his or her performance

Disagreements are most likely to come about because you think the candidate is not yet competent and the candidate thinks that his or her evidence is proof of competence. Your records should show you and the candidate the basis for your decision. It could be that you have misinterpreted some evidence given to you, in which case you can check that out, but the better course of action would be to involve your internal verifier, who can review your decision and verify its accuracy (or otherwise).

A1.3: PROVIDE FEEDBACK AND SUPPORT TO CANDIDATES ON ASSESSMENT DECISIONS

(a) Give candidates feedback at an appropriate time and place

It is not enough just to tell a candidate that he or she has been successful or not. Your role is also to let the candidate know why you have made that decision. This is why the assessor should always set aside a proper time for discussion with the candidate so that both have time to talk over the result and the assessor is sure that the candidate fully understands the reasons for the assessment decision.

For candidates who have not met the demands of the unit, it is particularly important that they are given specific indications of what they need to do, or how they need to improve, in a constructive way that will enable them to move forward to successful assessment. The reasons supporting the assessment decision should be noted in writing in the assessment feedback related to the relevant units. Ideally, this feedback will be given as soon after the assessment as possible, in a place where neither of you is likely to be disturbed. Arrangements for feedback should have been detailed on the assessment plan.

(b) Give candidates feedback in a constructive and encouraging way that meets their needs and is appropriate to their level of confidence

All candidates need to know how well they did and why and to know how they might improve. Candidates will have been judged on the standards – that is, they have met or not met the standard. However, they can be told what was particularly good about their performance or where their performance, though competent, could benefit from continued attention. Some candidates will have a good deal of confidence and competence. For other candidates, the feedback process is essential to motivate and move them forward. In all cases, the feedback should be seen as development and not just as an end in itself. Note down the key points of oral feedback for the candidate. They are often forgotten, as relief or anxiety can block the messages the assessor is giving. The relationship you established with the candidate at the planning stage will be crucial in ensuring that feedback is received positively and is useful to the candidate. Encourage discussion of the assessment and try to get the candidate to explain whether any changes to the process might help future assessment. In addition, your IV will need to know *how* and *what* you are feeding back to your candidate as he or she samples your decisions.

(c) Clearly explain your assessment decisions on whether candidates' evidence of competence is good enough

You need to be able to justify your decisions objectively, and you can do this only by referring to the range of evidence you have assessed and showing the candidate how you matched this to the performance criteria. The notes you took as you reviewed the evidence should help you here. You should be able, as a vocationally competent assessor, to reassure the candidate that you are assessing against industry standards and not your personal view of 'acceptable' work.

You may not have been prepared to judge the candidate competent on the evidence available. This could occur when the candidate has not provided evidence of sufficient quality. For example, the candidate has brought you a witness testimony written by a line manager, but it is so general that it does not back up the candidate's claim against specific elements. You might have to ask the candidate to get another, more specific statement, or you might decide that you will arrange to observe him or her at work instead.

Another situation could be that a candidate has enough evidence against the performance criteria but has not shown that he or she meets the range or scope of the unit. In this case, you will discuss in feedback what else the candidate needs to do.

Yet another example could be where a candidate has written answers to pre-set knowledge questions, but they are minimal in content. In this case, you might agree with the candidate that professional discussion will give him or her the opportunity to show greater depth and breadth of knowledge and understanding.

Whatever the problem is, candidates should be left with a clear idea of what they need to do, and the assessment plan should be updated accordingly. The written records will be used by the internal verifier in checking the accuracy of your assessments and your monitoring of candidates' progress.

(d) Give candidates advice when they cannot prove their competence and on how they can develop the necessary skills or provide more evidence

Candidates can be held up from proving their competence if their own NVQ candidates leave or are finding difficulty in completing their own units. Another problematic area is where a candidate is not linked into the centre's internal verification procedures in a satisfactory way. These circumstances can delay in particular the assessment opportunities for A1 and V1 candidates.

Assessors may be able to encourage the candidate to liaise more effectively with key centre staff (line mangers, internal verifiers) to ensure that suitable candidates are available and that internal procedures support the candidate's achievement. It is clear that thorough initial planning and liaison between assessor and centre can help to prevent these problems developing in the first place. Training, either one to one or group, may be available via the centre, the awarding body or the NTO responsible, and the assessor can help the candidate to access this. Assessors can also ensure that they have access to relevant texts and websites to help develop general subject knowledge and specific knowledge in assessment and verification (see 'Supporting Materials' at the end of the book for some useful references and websites).

(e) Encourage candidates to get advice on your assessment decisions

The relationship you have built should enable candidates to ask why or how you or others involved in their assessment arrived at their decisions, and to challenge those decisions if they are unclear or unhappy about them.

(f) Identify and agree the next steps in the assessment process and how candidates will achieve these

Go back to the assessment plan and check whether it needs amending or simply updating. If a complete unit has been signed off, a completely new plan for the next unit needs to be agreed.

(g) Follow the agreed complaints and appeals procedures if candidates disagree with your assessment decisions

You and the candidate will have gone through this procedure in your assessment planning session, and the candidate should have access to the written procedure. Hopefully, neither of you will need to implement it. If you do start to follow the procedure, keep careful notes of what you have done and said. You should of course have documentary evidence of all your planning, assessment decisions and feedback.

A1.4: CONTRIBUTE TO THE INTERNAL QUALITY ASSURANCE PROCESS

(a) Ensure your assessment records are accurate and up to date and can be followed by an auditor

You will have a number of documents to complete during the assessment process. These may be produced by your organization, or they may be documents produced by the awarding body. For each unit a candidate works through, you should have completed as a minimum:

- one assessment plan, reviewed and dated, with evidence of negotiation;
- a tracking document logging the various dates of achievement of performance criteria, range, scope, and knowledge and understanding, as detailed in the relevant standards;
- feedback sheets, dated and signed;
- records of achievement, dated and signed.

The best way of ensuring accuracy is to enter information as it is negotiated or fed back to the candidate and for both of you to sign and date documents there and then to confirm agreement and accuracy. These dates and signatures provide an audit trail that an auditor (ie an internal verifier or external verifier) can use to track any aspect of the assessment process against the appropriate standards.

The importance of meticulous record keeping cannot be overestimated in the assessment process. However, in order for the audit trail to work, the system needs to be simple, legible and credible. If mistakes are made in the recording, they should be altered clearly, and signed to indicate that the error has been corrected by the assessor and not altered without authority, much as you would initial a correction on a cheque. Correction fluid should not be used. You need to pass on records promptly to ensure that you avoid hoarding documents on your shelf, desk or filing cabinet, which would prevent other assessors, verifiers or any centralized recording system from inputting the information on candidates' achievements, therefore possibly preventing candidates' access to the qualification.

(b) Contribute to standardization arrangements so that your assessment decisions are in line with others'

An internal verifier should manage you in your organization. He or she should be regularly sampling all types of assessment decisions and should also hold standardization sessions where you will have the opportunity to check that you are making the same decisions on evidence as would other assessors. Often these meetings use anonymous photocopied unit evidence from real candidates, which is judged independently by each member of the assessment team. The results of the assessments are then compared and discussed, allowing differences of interpretation to be resolved.

(c) Give accurate and timely information on assessments

Your organization is likely to have at least three audit points in a year. Internal verifiers will need to know how you are progressing with your workload on a regular basis and will request quantitative and qualitative data from assessors.

(d) Contribute to the agreed quality assurance process

There will be centre verification procedures for both internal and external verification. Many organizations have their own system of recording, feedback, assessment decisions and candidate progress. Relevant details are then transferred across to meet external awarding body requirements. Discussions are usually held with external verifiers to ensure that there is no unnecessary duplication of information. All assessors should be included within the process. Contributions to the process could include attending meetings, providing qualitative and quantitative data (see Table 7.2, which shows the consequences of insufficient data regarding dates), being observed, discussing decisions and completing documentation accurately and promptly. Assessors may be requested to submit assessment decisions for sampling or for standardization purposes at any point during candidates' progress.

Whatever the quality assurance process used for verification by a centre, it should have been agreed with the relevant awarding body for each qualification offered.

7

Guide to Unit A2: Assess Candidates' Performance through Observation

Unit A2 has four elements:

- A2.1: Agree and review plans for assessing candidates' performance.
- A2.2: Assess candidates' performance against the agreed standards.
- A2.3: Assess candidates' knowledge against the agreed standards.
- A2.4: Make an assessment decision and provide feedback.

This award is for those assessors who carry out important but more restricted assessment than A1 assessors. They observe candidates carrying out competence-based tasks in the workplace and assess candidates' competence against performance criteria and the related knowledge. They cannot act as independent assessors for A1 candidates.

A2.1: AGREE AND REVIEW PLANS FOR ASSESSING CANDIDATES' PERFORMANCE

Remembering what is said about the different stages in the assessment process in Chapter 3, you will recognize A2.1 as the 'planning stage', where you reach agreement with your vocational candidate about *what* will be assessed, *how* the assessment will be carried out and *when* it will take place. You will be ensuring that there is no confusion about the suitability of the evidence and that all the arrangements for the assessment have been organized and agreed.

(a) Identify the best situations when you can assess performance

The assessor needs to help the candidate relate what he or she is doing as part of his or her normal work to the units and elements to be assessed so that together they *both* can identify the possible opportunities for assessment. The assessments should be done as part of a normal working shift, when the candidate is naturally carrying out performance tasks. Observations should be planned to cover as many elements and performance criteria as possible and the candidate needs to estimate the time likely to be taken. Issues to be considered will be the impact of observations on normal working, holidays and potential sickness, the preparation required, the commitments of the assessor, and the times when the candidate is most likely to be able to receive face-to-face feedback directly following the assessment.

(b) Use evidence that takes place in the workplace and ask relevant questions

Your assessment should be based on what the candidate is doing as a natural part of his or her work and on your observation of 'natural' performance. The starting point for discussion with the candidate is what evidence could be used to prove competence – that is, begin with what is already there in what the candidate is actually doing, rather than what needs more work to produce or design. Assessors need to check, through the use of open questions, any aspect of the planned observation that is unclear to them, so that risk of an ineffective visit is minimized.

(c) Choose opportunities for assessment that disrupt normal work as little as possible

Involving candidates' supervisors in the planning process should enable candidates to plan work-based assessment opportunities into their normal work routines with as little disruption as possible. Having an assessor around is likely to alter the dynamics of situations and increase the nerves of candidates (and *their* candidates, if the NVQ is process rather than product based). Of course, in some situations candidates will be used to being observed on a regular basis. For example, in a motor vehicle workshop, supervisory staff will be moving around all the time checking on work being done. Similarly, in an open-learning workshop, candidates will be used to staff circulating and being available for consultation. In situations such as these, candidates are less likely to be disturbed than in a situation where candidates are not used to being observed; for example, a candidate being assessed as a trainer may never have had an observer with him or her in the training situation.

The assessments should be organized so that candidates demonstrating their competence do not experience unnecessary disruption to their work routine. Assessors need to be conscious of the work environment and ensure that feedback and questioning following assessment keep within planned timescales.

(d) Choose opportunities for assessment that provide access to a valid, safe, reliable and fair assessment

See Chapter 3 for a fuller explanation of these terms. Safety must be considered in both the physical sense and the sense of being sure that the decision is sound. The only time an assessor should interfere in an assessment is if there is potential or actual harm to those involved. The assessor should have enough evidence to be sure that the candidate can perform competently and consistently over time.

(e) Explain the options open to the candidates clearly and constructively if somebody disagrees with the assessment plan

The candidates will need the opportunity to discuss the proposed assessment plan with workplace colleagues and their own candidates, but before they do this both of you need to clarify what is or is not negotiable in terms of the assessment. Rearrangement of time or place, choice of different units for candidates (and even of different candidates), materials to be used, types of evidence and witnesses are all negotiable. Non-negotiable for A2 is the agreed common evidence (detailed with all sets of the standards), which details the number of plans, reviews, records and statements to be provided by the candidate-assessor.

(f) Discuss and agree the proposed assessment plan with the candidates and other people who may be affected

Once candidates understand what is and is not negotiable, the plan needs to be shared with everyone who may be affected. The assessment plan should give a clear indication of *what* will be assessed, *how* it will be assessed and *when* it will be assessed. Only after this can the plan be finally agreed. Signing and dating by both parties is the convention used to denote agreement. It is important that this signing and dating is done as soon as the plan has been agreed. The other people who could be affected by the planned assessment will vary according to the work situation, but they might include:

- supervisors in the workplace who might need to adjust staffing rotas;
- witnesses who may be required to provide written statements;
- other tutors or trainers who need to coordinate their assessments with yours;
- technical staff, to make sure that the appropriate facilities are made available;
- the internal verifier, who will need to include you as an assessor and your assessments in his or her sampling plan;
- candidates' colleagues who might be affected by the presence of an assessor.

(g) Review and update plans at agreed times to take account of candidates' progress

One of the problems with working on assessments with candidates who are on a programme dependent on the progress and cooperation of others, possibly on different sites from the primary assessor, is the danger that they will feel isolated or let other work take priority. Assessors need to be aware of this and develop a system for keeping in contact, regularly reviewing progress. The way you decide to do this will depend largely on the experience of the candidate and the amount of support and motivation he or she needs from you.

As the candidate achieves targets, and as circumstances change, the plan will need amending and updating. It is crucial that the first workplace assessments take place as soon after the completion of the assessment plan as possible. This will enable the candidate to use feedback constructively and maintain motivation. The timescale for achievement needs to be realistic, and the assessor needs to help the candidate maintain progress via regular planned reviews and updates.

A2.2: ASSESS CANDIDATES' PERFORMANCE AGAINST THE AGREED STANDARDS

Having dealt with the planning for assessment, assessor and candidate can move on to the actual process of assessing performance evidence.

(a) Explain to candidates how the assessment of their work will take account of their needs

Different candidates will need different levels of support, depending on factors such as their maturity, their experience at performing the required tasks and their understanding of what they have learnt regarding the associated knowledge. Some candidates will have specific needs that should have been identified during the induction and assessment planning phases. Refer to Table 3.2 concerning barriers to access to be reminded of the range of special assessment needs.

All candidates will need to be reassured that the assessor will make some allowance for initial nerves. Assessors will start building relationships with candidates during the assessment planning process, which hopefully will lead to as relaxed an observation as possible.

(b) Watch candidates in a safe environment

The assessment environment must meet the requirements of the Health and Safety at Work Act. All participants in the assessment have a responsibility for reporting any unsafe environment, equipment or practices. The assessor must conform to any additional health and safety rules determined by the workplace, such as the wearing of protective clothing. The only time you, as assessor, should interfere with an assessment you are observing is if you, the candidate or his or her own candidates appear to be at risk.

(c) Use only the agreed criteria when assessing the evidence

You must not deviate from the agreed criteria when making your judgements. Even if you are convinced that receptionists should smile at their clients, but this is not included in the standard, then it is invalid and unfair to use it as a criterion for assessment. Make notes of any performance that appears to be *beyond* the requirements of the standards (eg smiling, in the case of the receptionists). This will be good for positive developmental feedback and may form good evidence for the candidate for another unit or even evidence against a future assessment at a higher level.

(d) Assess evidence fairly against the agreed criteria

Fairness in assessment is covered in Chapter 3. Assessors need to be sure that they are judging all candidates according to their performance against the identified criteria and not against what the assessor *thinks* they can do or thinks they *should* do. It is easy to want to give candidates 'the benefit of the doubt', but the candidates need to show they are competent at performing all the standards in their everyday work.

Just as unfair would be refusing to accept that a candidate is competent because of the lack of a skill that may not be required for the competence being assessed. Legibility of handwriting and the ability to speak fluently might be crucial to the achievement of competences for a candidate in administration, but might not be part of the standards for an IT candidate. Assessors need to be very familiar with the standards that are being used for the assessment.

(e) Identify and assess any other evidence that is relevant to the standards

The assessor should now have an idea of whether candidates have 'gaps' in their competence or knowledge. At this stage of the assessment process, the assessor will need to determine with the candidates how these gaps will be closed. A suitable method at this stage will be professional discussion, which if planned well and held at the candidates' workplace should enable candidates to explain, show or reinforce by activity any aspects of their performance or knowledge and understanding that are currently unclear to the assessor.

(f) Check that the evidence has come from each candidate's own work

Because performance evidence is generally generated through the observation of natural performance, the observational assessor should see candidates do the work and question them personally to establish competence or achievement across the range. However, there will be some situations where this is less clear cut. Safeguards will have to be in place to ensure that evidence from prior experience or learning is the candidates' own. For example, if a candidate in catering showed you a cake he had prepared, you might ask him to describe how he had made it, what ingredients he had used, and the temperature he had used while cooking it. In fact, you should ask as many questions as you need to ask to feel sure that he knows what he is talking about. You still might not be satisfied, so you might ask to talk to his supervisor, who could confirm that the candidate had made the cake or, if that was not possible, review a witness statement that stated that the cake was the normal standard of work of the candidate.

Assessors should check out any evidence, such as product evidence or APL, that has not been assessed by an accredited assessor.

(g) Watch candidates without interfering with their work

There is sometimes a temptation, when observing, to 'fit in' with the candidates and thus skew the dynamics of the relationship between the candidate and his or her own vocational candidates or work pattern. In order to assess accurately against the elements and performance criteria agreed in the assessment plan, assessors may need to be very close to the candidate for particular operations, perhaps to see what the candidate is doing or to hear what he or she is saying to a client. In cases like this, you may well be noticeable but not interfering. Assessors will obviously try their best to distract the candidate and his or her clients as little as possible. This will require discussion with the candidate and client, who can advise where the assessor should position him- or herself. What assessors must *not* do is contribute to the assessment in any way by offering information or advice, by asking questions or by showing how to perform tasks.

(h) Speak to the appropriate person if you or the candidates have any difficulties

Difficulties can occur at all stages of the process, owing to, for example, late arrivals, faulty equipment, client behaviour or the acoustics of the observation environment. If the assessment needs to be repeated for any reason, then the same people who needed informing the first time will need to be informed again. If any additional training or workplace adjustments need to be made, or the assessments need to be rearranged because of difficulties on either side, then again the relevant people will need to be informed.

(i) Give candidates feedback after you have watched them in the workplace

Candidates desperately need to know what they have achieved and how well they have done. They also need to know how to improve further (even if all performance criteria have been met). Just to tell candidates whether they are competent or not is not enough. Your role is also to let them know why you have made that decision. This is why the assessor should always set aside a proper time for discussion with the candidate so that both have time to talk over the result and the assessor is sure that the candidate fully understands the reasons for the assessment decision. Obviously, for candidates who have not yet achieved competence, it is particularly important that they are given specific indications of where they need to improve, in a constructive way that will motivate them for the next time they are assessed. See Table 3.4 for more information on this. Feedback is best given orally, as soon after the observation as possible. It should be backed up with written notes, with a copy for the candidate. If face-to-face feedback is not possible following the observation, written notes can be left with the candidate to read through, and a date and time fixed as soon as possible to go through the notes.

A2.3: ASSESS CANDIDATES' KNOWLEDGE AGAINST THE AGREED STANDARDS

(a) Identify which areas of candidates' knowledge have been covered by watching them in the workplace

All NVQ qualifications have defined knowledge that needs to be assessed as part of the candidates' competence. In some NVQs this knowledge is tightly defined, with model answers being provided for assessors. In others, there is more room for broader interpretation by assessors as to what the required minimum knowledge might be, particularly in the higher levels of qualifications.

When we look at someone carrying out an activity, we can usually tell that the individual knows how to do something under a particular set of circumstances. This may be sufficient for the knowledge requirements you are assessing. For example, in NVQ level 2 in Retailing, the element involving recognition of hazardous goods and substances has a knowledge requirement that the candidate should know the location and use of protective clothing and equipment. When assessing, you might observe the candidate go to a storeroom or locker and put on some protective clothing. It would then be quite reasonable to infer that the candidate had filled that particular knowledge requirement related to the element.

There are obviously difficulties in inferring knowledge from performance, particularly at higher levels. A notable exception to this is where the product evidence itself contains evidence of knowledge and understanding, such as a formal in-depth report on organizational training needs produced by a candidate involved in human resource development and presented as evidence for an NVQ in Learning and Development. Assessors need to be familiar with what their candidates need to know and be clear about whether this can really be inferred through observation or whether additional activities will need to be used to collect the evidence required.

Assessors will need to check off the knowledge evidence that has been assessed and note down candidates' responses if these are not in written form. Knowledge that has not been covered can be planned into professional discussion.

(b) Collect evidence of knowledge that has not been covered by watching the candidates in the workplace

Assessors will have anticipated in the planning phase what knowledge is likely to be evidenced through observation of performance. Estimates may need to be revised following observation, and further evidence sought. This may be just a matter of planning some additional topics into the professional discussion, or you may need to ask candidates to supply additional direct or indirect evidence.

(c) Use valid methods to assess candidates' knowledge

Knowledge has traditionally been assessed through tests and examinations. Assessing knowledge underpinning work-based performance is unlikely to involve either of these methods. Some inference of knowledge will be made by the assessor, but this needs to be backed up with questioning and professional discussion. Witness statements or judgements made by other assessors will help to give a rounded picture of the knowledge the candidate is demonstrating.

It is important to ensure that the assessment is on the knowledge, rather than factors connected with the evidence, such as communication skills. This is not, of course, to deny that communication skills are vitally important. It may be true that the candidate needs to address these, but unless they are clearly stated as being a prerequisite at a particular level, or are built into the standard in some way, they should not affect the knowledge judgement. With regard to the importance of removing barriers to access to assessment, candidates' particular needs should be taken into account, for example whether it would be fairer to test them in writing or orally. Someone who has worked for many years at a machine on a factory floor might not have had to do much writing. To test that person's knowledge by setting him or her a written test could be unfair (unless of course it was a requirement of the awarding body) and might not produce a reliable indication of what the person really knows.

Apart from this, you also need to consider the time and cost involved with different methods. Finding out what someone knows through professional discussion may be more time-consuming for the assessor than getting a group of candidates together for a written multiple choice test. However, it is likely to be quicker and more rewarding for the candidate or organization and, if planned to occur directly after observation, may take less time than anticipated. To check you are using these methods correctly, as usual talk with your internal verifier and be familiar with the awarding body guidelines. Table 7.1 gives a wide range of methods of assessing knowledge. A2 assessors are likely (and expected) to use the first three methods in the table.

(d) Ask clear questions that do not 'lead' candidates

If oral or written questioning is to be used, each question should be specific, easy to understand and not phrased in such a way that an answer is suggested or a bias on the part of the assessor is indicated. For example, a question such as 'Don't you think you should have cleared the work area before you began the next job?' is hardly a question at all, but an indication that the assessor thinks that the candidate has done something wrong. You will find more examples of different types of questions in Chapter 5.

(e) Speak to the appropriate person if you or the candidates have any difficulties

See A2.2(h).

(f) Give candidates feedback after you have asked them questions

Your preliminary questions will allow you to check out any areas of confusion and clarify why the candidate chose to perform his or her tasks in particular ways. Feedback should always be constructive, especially if candidates have not met the criteria, and should be accompanied by written notes of the points for candidates, even if you give feedback orally. See Chapter 5 for advice on giving feedback.

Table 7.1 Methods of knowledge assessment

Knowledge evidence gathered through:	Assessor needs to:
Observation of performance	Infer what candidate must know because of the quality of the performance.
Questioning	Determine the minimum level and breadth of acceptability for answers.
Professional discussion	Pre-plan discussion topics where clarification is needed. Encourage candidate to talk at ease about his or her role so he or she can show broad occupational competence. Ask probing questions where appropriate.
Witness statements	Check authenticity and recency. Check status of witness – what qualifies him or her to make a judgement? Match statement to criteria.
Qualifications	Check authenticity and recency; may need to look at whether updating is needed to bring candidate up to current occupational competence.
Personal statements and explanations	Check for coverage of scope and knowledge.
Assignments and projects	Assessment mark scheme needs clarifying and explaining to candidate prior to the start of candidate's work.
Simulation	Check the areas allowed by the NTO and the awarding body guidance prior to accepting.

A2.4: MAKE AN ASSESSMENT DECISION AND PROVIDE FEEDBACK

At this stage the assessor will have a good idea as to the candidate's overall competence, based not only on his or her own observations, but also from endorsements by other assessors and the internal verifier's statement showing how the assessor has contributed to internal quality assurance procedures.

(a) Base your decision on all the relevant evidence

The evidence must include that from all others involved in the assessment process. You will have observed the candidate yourself, received feedback and the judgements from other assessors, including the independent assessor, and have the internal verifier's statement. You will have the results of your professional discussion, and any additional work the candidate has done to provide sufficient evidence of knowledge. You make a positive decision about a candidate only when you have enough information to convince you that the candidate is able currently to meet all the criteria in the national standards.

(b) Give candidates clear and constructive feedback that meets their needs, after you have given them your assessment

The summative assessment needs to summarize the full extent of what has been achieved and to detail what the candidate needs to do next. All records used in making the decision need to be available for both the candidate and the internal verifier.

You may have decided to confirm competence cumulatively, as the assessment progressed. As soon as the candidates have received the final assessment of 'competent' or 'not competent', they need feedback. Candidates who are not yet competent will need advice on what to do before they re-present themselves for final assessment. Those who are competent will need to know what they did particularly well, how they can continue to 'put the icing on the cake' and what to do next.

(c) Encourage candidates to ask for advice on your assessment decision

Face-to-face feedback will help candidates to reflect on your decision and to raise questions. You will have all your records to show the candidates, and this should help them to understand the decision and what they need to do next.

When you have given feedback to a candidate, are you sure that he or she understands it? Are you sure that the candidate knows what to do with it? You may need to consider how you ensure that candidates have a proper opportunity to discuss the assessments with you, both in circumstances where they receive oral feedback face to face and where they receive written feedback. What means do you use in these situations to encourage them to discuss the assessment with you? How far are they aware of the feedback process and the active part they should play in order to get the most out of what they are told? All these are vital questions. The answers are not straightforward, but are bound up in the relationship that you manage to establish with the candidates.

(d) Make an accurate record of your assessment decisions

You need to check that all the details are entered on to the correct documentation and that you have signed and dated the assessment. Using the convention dd/mm/yy for dates will be useful where any records for electronic data entering have to be made, and will give much more accuracy as to the speed of a candidate's progress. Labelling the start of an assessment process merely as June 07 and its completion merely as August 07 gives an uncertainty of two months regarding the time taken to achieve it (see Table 7.2).

Table 7.2 Completion times possible when names of months only are given (June 07 to August 07)

01.06.07	01.06.07	30.06.07
31.08.07	01.08.07	01.08.07
3 months	2 months	1 month

(e) Pass on records that are accurate and easy to read to the next stage of the process

The importance of meticulous record keeping cannot be overestimated in the assessment process. In order for the records to be useful, all those entitled to see them, including verifiers, other assessors, appropriate administrative personnel and the candidates themselves, should be able to access and make sense of them. Handwritten records must be legible. Any mistakes made in the recording should be altered clearly and signed to indicate the error has been corrected by the assessor and not altered without authority. Results should be entered into records at the time the judgement is being made. Paper records might need to be transferred to electronic recording systems; this should be done as soon as possible, and the original paper record should be kept until at least after the next audit and the candidate has received his or her certificate. Many organizations and awarding bodies recommend that file copies be kept for three years before destruction. Records should be passed on promptly, as not doing this could hold up a candidate's assessment, especially if the observational assessor records form just part of a candidate's unit assessment. Records also provide the evidence for the sampling and monitoring activities carried out by the internal verifier and hence must be kept up to date so that internal verification can take place throughout a candidate's progress.

(f) Follow the agreed complaints and appeals procedure if candidates do not agree with your assessment decision

Each organization should have its own complaints and appeals procedure, and both candidate and assessor should be familiar with this. In addition, awarding bodies will have their own complaints and appeals procedures, which should also be understood by candidates and assessors. These will be used if matters cannot be resolved locally.

8

Guide to Unit V1: Conduct Internal Quality Assurance of the Assessment Process

Unit V1 is for those who undertake the role of internal verifier for a centre. The internal verifier candidate will also be expected to be competent in assessing using a wide range of sources of evidence and will have already obtained D33 or A1. The candidate should have practised as an assessor for a minimum of 12 months prior to undertaking the internal verifier role. The internal verifier role is a management function and therefore is at NVQ level 4, unlike A1 and A2 (and D34), which are at NVQ level 3.

The NVQ Code of Practice and the Joint Awarding Body (JAB) guidelines are invaluable documents for internal verifiers (IVs). All IVs should be fully familiar with their contents and have discussed their implications with centre colleagues and assessors and their external verifiers (EVs). All the explanations that follow should be read in conjunction with the JAB guide and the NVQ Code of Conduct.

There are four elements to V1:

- V1.1: Carry out and evaluate internal assessment and quality assurance systems.
- V1.2: Support assessors.
- V1.3: Monitor the quality of assessors' performance.
- V1.4: Meet external quality assurance requirements.

V1.1: CARRY OUT AND EVALUATE INTERNAL ASSESSMENT AND QUALITY ASSURANCE SYSTEMS

(a) Put your organization's requirements into practice for auditing internal assessments and those of the external awarding body

A simple phrase that covers a lot of work! Organizations, particularly large organizations, have their own, often standardized, procedures for auditing assessment. These need to be followed irrespective of any awarding bodies that may be involved with the centre. However, you will also need to ensure that the centre's procedures are acceptable to each awarding body with which you deal. The EV will expect you to explain the centre's systems and indicate why these meet the awarding body's specifications. You will have been given details of these specifications when the centre applied for registration. In rare cases, IVs may need to carry out some additional procedures to ensure that the awarding body's requirements are met.

You may need to liaise with others in the organization to obtain all the data you need. For example, in a large training organization there may be staff responsible for recruitment and enrolment with whom you need to liaise in order to get an idea of candidate numbers and expected timescale for completion. Similarly, you may need to give details of when you expect visits from the EV, and the status of the centre in terms of being able to make direct claims without waiting for an EV's visit.

It is your responsibility as the internal verifier to ensure that the requirements are acted upon, so you will need to show how you do this. Most IVs compile a centre file containing records of all the activity for which they are responsible.

(b) Identify the outcomes needed by the agreed standards and their consequences for internal auditing

The requirements of each NVQ will make resource demands on the organization. If there are too few qualified assessors or problems with centre management information systems, for example, registration, assessment or certification could be held up. Most candidates will produce witness statements, and centres will need to have internal audit procedures for checking their authenticity and sometimes for induction of witnesses. There will need to be safe and secure storage for candidate portfolios. Candidate-assessors and -verifiers will need to have all their decisions countersigned by qualified assessors. Sampling plans will need constructing and auditing, as will assessment tracking documents and assessment plans.

Where centres have been used to end-loading verification and sampling only completed qualifications, practice will need to change to continuous sampling processes and cover all assessment activity, including observation and the assessment of independent assessors and of professional discussion.

(c) Carry out appropriate administrative and recording arrangements to meet external audit requirements

Previous EV reports should show how well the centre is doing in terms of administration and recording and whether there are any current action points that the internal verifier should be following through. Current records will be needed to show that the necessary action is being taken. IVs need to be able to access relevant records on assessment practice and internal quality and be able to give information swiftly. This information will include candidate/assessor allocation, sampling, tracking and standardization, numbers of registered, certificated and 'in progress' candidates, and the correct codes for courses, and will involve reviewing organizational policies to see whether they need updating with respect to assessment and verification.

(d) Identify the agreed criteria for choosing and supporting assessors, and ensure they are applied

The NTO assessment strategies for each NVQ will need to be matched to each assessor and IV. All those assessing and verifying A1, A2 and V1 will need to meet the assessment strategies of both the vocational awarding body and ENTO. You will need to be able to show that your records are regularly reviewed and updated. Since all awarding bodies require proof of relevant qualifications, a central file containing original certificates for vocational and assessor/verifier awards, with an accompanying CV, is very useful. If candidates do not wish their original certificates to be lodged with the centre, a photocopy endorsed by a qualified EV and the quality manager for the centre will be an acceptable substitute.

Each centre will have its own arrangements for supporting assessors, and these should be clear to all parties.

Some methods of supporting assessors are:

- a library of documents, awarding body publications, QCA publications, training videos, books on assessment and quality assurance, and supporting information on vocational NVQs offered;
- lists of training courses offered internally and externally;
- mentors for newly qualified assessors;
- a programme of meetings for the year, including general information, standardization and monitoring;
- a 'buddy' system for qualified staff;
- a monthly information sheet, containing updates on assessment practice;
- training needs analysis and continuing personal development plans for staff.
- written feedback on assessment decisions and observation monitoring.

(e) Carry out assessment standardization arrangements

Carrying out assessment standardization arrangements will include holding meetings with assessors at which they all assess the same evidence and assessors assess evidence from each other's candidates. Careful records need to be kept of attendees, the units sampled and the evidence used. Reports of the findings need to be made and distributed. The EV will want to see evidence of standardization activities related to assessment decisions.

(f) Ensure that a procedure for complaints and appeals is in place

The procedure for complaints and appeals must meet the requirements of the awarding body and must be followed where necessary. The organization's own complaints and appeals procedure needs to be checked against that for the relevant awarding body, to see whether any adjustments need to be made. There needs to be a clear procedure for recording complaints and their outcome, and how the organization or individual would action a complaint that needed referral.

(g) Identify and use internal and external measures of performance to adjust internal systems

The measures of performance are likely to be both quantitative and qualitative (see Table 8.1).

Table 8.1 Some measures of quality

Quantitative measures	Qualitative measures
Numbers of enrolled, 'in progress', withdrawn and completed candidates	Availability of resources
National benchmarking data for the qualification	Policies and procedures
Time taken from enrolment to completion	Feedback from assessors and other centre staff
Audit trails checking compliance	External verifier reports on process
Data from satisfaction surveys	Internal verifier or other internal quality reports
Records of complaints	Reports from other examiners or inspectors
Equal opportunities monitoring data	Staff CPD records

(h) Make recommendations to improve internal quality assurance arrangements and develop a plan to put these improvements into practice

Having surveyed the data, both qualitative and quantitative, that are available to you, you need to summarize the information, preferably in both written and numerical/graphical format. The report should be available for external auditors such as EVs and inspectors, as well as for internal quality managers. Its findings need to be shared with assessors in order to develop and maintain good practice and determine the action that needs to be taken to maintain and/or improve performance.

V1.2: SUPPORT ASSESSORS

(a) Ensure that assessors have appropriate technical and vocational experience

Relevant and recent work-based experience is important for all assessors (and trainers), so work experience placements in industry, as well as training candidates in their vocational subjects, can help to keep assessors updated. This is particularly important for assessors who are based in colleges or training companies, who may spend much of the week away from the work environments attended by their candidates. Assessors of fast-moving vocational subjects such as engineering, IT or media will need to be familiar with technical developments in those areas.

In addition, assessors need to have a good range of information and communications technology (ICT) skills, so that they can take advantage of e-mail, electronic recording systems and information on the internet from NTOs and awarding bodies. The ability to word-process, photocopy and scan material is now a key workplace skill, as is the ability to keep updated filing systems. The introduction of professional discussion, which must be recorded, means that assessors need to be able to use video equipment, audiotape equipment and possibly digital or other camera equipment. In addition, there are now IT-based initial assessment and diagnostic Key Skills packages that assessors can use at induction to enable them to give sound advice to candidates.

(b) Ensure that assessors are familiar with and can carry out the specific assessment and follow the recording and internal audit procedures

Centre induction will have provided assessors with the necessary initial information they need, including an introduction to the documentation and administrative systems they will be required to use. All assessors should have the opportunity to attend updating sessions, whether provided by the awarding body or cascaded through the internal verifier. You need to check that they have understood their training and are able to follow the systems. Keep records of your monitoring and of assessor attendance at training sessions.

(c) Identify the development needs of assessors in line with assessments, the needs of candidates and technical expertise and competence

Assessors can make self-assessments of their perceived needs that can be compared with the skills they need to perform their role. These can be checked against the requirements that the IV has identified as being mandatory and advisory to the centre's good-quality practice, and action plans for each assessor drawn up on this basis. Most organizations have annual appraisals where individuals negotiate yearly action plans with their line managers. These may not cover the detail required here related to assessment, so the IV will need to conduct his or her own needs identification.

(d) Give assessors the chance to develop their assessment experience and competence and monitor their progress

Giving assessors this chance will require matching experienced assessors with those new to assessing itself or new to assessing in a particular vocational area. Support may be required for all assessors as they work with the new A standards, until you are satisfied that they have successfully updated their practice. Keep records that show as a minimum who, how, what and when you have monitored concerning the assessment practice of your assessors. Experienced assessors may wish to explore new ways of recording assessment activity, such as by using digital equipment (PDAs) and online recording systems.

(e) Ensure that assessors have regular opportunities to standardize assessment decisions

There should be a planned timetable for assessors to get together to standardize their assessment decision. It might be helpful to plan the timetable so that there is always some standardization activity between EV visits, indicating who will be required to attend, so that assessors understand their commitments. Standardizing observation practice can be done using video evidence of candidates performing tasks, which can be viewed at leisure or alongside other assessors, and by having assessors complete assessment observation forms and then reviewing them. Different types of portfolio evidence can be copied for assessing by a number of assessors, and a range of completed units can be assessed by different assessors, allowing differences and similarities in assessment practice, ways of giving written and oral feedback, and recording to be reviewed. It is also instructive to ask assessors to consider the minimum knowledge they require for the successful assessment of knowledge, by using a range of the questions in the standards and asking for written responses.

Your standardization plan, attendance sheets and standardization reports from each session need to be available for quality assurance and EV scrutiny.

(f) Monitor how assessors are capable of maintaining standards

Your monitoring of assessors needs to be planned over time, so that you are confident that standards are maintained and do not decline. It is equally important that both weak and over-rigorous assessment are addressed.

You will do this through a combination of all your activities as an internal verifier.

V1.3: MONITOR THE QUALITY OF ASSESSORS' PERFORMANCE

The following criteria will be demonstrated by showing that you are checking that assessors are working to the A1 and A2 standards. You will need to work to these yourself in order to 'assess' the quality of the assessor performance for which you are responsible. Much of this work will be done through the implementation of your sampling strategy, where you monitor the assessment practice of assessors on a regular basis by dipping into assessments at all parts of the process. This will involve monitoring, for example, the assessment planning process with a newly registered candidate, as well as the monitoring of independent assessments, of observational assessors and of final unit assessment and feedback to candidates. Sampling of finally assessed units is just one of the many parts of this process.

(a) Ensure that individual assessors are preparing for and planning assessments effectively

Ensuring that individual assessors are planning and preparing effectively can be done by viewing copies of assessment plans and by talking to assessors, candidates and workplace supervisors. You will need to check that the assessor has considered the effectiveness in terms of both cost and estimated completion time of conducting the assessments. The separation out of training and assessment costs might need to be considered. The IV will need to monitor that assessors are making best use of workplace visits by well-planned assessments that cover a wide range of performance indicators, and that professional discussion is similarly effectively planned. The IV will also need to look at the use of observational and independent assessors, witness statements, postage costs, and the times taken by individual assessors to support candidates through to completion.

(b) Ensure that individual assessors have effective processes for making assessment decisions

You will need to check that assessors are assessing against the standards, rather than their perception of what is acceptable, and that their recording against criteria is done accurately and cumulatively. Candidates should know how much they have achieved from each assessment. These processes will be the ways in which individual assessors deal with the portfolio evidence, matching it to elements, performance criteria and knowledge, and checking their assessment against any claim the candidate may have indicated prior to making their assessment. Assessors need to be supported to justify their decisions against the standards. Simple tick statements such as 'The evidence clearly meets the requirements' are not enough. The IV needs to be clear as to *why* the assessor believes this is so, and should be able to check the assessor's decision-making process and see exactly how the assessor has come to his or her decisions.

(c) Ensure that individual assessors understand the necessary outcomes

Assessors' understanding of the NVQ or unit requirements needs talking through. For example, there has been a perception that, to get A1, an assessor needs to have seen a candidate through to successful completion of a unit. This is not so. The standard requires the candidate *to submit for summative assessment*; whether the candidate is judged competent or not yet competent is irrelevant.

(d) Ensure that individual assessors apply safe, fair, valid and reliable methods of assessing candidates' competence

The standardization activities you implement will help to ensure this, as will asking assessors to give verbal or written reports that indicate the measures they undertook to meet these criteria.

(e) Check individual assessors' judgements to ensure they are consistent over time and with different candidates

The checking process includes watching individual assessors carry out assessments and checking a sufficient number of assessors to ensure consistency between assessors over time and with different candidates. This is where you implement your sampling strategy, using the principles outlined in the JAB guidelines. A timetable of dates for sampling, with no strategy, is inadequate, as it is not linked into any programme of continuous improvement.

(f) Check a sufficient number of assessors to ensure consistency between assessors over time and with different candidates

Checking a sufficient number of assessors should not be a problem in centres with just a few assessors. In larger centres, the sampling plan will need to be robust enough to ensure that all assessors are making similar judgements against the standards and that their judgements are not swayed by the particular needs of individual candidates. The IV needs to include all assessors, including independent assessors, in his or her sample. The IV should agree the sampling plan with the EV.

(g) Check different assessment sites to ensure that assessment decisions are consistent

It is important not only to sample documentary assessments from different sites, but also to visit different sites (eg sub-centres or satellites), as factors impinging on the assessments may not be apparent from the document without a visit. Resources, the nature of the candidates and the skills and experience of assessment staff can all affect assessment decision-making processes.

(h) Ensure that assessors set up and maintain effective working relationships with candidates at all stages of the assessment process

The key to ensuring effective working relationships will be assessment planning and review documentation, and any written feedback between candidate and assessor. More detail can be gained by contacting a sample of candidates, looking at any centre quality feedback forms, checking complaints, and reviewing assessment plans and feedback forms, particularly those on which the candidate responds to the assessor's feedback. Another measure of a good working relationship is the number of sound completions within the original estimated time that individual assessors achieve with their candidates. Slippage from this may indicate a misplaced reluctance on the part of the assessor to keep candidates to deadlines or to motivate candidates, or poor communications between candidate and assessor.

(i) Ensure that assessors apply relevant health, safety and environmental protection procedures, as well as equality and access criteria

Assessors must be aware of their responsibilities under the Health and Safety at Work Act, the Disability Discrimination Act and the Mental Health Act, and the requirements in the *Access to Assessment* document published by the QCA. They need to show you how they have interpreted and applied these requirements, by providing themselves with the right clothing, conforming to the requirements of each particular workplace they visit, reporting situations of risk, and planning assessments to minimize barriers to access. The Data Protection Act will also need to be followed, as confidentiality regarding candidates needs to be maintained.

(j) Monitor how often assessment reviews take place and how effective these are

There must be a minimum of one assessment review per complete unit, but this is probably inadequate for all but experienced candidates. If assessors can indicate in their plans when they think reviews should be held and keep records of whether these were implemented, monitoring should be fairly easy. It is important to separate out any meetings that assessors have with candidates that are focused on pre-assessment planning and training, either for the vocational NVQ or for the requirements for A1 and A2. Assessors occasionally get over-involved in support and training activities and fail to move candidates on in assessment.

(k) Monitor how often assessors give feedback to candidates and how effective this is

When sampling, IVs will look for written records that are signed and dated. It will be important to see whether candidates have acted on assessors' advice and also whether the assessors are following through actions that they have asked candidates to undertake. If there is no evidence of written feedback in candidates' portfolios, the IV will need to check whether oral feedback is going unrecorded, and plan with the assessor how to formalize its recording.

(l) Monitor how accurate and secure assessors' record keeping is

Recording of achievement needs to be in duplicate. The candidate needs a copy, and the assessor needs a copy. Assessors' copies should be kept in such a way that they and others are unable to alter the documentation. Dating and signing all entries helps this process. Online systems prevent any changes to a candidate's evidence or an assessment decision once data have been entered.

(m) Give assessors accurate and helpful feedback on their assessment decisions

Moderating your decisions on an assessor with those of other IVs can help to reassure you that your decisions are sound, as can the feedback from your external verifier or taking part in standardization exercises yourself. Feedback should be given in a way that enables the assessor to get credit for what he or she is doing well and to act on any identified points for improvement that have been found to be needed. All feedback should be constructive.

V1.4: MEET EXTERNAL QUALITY ASSURANCE REQUIREMENTS

(a) Identify how internal assessments will be checked externally and the information needed for this purpose

The documentation received from the awarding body, together with previous external verifier reports, will provide guidance on this. Note the scheduled date of the next planned visit from the EV. You are likely to have to supply a range of material to the EV at least 15 working days before his or her visit. If the EV has not contacted you 30 days before the planned visit, it is advisable to contact him or her to confirm dates, times and what is wanted. Evidence of action to be taken by the centre following the last visit will definitely be required, as will details of any changes in the centre that affect assessment, such as new staff or assessment schedules.

   If there is an internal verifier coordinator (IVC) for the centre, that person is likely to be the point of contact with the external verifier. You will need to liaise with him or her to check that you understand the part you will be playing in the process and what information will be required from you regarding the assessors for whom you are responsible.

(b) Plan, collect and analyse information on internal assessment decisions

You will need data from all the internal verification activity you have undertaken in the period since the last external verifier visit, assuming that the period you have taken to show your competence as an internal verifier has been at least this long so that your assessors have had time to develop through your monitoring processes.

It will probably be most helpful to present this information in a succinct, detailed written report, attaching any helpful data in the form of appendices. These might include lists of assessors and their candidates, tracking documents, or reports of standardization exercises. You could present data relating to the numbers of active and completed candidates for whom your assessors are responsible, and analyse the data, looking for trends such as candidates who are slow to achieve. This may well lead you to take action in the form of supporting certain assessors to be more effective.

(c) Agree the timing and nature of external assessment audit arrangements

You will need to consult with your assessors and their candidates if the EV requests to observe assessment or visit assessment sites other than the main centre. Give estimates of the activities that are likely to be occurring, and check that staff will be available and how long centres will be open before confirming dates and times.

(d) Give supporting background information to external auditors about the assessment process

The EV will normally request exactly what he or she wants. An overall written report is very helpful and shows that you are studying the results of your IV activity, are analysing what has happened and are aware of actions that have been or need to be taken.

Your report can also highlight unusual circumstances that have arisen and affected assessment activity, for example a large increase in the number of candidates following an award for excellence that has been won by the centre, or building activities or illness that has slowed down the assessment opportunities available to candidates.

(e) Explain any issues raised by external auditors and give them supporting information as necessary

During the external verification visit, you may be asked to supply missing or additional information or to justify any of the documentation or decisions that you have supplied. All candidate portfolios not included at the last verification should be available for the verifier, so that he or she can take additional samples. This may involve asking candidates to bring in their previously assessed work, a process that you will need to start some weeks before the verification.

(f) Raise concerns and disagreements about external audit decisions in a clear and constructive way

External assessors may make decisions that indicate that practice needs improving in some way. If you have not supplied relevant evidence or what you have supplied is open to interpretation, then their judgements may need to be revised in the light of additional evidence that you or others can supply. Disagreements and concerns are often resolved in this way. However, the EV may have identified areas for improvement that surprise you, and these need to be carefully clarified, bearing in mind that the EV should be able to justify his or her decisions against the NVQ Code of Conduct. This contains a table of sanctions (see Appendix 2), of which all assessors and verifiers should be aware. The EV should be pleased to advise you on how to meet the code if there are problems.

(g) Refer to the awarding body any questions or concerns that could not be dealt with internally

The centre contact or IVC (who may be different from yourself) is probably the best person to raise matters with the awarding body, which needs to limit, in a structured way, the contact with centres to ensure that key messages are transmitted to the right people. The 'awarding body' is likely to be, initially, the EV or the administrative centre.

(h) Give assessors feedback on external audit decisions

The centre will have a copy of the EV's report, either left at the time of the visit or sent soon afterwards by the awarding body's administrative centre. The action plan from this needs to be available to all assessors. The IV will need to feed back to individual assessors who have had their decisions sampled, so that they are clear as to whether their judgements have been verified as correct or whether they need to reassess any assessment decisions already made.

(i) Ensure that external auditing decisions are included in internal reviews of procedures

The organization needs to consider the outcomes of EVs' decisions and show that it has taken these on board. Colleges and other training organizations supported via the Learning and Skills Council will need to incorporate the findings into the self-assessment report, so as an internal verifier you need to show that you know this has been done. Other organizations will have different reporting arrangements, but again they will need to show how the results have been communicated beyond the assessment team and that they are part of the centre's overall review of quality.

9

Standards for V2: Conduct External Quality Assurance of the Assessment Process

External verifiers are recruited and trained by awarding bodies. They are experienced assessors in their vocational areas. External verifiers of Learning and Development awards, which include the A&V awards, are also qualified and experienced in the area of Learning and Development. All external verifiers need to hold V2 or update from D35. Awarding bodies offer V2 to their verifiers.

External verifiers appointed to centres offering NVQs monitor and audit those centres to ensure that they are complying with the NVQ Code of Practice, the national occupational standards being used, and the awarding bodies' own conditions of approval. They also offer support and advice to centre staff and act as a channel of communication between centres, awarding bodies and lead verifiers.

Part of the monitoring role is to sample the centres' internal verification process. To do this, EVs need to sample all aspects of the internal verification and assessment systems. This means that an EV may need to attend standardization activities, accompany verifiers on observation visits, and talk to assessors or candidates, as well as verify that the assessment decisions made by assessors are accurate. They do *not* reassess candidates' work and will sample only the work of candidates registered with the awarding body.

External verifiers normally act on a consultancy basis for their awarding body, and as such their work is part time, on a daily basis.

V2.1: MONITOR THE INTERNAL QUALITY ASSURANCE PROCESS

(a) Monitor the organization's arrangements for auditing internal assessments.

(b) Plan and apply the monitoring procedures that the awarding body needs.

(c) Monitor how effective the chosen methods are against the necessary outcomes.

(d) Monitor how accurate internal administration and records are.

(e) Monitor the criteria used for choosing assessors.

(f) Recommend how the organization can comply with all relevant audit processes and procedures.

(g) Review how the internal assessment audit system is evaluated to ensure that the organization can comply with all processes and procedures.

(h) Give the awarding body accurate reports on the internal assessment process and any changes that may be necessary.

V2.2: VERIFY THE QUALITY OF ASSESSMENT

(a) Check to ensure that assessors and internal verifiers/auditors have the technical and vocational experience necessary to assess the agreed standards.

(b) Monitor the quality of induction and support procedures for assessors.

(c) Check that assessors have applied relevant health, safety and environmental protection procedures, as well as equality and access criteria, when carrying out assessment.

(d) Check the decisions made by a number of assessors to be sure that each is applying the assessment requirements consistently over time, with different candidates and in different places if necessary.

(e) Get evidence of how effective working relationships between assessors and candidates are, along with assessment reviews.

(f) Review how accurate, prompt and secure individual assessors' record keeping is.

(g) Check that assessors have been given accurate and helpful feedback on their assessment decisions and performance.

(h) Identify concerns over assessors' decisions and review these with internal verifiers and auditors.

(i) Make a record of the results of the audit, using agreed procedures and documents.

(j) Agree and make a record of a course of action to put things right if assessment arrangements have not been satisfactory.

(k) Follow the agreed complaints and appeals procedure that the awarding body needs if improvement and other related issues have not been sorted out.

(l) Identify and highlight good practice and ensure you give positive feedback.

(m) Give the awarding body full and accurate reports on the internal assessment process and any recommendations for changes to it.

V2.3: PROVIDE INFORMATION, ADVICE AND SUPPORT ON THE INTERNAL QUALITY ASSURANCE OF ASSESSMENT PROCESSES

(a) Make early and regular contact with internal verifiers/auditors at all stages when developing assessment systems and procedures.

(b) Identify concerns over the internal audit process and review these with internal verifiers/auditors.

(c) Ensure that effective administrative arrangements are developed to support the internal audit and assessment process.

(d) Agree how internal assessments will be externally audited, and the information needed for this purpose.

(e) Give information and advice on the timing and nature of external audit arrangements.

(f) Give the centre details concerning the people to be interviewed or involved in the audit process.

(g) Identify and explain any issues concerning understanding of the awarding or accrediting body's criteria and requirements.

(h) Raise concerns about internal audit procedures and assessment decisions in a clear and constructive way.

(i) Give constructive and helpful feedback on external audit decisions.

(j) Identify opportunities to improve internal audits and assessments, and give advice and support to help put these improvements into practice.

(k) Carry out the appropriate complaints and appeals procedures if you are not able to resolve disagreements or concerns.

V2.4: EVALUATE THE EFFECTIVENESS OF EXTERNAL QUALITY ASSURANCE OF THE ASSESSMENT PROCESS

(a) Identify and use internal assessment audit information to evaluate the systems and procedures of awarding bodies.

(b) Contribute to the awarding body's standardization arrangements.
(c) Evaluate how effective the process of candidate assessment is as part of the internal quality assurance process, and report back to the awarding body and internal auditors.
(d) Review recording and administrative arrangements against information needed by the awarding body.
(e) Contribute to the awarding body's reviews of external auditing arrangements.

Section 2

The Requirements of the Standards for Teachers, Tutors and Trainers in the Lifelong Learning Sector (STTTLLS): Domain E: Assessment

Introduction: The Lifelong Learning Sector

Section 2 explains the knowledge requirements of Domain E (Assessment) of the Professional Standards for Teachers, Tutors and Trainers in the Lifelong Learning Sector (STTTLLS) and is for anyone interested in understanding current ideas on assessment throughout the sector. Chapter 10 has been written so that it can stand alone, but as the whole book is about good assessment practice we would encourage readers to look at other relevant sections. For that reason and also to avoid duplicating information, we have cross-referenced some of the text in the chapter to other chapters of the book.

The STTTLLS have been formed into different units by SVUK, and Chapter 10 is of relevance to the level 3 and level 4 units Principles and Practice of Assessment, in that it provides the underpinning knowledge and understanding of assessment for these units. However, it also underpins parts of some other units as well. See Appendix 5 for the Principles and Practice of Assessment Units at L3 and L4.

In Chapter 10, we will be looking at assessment across a range of qualifications and, rather than focusing just on work-based assessment, as with NVQs, we will be looking at the assessment that takes place in more formal teaching or training situations. Unlike NVQs, which focus on accreditation of competence rather than evidence of learning, assessment and learning are closely linked in more formal teaching environments. In order to reflect this different emphasis and also to use the language of the STTTLLS, in this section we will refer to 'learners' rather than 'candidates'.

We will also draw on ideas of good practice in education and training that have emerged from DfES, Ofsted, other government bodies and various research projects, which have influenced the thinking behind the standards. A key feature of many current ideas on good practice is an emphasis on 'personalized' learning, which means: 'working in partnership with the learner and employer – to tailor their learning experience and pathways, according to their needs and personal objectives – in a way which delivers success' (DfES, 2006, *Personalizing Further Education: Developing a Vision*, p 7).

This is the context for the following discussions on different aspects of assessment as required in the STTTLLS.

10

Knowledge Requirements for STTTLLS Domain E: Assessment

THE LIFELONG LEARNING SECTOR

The name 'lifelong learning sector' (LLS) recognizes that learning does not take place just at one point, but carries on throughout people's lives, both formally and informally, and that there are a number of different types of formal learning environments where this learning is assessed and accredited. These are often funded through the Learning and Skills Council (LSC), although other sources of funding may also be used.

Examples of different environments and types of assessment situations could include:

- *learners in colleges of further education* taking:
  - NVQs
  - other vocational qualifications, such as BTEC or City and Guilds certificates or diplomas
  - more advanced vocational qualifications such as foundation degrees
  - academic qualifications such as GCSE and A/S or A levels;
- *trainees in Private Training Organisations* taking:
  - NVQs
  - other vocational qualifications, such as European Computing Driving Licence (ECDL);
- *trainees in public sector organizations*:
  - NVQs and Apprenticeships (eg in the Health Service)

- skills for life qualifications (eg prison service, probation service, young offender institutions);
- *Job Centre Plus programmes;*
- *trainees in private sector organizations* (including large or medium-size industrial or commercial companies) taking:
  - NVQs and Modern Apprenticeships
  - 'Train to Gain' employer-supported training;
- *learners in adult and community learning* taking:
  - courses accredited by accrediting bodies such as the Open College Network
  - skills for life qualifications;
- *learners with learning difficulties or disabilities* taking a whole range of qualifications at different levels with appropriate support.

This is by no means a complete list and is only intended to give a flavour of the kinds of places and types of courses that are covered in the LLS.

KNOWLEDGE REQUIREMENTS FOR STTTLLS DOMAIN E: ASSESSMENT

EK 1.1[1] Theories and principles of assessment and the application of different forms of assessment, including initial, formative and summative assessment in teaching and learning

Assessment theories

A theory is a framework that helps us in understanding, explaining or predicting some area of interest or concern.

Theories of assessment are usually concerned with exploring the different types and purposes of assessment and how various types and methods of assessment can help or hinder those purposes. A helpful distinction here is between assessment that is solely or mainly for *testing* learning and assessment that is mainly for *helping* learning.

Some assessment theory may be closely linked to other types of theory, including:

---

[1] Values and criteria are prefixed by letters. K = knowledge, P = practice and S = scope.

- *Theories of learning:* behaviourist, cognitivist, humanist, social. So, for example, if you favour a humanist theory of learning, where learning is about the development of the whole person, you are likely to consider types of assessment that address broad and complex aspects of thought and emotions and that are used as a process of development for the learner.
- *Theories of intelligence:* one example here is Gardner's theory of multiple intelligences. If you accept that people have different types of intelligences, then you will consider how different types of assessment might be used to test or develop those intelligences.
- *Theories of motivation:* an important educational notion is that good assessment practice can motivate learners. If you accept this idea, then considering different types of motivation, as well as barriers to learning, could also help with determining appropriate types of assessment.
- *Theories of communication:* good assessment involves good communication. Assessment tools need to take into account the language and communication levels of the learner and attempt to communicate as unambiguously and effectively as possible. Good assessment feedback needs to take into account the audience for which it is intended, eg is it the learner or is it an external moderator?

Principles of assessment

Principles of assessment are the common processes and ideas that underpin the different purposes and types of assessment and are drawn from theory and practical experience.

There has been a shift in the way that assessment has been understood and theorized over the last couple of decades:

- Previously the emphasis was on assessment as a separate process, concerned only with measuring attainment. Currently the emphasis is on assessment as an integral part of the learning process.
- Previously, the emphasis was on a few highly standardized methods of assessment, which were applied to everyone. Currently the emphasis is on exploring a whole range of different types of assessment and trying to fit the assessment not just to the purpose but to the learner and learning situation.
- Previously, only the teacher was involved in assessing the student. Currently, wherever possible, the learner is involved in his or her own assessment.

Good practice in assessment involves certain key principles:

- Teaching, learning and assessment are integrally linked together.
- Everyone has the capacity to improve.
- As far as possible the type of assessment should take into account the needs of the individual learner.
- As far as possible the learner should be actively involved in his or her own assessment.
- Both the teacher and the learner should be clear on what is being assessed and how it is being assessed.
- The assessment should be fair and unbiased.
- The type of assessment used should match the purpose for which it is intended (validity of assessment).
- The assessment should be consistent (reliability of assessment).

Purposes of assessment

When considering what and how to assess, it is very important to be clear about the purposes for the assessment. Some typical purposes of assessment would include one or more of the following:

- to find out the learner's current level of capability in the subject or skill area;
- to find out what support the learner might need in order to be successful in his or her learning;
- to find out what methods of teaching and learning would be most appropriate for the learner;
- to provide the teacher with information about what the learner is learning during the course and how he or she can be helped to improve;
- to provide the learner with information about what he or she is learning and what help the learner thinks he or she needs to improve;
- to motivate the learner to continue;
- to motivate the learner to do better;
- to motivate the teacher to try different ways of helping the learner learn;
- to provide the teacher with evidence of what the learner has learnt;

Table 10.1 Three categories of assessment

Initial assessment	Finding out about the learner.
Formative assessment	Helping the learner towards his or her goal (see also Table 5.1).
Summative assessment	Measuring what the learner has achieved.

- to provide other stakeholders (eg awarding bodies, parents, potential or existing employers, universities) with evidence of what the learner has achieved.

Initial assessment

The idea of initial assessment is based on the following: 1) in order to help someone to learn more, both teacher and the learner need to be aware of what the learner knows and can do already, and what he or she still needs to learn; 2) both teacher and learner need to be aware of how the learner likes to learn. In other words, people learn by building on the knowledge and skills they already possess and people like to learn in different ways. Initial assessment can provide important information in both these areas.

The term 'initial assessment' means what it says, ie assessment at the beginning of something, but the term can be used to reflect different situations, and this can sometimes be confusing for the new teacher. It is important that you know the various ways the term is used, and are clear how it is being used in your own work context.

Examples of initial assessment in the lifelong learning sector include the following:

- Initial assessment might be part of the process by which a learner is guided on to a course by specialist advisers at certain FE colleges. Here the learner might be given an initial assessment that would enable the adviser to guide the learner on to a particular level of course. This assessment might include gaining information about the learner's interests and abilities, as well as identifying any general issues of support necessary for this learner. For example, if the learner already knew he or she was dyslexic, then this could be recorded straight away and taken into account during the guidance and discussion on what extra support the learner might need, whichever course he or she chose.
- Initial assessment might take the form of an entry test designed to test an applicant's ability to deal with a specific course. For example, a subject such as plumbing requires the ability to solve problems, so the entry test questions might be designed to represent situations and problems that the learner might meet on the actual course and would test his or her potential to deal with these.
- Initial assessment might also be used right at the start of a course, this time more specifically, to help the teacher identify the learner's current level of knowledge and skills and also to identify any additional support needs.

Throughout the LLS, a key aspect of initial assessment includes assessing literacy and numeracy skills to ensure that, where necessary, the correct specific support is put in place for the learner. Literacy assessment would probably include assessment for both reading and writing skills as these are essential for most courses. However, in some cases, the teacher might decide to focus on certain aspects of a learner's ability during an initial assessment and assess other aspects of his or her ability on an ongoing basis during the first few weeks of a course. One example of this would be where a teacher decides that a learner's ability to read a certain level of information needs to be assessed straight away, because without that ability he or she cannot even begin the course, but that the learner's writing ability can be assessed more naturally during the first piece of written work.

Individual learning plans (ILPs)

Following initial assessment, learners will usually formulate an individual learning plan in discussion with the teacher, which identifies the goals the learner wishes to achieve and the support required for him or her to achieve them. The initial assessment provides some important detail to inform this plan, which is then reviewed on an ongoing basis to monitor the learner's progress and identify any subsequent support needs.

Confusion between 'initial' and 'diagnostic' assessment

You may encounter the terms 'initial assessment' and 'diagnostic assessment' used in different ways. This can be confusing, but there is no clear and consistent way that these terms are used:

● Initial assessments are used to 'diagnose' learners' needs and so sometimes the terms 'initial assessment' and 'diagnostic assessment' are used to mean the same thing.
● Sometimes the two terms are used together, ie 'initial diagnostic assessment'.
● However, sometimes they are used to mean different stages of the same process, where the initial assessment provides a certain level of detail, but a diagnostic assessment provides a greater level of detail. An example of this is where a teacher carries out an initial assessment and identifies that the learner has problems with writing. The learner is then referred to a literacy specialist, who carries out a diagnostic assessment that identifies the particular problem areas in specific detail.

The only advice we can give here is always to check out what the terms mean in the context where you meet them!

Formative assessment

In Part 2 we cover formative assessment in relation to NVQs, and you should find that part useful. The principle of formative assessment is that it 'forms' the learner towards a desired goal. In NVQs this is fairly straightforward – formative assessment is geared to helping the candidate become competent and meet specific performance criteria. However, formative assessment may serve a number of different purposes in the range of qualifications and contexts in the LLS.

Examples of formative assessment in the LLS are:

- A joinery teacher walks around the workshop in a private training organization while learners are carrying out a specific joinery task. The teacher observes each student and stops where necessary, pointing out how the students might improve what they are doing or correcting mistakes. The purpose here is to provide immediate and ongoing feedback to help learners in the task they are actually performing, and in this case there is little distinction between formative assessment and teaching.
- A teacher on a foundation degree in educational administration offered in an FE college receives the first draft of a learner's written assignment. The teacher sends back the first draft accompanied by a completed formative assessment sheet, which includes specific comments on how to improve academic writing skills. The purpose here is to provide clear and detailed guidance on how to improve, giving the learner an opportunity to read the feedback in his own time and ask for clarification on any points he does not understand.
- A basic skills teacher working in a community centre has a progress tutorial with a learner, where they look in detail at the initial learning goals identified in the ILP. During this process the learner identifies what she thinks she has achieved so far and, in discussion with the learner, the teacher gives formative feedback on the learner's development and what she needs to do to improve or develop further. The purpose here is to provide clear guidance and action planning for further development, but also to model a process in which the learner is actively involved in her own assessment.

As well as providing learners with information, it is also important to remember that formative assessment gives teachers information about their own teaching and how they may need to adjust, clarify or even radically alter their approach.

Summative assessment

Whereas formative assessment relates to development, summative assessment relates to what has been achieved at a particular point or at particular points in a course of study. This may take many forms, including a written examination, a module assignment, an online test or an observed practical task. The main purposes behind summative assessment are to measure the learner's performance against an expected standard and to draw conclusions about how well he or she has performed.

Sometimes summative assessments occur at various times during a course, as for example in end-of-unit tests. However, even at the end of a course, summative assessment is not really 'the end' in that it can provide information for learners to decide on their future learning and directions for development.

EK 1.2 Ways to devise, select, use and appraise assessment tools, including, where appropriate, those that exploit new and emerging technologies

An assessment tool is the method or resource you use to carry out an assessment. From the discussions in the previous sections, you will be aware that it is important to consider the purpose of the assessment and how you can devise or select the best 'tool' for the job.

In assessing NVQs, the two main types of assessment tools are direct observation of performance and product, and oral questioning. Other types of NVQ assessment are covered in Chapter 5. As we discuss in Chapters 11 and 12, there is a move towards paperless portfolios in the form of the increased use of e-portfolios and a greater reliance on the assessor to provide more in-depth evidence of assessment and to record professional discussion.

However, in the LLS as a whole, a far wider range of assessment tools may be used, although teachers may be restricted in some of the assessments they use. For example, learners may have to sit a formal written examination at the end of a course because this is prescribed by an awarding body.

Deciding on assessment tools

Some assessment tools are prescribed by awarding bodies, and the teacher may have little choice but to use them. However, it is worth remembering that awarding bodies are made up of human beings and often include ex-teachers. Comments and ideas for change from teachers in the 'field' having difficulty with particular assessment systems should be taken seriously and used to help improve what is on offer.

In some circumstances, the teacher can make a choice about which types of assessment tools to use, especially in formative assessments.

Key questions in deciding on appropriate assessment tools are:

- Why is this learner being assessed (what it the purpose of this assessment)?

- What knowledge or skills is the learner being expected to learn?
- What are the best ways of finding out if the learner has learnt them?
- What is the most appropriate assessment tool for this learner in this situation?
- How can I use this information to help the learner learn better?
- How can the learner use this information to help him or her learn better?
- How can I use this information to help me teach better?
- Are there any creative ways that I could use new technology?

In these questions, you will probably have noted that we focus on 'the learner' rather than 'the learners'. This is because personalization of learning does imply some differentiation between different learners.

In practice, much of the time, the teacher will have to use the same assessment tool with all the learners, as being more time-efficient and more consistent. This will be especially true for summative assessments. However, in initial assessments and, particularly, in formative assessments, it may be more appropriate and less difficult to customize the assessment tool to the individual learner, and the teacher may think of more creative ways of finding out what the learner has learnt. The ideas below take into account the notion that people learn in different ways and have different strengths and abilities, which traditional methods of assessment may not allow them to demonstrate. When you read them, you will probably have many more ideas on how they could be used.

Currently in the LLS, it is also important to take into account the requirements of the minimum core for literacy, numeracy and information and communications technology (ICT) when designing assessment tools. The minimum core requirements are those that teachers themselves need in these three areas in order to be able to understand the background of their learners and work effectively with learners to develop their skills in a holistic way. The minimum core standards are still being developed at the time of writing. See 'Supporting Materials' for a useful website.

EK 1.3 Ways to develop and promote peer and self-assessment

We have already mentioned the different purposes of assessment and have emphasized that assessment is about helping people to learn as well as about measuring the standard they have achieved. The teacher is there to help in this process, but the ultimate goal of education must be that the learner has learnt how to learn independently and hence is able to develop and progress on his or her own after any formal input has ended. This is essential if the individual is to be involved in lifelong learning.

Table 10.2 Some possible assessment tools, including some suggestions for their potential for including minimum core language, literacy, numeracy, and information and communications technology

Type of assessment tool	Some examples of what this assessment tool can test	Minimum core
Written assessments		
Examination	Knowledge, understanding of concepts and ideas, factual recall, ability to construct a logical argument, ability to provide clear and logical written answers in strict timescale	li, la, n
Short answer test, online testing	Knowledge, factual recall, superficial understanding of concepts and ideas	li, n, ICT
Essays	Knowledge, understanding of concepts and ideas, factual recall, ability to construct a logical argument, ability to provide clear and logical written answers	li, la, ICT
Assignments	Knowledge, understanding of concepts and ideas, ability to research different types of information, ability to organize material, ability to manage own time	li, la, n, ICT
Writing articles	Knowledge, understanding of concepts and ideas, ability to summarize for a specific audience	li, la, n (statistics), ICT
Writing leaflets, producing leaflets in electronic formats	Knowledge, understanding of concepts and ideas, ability to summarize for a specific audience, ability to lay out information in a way that is easy for others to understand	li, la, ICT
Online discussions, blogs	Knowledge, understanding concepts and ideas, ability to present an argument, ability to interact online with other people, ability to present information, ability to use ICT for online discussion	li, la, ICT
Portfolios, e-portfolios	Evidence of skills, knowledge, ability to organize and present verbal and visual material in an accessible way; e-portfolios – use of ICT	li, la, n, ICT
Reflective journals	Ability to evaluate own and others' practice and to use information and ideas from practical experience to develop and improve	li, la

Type of assessment tool	Some examples of what this assessment tool can test	Minimum core
Oral assessments		
Learner answering questions	Factual knowledge, knowledge of processes and procedures, ability to give answers quickly and clearly	li, la, n
Learner devising questions	Factual knowledge, ability to consider level of audience	li, la, n
Learner presentations	Knowledge, skills in presentation, ability to construct a logical sequence of ideas or information, ability to summarize, ability to consider level of audience, ability to construct interesting visual resources	li, la, n, ICT
Role plays	Ability to perform real-life skills when it is not possible to assess in a real-life situation, ability to put self in place of others	la
Participation in group discussions	Ability to put forward ideas or arguments orally, ability to listen to others	li, la
Debates	Ability to construct and deliver a logical oral argument from a particular viewpoint, ability to argue against others' ideas, ability to use emotive language	li, la, n (statistics)
Song, rap lyrics	Ability to use language creatively, ability to link words and music, ability to use language to suit a particular audience	li, la
Audio-visual assessments		
Poster displays	Knowledge, ability to summarize using a combination of visual and verbal media, ability to create an interesting display for a particular audience	li, la, n, ICT
Art work – drawings, paintings, graphics, 3D designs	Practical skills, ability to use visual media creatively, ability to create an interesting display for a particular audience, spatial ability	n (calculations), ICT
Art or design objects	Practical skills, spatial ability	n (calculations)
Photographs, using camera or mobile phone	Practical skills, ability to use visual media creatively, ability to summarize using visual rather than verbal media	li, la, ICT

Table 10.2 *(Continued)*

Type of assessment tool	Some examples of what this assessment tool can test	Minimum core
Production of DVDs or videos	Practical skills, ability to use visual media creatively, ability to summarize, ability to produce for a particular audience	li, la, ICT
Interactive whiteboard displays, web displays	Practical skills, ability to use visual and verbal media, ability to summarize, ability to produce for a particular audience, presentation skills	li, la, n, ICT
Production of radio programmes, podcasts, group texts using mobile phone	Practical skills, ability to use verbal media, ability to summarize, ability to produce for a particular audience, presentation skills, ability to use ICT	li, la, ICT
Production of piece of music	Creative skills, ability to produce for a particular audience	n, ICT
Practical assessments		
Practical workshop tasks	Practical skills	n, ICT
Practical demonstrations	Practical skills, oral skills, ability to present practical skills so that other people can understand	li, la
Project work, community-based work, event organizing	Research skills, organizing skills, skills of working with others, verbal and oral presentation skills	li, la, n, ICT

Key: li – literacy; la – language; n – numeracy; ICT – information and communications technology.
You will find more detailed discussion of some NVQ assessment tools in Chapter 5.

If we want a learner to become independent, then we need to think about how assessment can help that process. In many types of assessment, it is someone else who decides how well the learner has performed, for example the person marking GCSE scripts for the exam board, the work-based assessor watching a practical task being carried out, or the teacher assessing an assignment. In these cases, we could say that assessment is being 'done' to the learner, rather than the learner having a chance to take part and begin to learn to understand the standards required. Current good practice emphasizes how learners might be involved, by using self- or peer assessment.

Self-assessment

Teachers can help learners to learn how to self-assess so that the learners can take ownership of the standards they need to achieve. The eventual aim is that they will become independent learners with the ability to become self-directed in developing new skills and knowledge. This self-assessment needs to achieve three goals: It needs to:

1. be realistic;
2. be accurate;
3. recognize strengths as well as areas for improvement.

The following are examples:

- In the induction for a BTEC diploma in travel and tourism, the teacher talks through with the whole group how they will be assessed, the criteria that will be used and how feedback will be given. The teacher then carries out a pair work activity where each pair is encouraged to use Post-its to jot down any questions about the work they will have to do and how it will be assessed. The teacher then collects the Post-its, sticks them up and answers each of them in turn, making sure that all the learners' queries are answered fully.
- In a City and Guilds level 2 plumbing course, learners have to self-assess their practical work before the teacher assesses the work, using an assessment sheet that they have helped devise based on the awarding body criteria. By doing this, they are given the opportunity to look at their own work with a critical eye and also to have the chance to correct any mistakes before the teacher is involved.
- In the first module on a foundation studies degree for teaching support assistants, the teacher carries out an exercise where learners have to 'mark' two short sample (fictional) assignments – one poor and one excellent. They then discuss with the teacher how they judged the assignments. This exercise raises a number of issues about standards in academic writing and provides a model of good practice that can help the learners to become aware of the standards they should aim for themselves.

Peer assessment

Involving learners in peer assessment through providing opportunities to assess each other's work can also help to develop independence from the teacher and, if done in a constructive and cooperative way, can be a rewarding experience. However, if handled badly, peer assessment can sometimes be a demotivating and damaging experience for particular learners. Teachers can help to make peer assessment a positive experience in the following ways:

- Give plenty of opportunities for learners to become aware of good practice in assessing and giving feedback. This can be done through teachers presenting a model of such good practice themselves, but also by drawing learners' attention to the principles of giving constructive feedback.
- Give some opportunities for practice in giving helpful feedback under supportive and controlled conditions, before allowing full peer assessment to take place.
- Set down clear ground rules for peer assessment.
- Carefully choose the composition of the pairs or groups that will peer-assess.
- Create structures for giving feedback that build in comments on strengths as well as areas for improvement.
- Ensure that feedback focuses on the work and not the person.
- Praise and value good skills in peer assessment and giving feedback.

See also the section on feedback in Chapter 3.

EK 2.1 Issues of equality and diversity in assessment

The two terms 'equality' and 'diversity' are often used together and are closely associated, although they do not mean the same thing. There has been increased emphasis on the way that equality and diversity issues are handled in education and training and also the importance of staff development in these areas. The LSC currently has in place a National Equality and Diversity Strategy 2004–2007, which sets out six core priority areas – leadership, reaching learners including those who are disengaged, supporting compliance with regulations and legislation, personalized learning, working with employers, and measuring outcomes. Ofsted inspections now include consideration of how equality and diversity are addressed. The 'Every Child Matters' national framework is also a key driver in this area.

The term 'equality' refers to the importance of treating people equally and giving people the same opportunities, whatever their background, age, ethnicity, religion, gender, disability (mental or physical) or sexual orientation. However, treating people equally does not mean dealing with people in exactly the same way. The term 'diversity' refers to the differences between individuals, and the importance of appreciating those differences and acting accordingly. So you may want to give learners equal opportunities to achieve a qualification, but because of their diversity you may have to offer each of them different kinds of input or support for them to achieve the same eventual goal.

Some examples can be found in Chapter 3.

EK 2.2 Concepts of validity, reliability and sufficiency in assessment

These concepts are also covered in Chapter 3.

Table 10.3 Assessment concepts

Sufficiency	Whether the assessment method gives you sufficient evidence to make a judgement.
Reliability	How far the assessment method can give consistent, dependable results.
Validity	How far the assessment method can test what it means to test.

You may come across terms relating to different aspects of validity:

- *Face validity:* 'on the face of it' the test looks all right, seems suitable for the purpose and fits the culture of the teaching environment.
- *Content validity:* covers a relevant sample of the overall knowledge and skills expected to have been learnt (eg it tested some aspects of the syllabus).
- *Construct validity:* the method is as close as it can be to testing what it is intended to test.
- *Predictive validity:* the method has some capacity to predict future performance (eg in another environment), not only current performance.

Balancing validity and reliability is a juggling act, especially when you bring in the importance of providing equality of opportunity and addressing the diverse needs of learners. Good practice means that all of these components need to be taken into account.

EK 2.3 The principles of assessment design in relation to own specialist area

The DfES and Ofsted have now placed a great deal of importance on the subject specialist knowledge and skills of teachers in the LLS.

Different specialist subjects and qualifications often favour a particular method or methods of assessment, and teachers within that specialist area need to become familiar with that approach to assessment. Remember that what is valid assessment for one specialist area might not be valid for a different area.

Bearing in mind your specialism, when designing an assessment tool it is important to consider the following questions:

- What methods have I already used, observed in use or been assessed in myself in this specialist area?
- How valid and reliable have these methods been?
- What is considered good practice in assessment by teachers and awarding bodies in my specialist area?
- What do I consider good practice in assessment in my own specialist area?
- What assessment ideas, tools and pro formas that already exist can I, or must I, use?
- How much freedom have I got to adapt or improve on existing assessment tools – to make them more valid or reliable, or to make them more suitable for personalized learning?

EK 2.4 How to work as part of a team to establish equitable assessment processes

In order to make sure that assessment is reliable, there are various ways in which other people in the teaching and assessment team are involved. These can be processes such as joint design of assessment tools or discussing learners' work on an informal basis, for example asking the opinion of a more experienced colleague on a piece of work that you think should fail, but you want to make sure. There will also be formal processes to ensure consistency of assessment, such as double marking, internal moderation and external moderation or external examination. In NVQs the terms used are 'standardization', 'internal verification' and 'external verification', and Chapters 4 and 13 give an overview of the processes involved. However, in other education and training contexts you will sometimes see other terms.

EK 3.1 Ways to establish learners' involvement in and personal responsibility for assessment of their learning

Some examples of getting learners involved in assessment have already been suggested in the sections on self- and peer assessment. Important aspects of increasing learner involvement include the following:

Table 10.4 Processes to ensure consistency of assessment

Internal and external verification	See Chapters 4 and 13
Double marking	One assessor marks a piece of work. Another assessor then marks the same piece of work. The mark is then compared and adjusted, if needed. Usually used where grades or numerical marks are involved.
Internal moderation	An agreed sample of marked student work is presented for internal moderation by internal moderators. Internal moderators are designated moderators within the organization or course team whose role is to look at work, based on an agreed sample, and to agree or disagree with the decisions. In some courses, the internal moderator may have the right to recommend that assessment decisions, marks or grades are changed, but in all cases will have the role of identifying any general issues of quality that have arisen from the moderation.
External moderation	An external moderator is someone outside the organization who has the professional ability to look at an agreed sample of marked work, give informed advice on the quality of the assessment processes and confirm or query the assessment decisions made by the assessors. Generally the external moderator produces a formal report.
External examination	This term is used in HE programmes. An external examiner generally carries out the same work as an external moderator. Generally the external examiner produces a formal report.

- Making sure that learners can understand the processes of assessment, by sharing how you approach it and what you look for when you are assessing.
- Making sure that the assessment tools are as relevant and fair to learners as possible.
- Taking the learners' views seriously. So, for example, if they self-assess, discuss their ideas with respect, rather than immediately imposing your own. They may have important perceptions about what constitutes good practice that can help the learning and assessment process. If their self-

assessment is very different to your assessment, explore why this has occurred – it could provide important information for you to help them.
- Don't throw learners in at the deep end. As with any other learning process, you should devise strategies to increase their levels of responsibility gradually, moving from quick informal assessments to more detailed evaluative reflections.

EK 3.2 Ways to ensure access to assessment within a learning programme

This has been covered in Chapter 3. A key aspect to remember is that, if possible, we would like all our learners to succeed, although we work within the constraints of assessment systems and organizational requirements, which set the standards that must be met. Hence if there are ways in which we can help learners to be assessed fairly and according to their individual circumstances and needs, then it is our professional duty to explore them and provide personalized opportunities where resources and time make them possible.

EK 4.2 The role of feedback in effective evaluation and improvement of own assessment skills

For NVQ assessors working towards the A units, there is an established structure in place that means they need to be observed actually assessing and giving feedback and they are then given feedback on how they perform and how they could improve.

Given the close relationship between different types of assessment and ways to enable learners to develop and learn, it is important that a teacher's skills in assessing, both informally and formally, are also given a chance to improve through specific focus on this area of development.

Ways of getting feedback on your assessment skills include the following:

- Get an experienced colleague to observe you.
- Ask your tutor on a teacher training programme to focus on how well you assess during one teaching observation.
- Identify actions to improve your assessment skills in discussion with your mentor.
- Get feedback – formal and informal – from your learners on different types of assessment you use and how these could be improved.
- Write reflections to explore and evaluate the different ways you assess, using information from some or all of the above, as well as the actual experiences and results related to the assessments you use with learners.

Confusion between assessment and evaluation

Sometimes the terms 'assessment' and 'evaluation' are confused. 'Assessment' is judging performance against an agreed standard. 'Evaluation' is judging the value of what has been experienced or achieved by considering a range of sources of information, including your own opinion and the opinions of others, as well as practical outcomes, such as assessment results.

EK 5.1 The role of assessment and associated organizational procedures in relation to the quality cycle

The results of formal assessments are seen as an indicator of the quality of a course, in a number of different ways:

- If a large number of students achieve certification, then the course has a good chance of meeting its targets for retention and achievement. These results feed into the results for organizational targets, which have been set to meet government targets, and these results in turn affect the funding received by the organization in future.
- If a high proportion of students achieve qualifications, then it is seen as one indication that the course is being taught well and the learners are learning effectively.
- In many organizations, the course leader writes an end-of-course review, which is received and monitored by a member of senior management or by a review panel. Student results will form part of the end-of-course review and will give an indication of whether there needs to be any radical intervention or whether there could be anything done to improve already good-quality provision. The appropriate person (people) will then take action, and this action will be reported and monitored.
- In most organizations the external moderator or external examiner reports are considered in detail, actions are identified and responses are reported and monitored.

EK 5.2 The assessment requirements of individual learning programmes and procedures for conducting and recording internal and/or external assessments

All teachers have the responsibility to keep up to date with the assessment requirements on all their courses and for all their learners. You can get some of this information from more experienced colleagues, but beware! Assessment regulations and procedures can change, and it is important that you have the latest information. Most awarding bodies send out regular newsletters and updates to those on their mailing list. There are also websites you can access, but in some cases there can be a time lapse between a new assessment procedure or regulation and its appearance on a website.

Although teachers complain (with some justification) about the amount of paperwork they need to fill in, the accurate recording of assessments is extremely important. This is for learners, who in most cases will have invested considerable time and effort in trying to achieve success, and for the organization, which is accountable to a range of outside bodies.

EK 5.3 The necessary/appropriate assessment information to communicate to others who have a legitimate interest in learner achievement

- In normal circumstances, the Data Protection Act 1998 prevents information about individual assessments being released to any outside stakeholders, such as employers. The major exception here is students who are under the age of 16, where information about assessments can be released to the parents or legal guardians.
- However, outside stakeholders such as the LSC or DfES have a legitimate right to gain statistical assessment information from the organizations involved, and each organization must have proper systems in place to ensure that accurate and comprehensive statistical information is received by these stakeholders.
- As part of their inspection processes, Ofsted inspectors will consider statistics on student achievement and will also consider reports from external and internal moderation processes.
- Awarding bodies may also have a right to statistical information on those learners who have taken their qualifications.

SUMMARY

This chapter has given an overview of some of the major aspects of the STTLLS standards in Domain E: Assessment. It is intended as a starting point for you to reflect on how you assess and to find out more about assessment by observing others, asking questions of colleagues and learners and undertaking further reading on the theory, policy and practice of assessment.

Part 4

Preparation and Planning for Assessment and Certification

Introduction: A Candidates' Guide to Effective and Efficient Working

Part 1 has information on the need for skills training and good assessment, NVQs and vocational qualifications, and the organizations connected with the development, delivery and quality assurance of NVQs and vocational qualifications. In Part 2, we describe the procedures, processes and people involved in the assessment of NVQs and vocational qualifications. Part 3 explains the performance criteria of the standards to which assessors and internal verifiers must work and gives details of the specific assessment and verification units. The three chapters in Part 4 should provide learners, candidates and trainers with underpinning knowledge for assessing in general, as well as the essential knowledge for the PPA and the A&V awards.

In earlier editions of this book, we described in some detail the ways that candidates could present their (assessor/verifier) evidence for assessment. Awarding bodies now give detailed guidance on this subject, and many have developed their own preferred documentation and systems. However, we have always followed a common-sense and minimalist approach to the selection and presentation of evidence, particularly as it relates to the assessor and verifier awards. We are pleased to see that ENTO has followed our line, as shown in their 'Back to Basics' approach.

We are assuming that many people reading Part 4 will be taking or intending to take the assessor/verifier qualifications or the PPA qualification themselves. Each chapter focuses on some of the aspects of each role that we have noticed that candidates (and sometimes qualified assessors/verifiers) can find difficult. These chapters will also be useful for qualified staff who want to check through potential trouble spots in order to familiarize themselves with a new environment.

There is a lot more help and support available now for anyone working with NVQs or VQs. In particular, the web links and the ENTO publications listed in 'Supporting Materials' are worth exploring.

Candidates for any qualification know that there will be some type of assessment process they will need to undertake in order to get their qualification. There are some learners who enrol on to courses for the joy of learning and have no need for a qualification, and so sometimes opt to do limited assessments, but, for the vast majority of learners, assessment of their work is a crucial part of their study.

11

The Candidate as an Active Participant

The more prepared you are before you start your course, the better you will be able settle down to the work involved. A day spent 'finding out' before you register for a qualification can save you wasting precious time later. It can feel strange going back to learning as an adult, but we can assure you that you certainly won't be the only one wondering what is going to happen and how you will cope! The more you understand about what might happen, the better able you will be placed to ask any necessary questions. You may also find you take in much more in the first few sessions. Many adults forget most things they have been told in the first few weeks because it's all so new! Once you are committed to a qualification, then being proactive in setting yourself targets, checking your progress regularly with assessments, and meeting deadlines will give you positive feedback and the motivation to finish with a flourish!

MAKING A GOOD START

There are three parts to the introductory phase of starting a course or qualification: pre-course information, guidance and advice; initial assessment; and enrolment and induction.

Pre-course/qualification information, guidance and advice

Your accredited centre should be able to provide you with information on your course or qualification and the entry requirements, and also on the assessment scheme, the type of assessments and when they are to be done. You will need details of costs and whether you are exempt or can access funding from elsewhere. You may find this information on the centre's website. Many centres have open days or general information sessions. You may need to book an appointment, or there may be a queuing system. It is usually possible to drop in to centres and talk to someone about general issues, though specialist trainers or teachers may not be available. Candidates for assessor/verifier and the PPA units should ensure they are qualified (usually to at least L3) and/or well experienced in their *specialist vocational subject*, such as construction, health care or cleaning, before they plan to take their assessment qualification. Access to bona fide candidates will also be needed.

Candidate-assessors or -verifiers who will be assessing or verifying Learning and Development NVQs, including those who may be assessing the A&V units as part of another vocational NVQ, need to meet ENTO's assessment strategy for Learning and Development. This includes competence in the vocational area of Learning and Development itself, usually taken as holding a teaching or training qualification at L3 or above. The assessment strategy for Learning and Development is reproduced in Appendix 4.

Initial assessment

This takes place ideally before enrolment with an accredited centre, so candidates can check their suitability for a chosen qualification. NVQ prospective candidates may be asked to complete a self-assessment of current job role against the standards towards which they intend to work. This latter may take the form of a self-assessment checklist of your familiarity with performing tasks in each NVQ unit, and will help to identify whether you need any further training or experience before undertaking assessment. Potential candidates will probably be asked to take tests to check their Key Skills and preferred learning styles. Candidates who have problems with literacy, numeracy and/or ICT at the required levels should be advised at this stage whether they would be better improving their Key Skills before progressing with the course/qualification or whether there will be sufficient support available for them to progress at the required rate and achieve at the required level. If your vocational qualification involves written work or study at L3 or above and you are a bit 'rusty', a study skills course taken *before* you start your course might make all the difference to the ease and enjoyment of your subsequent assessments. The access arrangements for each awarding body should be available to clarify any identified potential problems.

It is now normal for candidates to present much of their written work in word-processed formats, and for course information for candidates to be presented on internal websites. Candidates need to know how they will access the required resources if they do not possess their own computers or internet access.

Enrolment, registration and induction

Enrolment with the accredited centre that will support you through your studies usually takes place before registration with the awarding body that will eventually award you your qualification. Enrolment and registration involve the completion of several forms, and payment can take some time. If your fees are being paid for you, perhaps by your employer, the centre will need proof of this when you enrol and/or register. The forms are often quite complicated. This is because much of the information on them is used to provide data to the LSC. Check the small print – often you have the right to withdraw from a programme within the first couple of weeks of a course if you find it is not what you expected, and get your money back. It should be clear at the outset exactly what procedures are involved in your assessment process, and what associated costs there are, such as equipment or additional assessment costs, particularly if there is an hourly, instead of a flat, rate for assessment.

You may be asked to enrol just for the taught part of the course at this time. Some awarding bodies ask candidates to register for the qualification within a certain number of weeks of the start date of the programme. Your registration for an NVQ may be valid for several years. However, your centre may well expect you to complete within say one year, as their funding will be for just one year. You need to be clear on what the financial arrangements would be in the event that you fell behind with your work and had to complete some of your assessments the following year.

At induction, you should find out about the centre and about the resources you are entitled to use and any others you will be expected to provide yourself. For instance, if written documents are available to you online, you may need to purchase paper or photocopying cards if you prefer to read from paper rather than a screen. The requirements of the course and the qualification will be explained, and candidates should receive all accompanying documentation, including details about both the centre and the awarding body's complaints and appeals systems, and have these explained. It is useful to have the web addresses of your awarding body and your centre, plus any centre student guidance.

USING A MENTOR

Candidates are often advised, or required, to have a mentor. The mentor does not need to be your line manager. Mentors may need to be specialists in your vocational subject and be recognized for their experience and be regarded as role models. They also need to understand the context of your qualification or course and your work, and should be able to point you to useful additional sources of information and advice. Your mentor does not need to be in your organization, and may even have retired, though you need to check that he or she is currently up to date. Normally the relationship is of 'wise and experienced professional' with the 'new or aspiring role holder'. Mentors rarely receive payment for the time they give, so you probably need to negotiate at the start of your qualification what might be needed and what is reasonable. Mentors should not be involved in your assessment, but they might be prepared to observe you on an informal basis to give you some feedback before a formal assessment. They will need to give their details, including their qualifications and experience, to your centre, and the centre may invite them to briefing sessions and should provide them with documentation about your qualification and its requirements. It is best to seek out a potential mentor before you enrol for your course – he or she may be able to provide you with useful information when you go for interview and initial assessment, and you will find that you get into the swing of things much more quickly.

ASSESSMENT PLANNING

The most important thing to remember as a candidate is that you need to know how well you are doing. You cannot get any feedback from your assessor on this until you have given him or her something to assess, whether this is a workplace assessment, test answers or a piece of written work. Don't put off doing your assessments because you feel the work isn't as good as you could do, or because you aren't sure what the assessor wants, or because you won't be good enough yet (all reasons we have heard from our candidates). Have a go! Assessors are there to give you constructive feedback and tell you what you have done well and how you can improve where necessary. Assuming you have had the necessary training and practice, it is better to get stuck in and get it 60 per cent right within the due dates (especially if there is an option to rework and improve) than to put off assessment until you feel you are 'ready'. You could get so behind that you never catch up and, worst of all, you are not building the positive feedback relationship between you and your assessor that will help you to progress.

Most candidates will undertake a period of learning before they are ready to tackle assessment, but it is always a good idea to have an overview of the assessment requirements before you start, so that you can see how your learning applies not just to your work role but also to the assessments. Normally, your assessment will be 'continuous', as there will be a number of occasions on which you meet with your assessor for the purpose of checking work-based competence. There will also be a summative assessment when all your claims to competence are checked through and the complete units are finally signed off.

You should not be put in the position of negotiating and agreeing any assessment plan before you are fully familiar with the assessment scheme or process for your awards and for your centre's operation of its qualification.

NVQ candidates

If you are taking an NVQ, your first assessment planning meeting with your primary assessor should give you an overview of how the assessment for the whole award is envisaged and should result in the detailed planning for the assessment of at least one complete unit. Experience has shown us that candidates who plan for their option units first are likely to finish their award most quickly. This is because, as the option units are completed, the candidate will also meet many of the criteria in the mandatory awards. It also means that the candidate has longer to develop any new skills needed for the options. For each NVQ unit, your negotiated plan should cover the (minimum of four) methods that will be used to assess your knowledge and competence, what you will need to do or present to demonstrate knowledge and competence, what this will involve, who will be involved, and the planned timescale.

PPA/vocational candidates

As a candidate for this type of qualification, you are quite likely to have a number of written assignments given to you at regular intervals throughout your course. If you are not given a schedule, ask your tutor/assessor for the due dates of the assignments and any tests or examinations, and the dates you should expect marked work to be returned. Most organizations have a policy on this, commonly a maximum of 15 working days. This will enable you to plan your life, though you should always allow leeway for the unexpected to get in the way of your work, as we all know it does sometimes, and you don't need to spend your holidays doing assignment work. Neither do you want the even worse scenario, where the course has finished, you have no more tutorial time due to you, and the work is still not completed. That's bad for both you and your tutor/assessor.

Unit for assessment: A1
Candidate: I Swilling
Primary Assessor: A Body

Methods agreed for assessment: observation, professional discussion, written questions, prior qualifications and experience, witness statements

Persons who will make assessments/judgements: A Body (primary assessor), B Kind (observational assessor), C Tuit (independent assessor, contact no. 01234 567890, D Pending (candidate's line manager and witness), Z Carr (centre internal verifier)

Candidate-assessor's vocational candidates, NVQ and units for assessment:
E Longate, F Ahma, G Force all taking NVQ2 in Care
   U 2   U 10   U 2

Process

Assessment Activity	Target Date
IS	
• to make unit plans with each of the three candidates	
• to arrange with DP when she can be available for assessment	
• to contact BK and arrange observation date	by end of week 1
• to conduct assessments with EL, FA and GF	by end of week 5
• to ask DP for statement covering A1.3, A1.4	by end of week 3
• to find vocational qual cert, CPD record	
• to complete answers to written questions relating to underpinning knowledge	
AB	
• to receive observational assessor report, witness statement, written answers, assess against standards, make judgement and provide feedback on 1:1 basis to IS	Thursday afternoon, 2–4 pm week 6 in IS's office
• to update assessment plan and provide copy of assessment judgement and feedback to IS	
IS	
• to inform BK and AB when one of the three candidates is ready for unit assessment	Week 8
• arrange observation of unit assessment and feedback to candidate; review assessment plan for candidate	
• contact CT and arrange to send completed and reviewed assessment plan for assessment	Week 10
• complete assessments with other candidates; arrange date with AB for workplace visit	
AB	
• plan professional discussion and arrange loan of video camera	Week 10
• visit IS in workplace; view evidence of the three candidates; conduct professional discussion	Week 11, 3 hrs
• make assessment judgements, give feedback and review assessment plan; update tracking document	
• arrange date for summative unit assessment	Week 12
IS	
• organize portfolio of evidence and pass to AB for final assessment	Week 14, 1 hr
AB	
• meet with IS at workplace for feedback; update assessment plan; pass result to ZC for results processing	
	Estimated 1:1 time with assessor: 8 hours

Signature	Assessor	Date	
Signature	Candidate	Date	Time taken 1.0 hr

Figure 11.1 A combined action and assessment plan for an A1 candidate

BEING QUESTIONED

Irrespective of your position and experience, being questioned by an assessor can still be a stressful occasion, if only because you may be highly practised and knowledgeable and will be *expecting* to be deemed competent!

The assessor may ask you to describe or explain your evidence, so refer to any product or paper-based evidence to save time. Often the focus will be on exploring how much knowledge is covered by the activities the assessor has seen you carry out in workplace practice, or asking you what performance criteria/performance indicators or range you think is met by some of your evidence. The assessor should, following good assessment practice, have a pre-prepared list of questions, from which an appropriate selection is made, and should record your answers. (See Chapter 5 for help on devising questions to check underpinning knowledge and understanding.) The box gives a sample list of questions that could be used by an assessor or verifier assessing natural performance.

Sample questions for use with assessment observations are:

1. How has this assessment been agreed with your candidate?
2. What determined the physical arrangements, eg where you stood, when you asked questions?
3. What did you do to encourage the candidate to select and present relevant evidence?
4. How did you decide/construct the questions you asked orally? Are the questions written down?
5. What is your definition of a 'leading question'? How can you avoid asking them?
6. Why did you ask the number of questions that you did?
7. How are you sure that you can infer competent performance in other situations where the task/activity might occur?
8. In what ways can you involve candidates in their own assessments? How effective was the candidate's performance in this case? How might it be improved?
9. What rules do you follow when giving feedback?
10. How do you encourage individuals to ask questions as a natural part of the feedback and evaluation process?
11. What makes this assessment fair, reliable, valid and sufficient?
12. Did this candidate have any special needs for which you had to cater? What special needs might candidates have and how would you accommodate these?
13. Are there any aspects of my assessment of you about which you are unclear or which you wish to discuss further?

Some questions might be of the 'closed' variety, particularly if the assessor is checking fact, eg 'What was the tolerance on that measurement?' Others are likely to probe processes, such as 'How did you help the teacher to plan that work?' or 'What is the basis on which you have drawn up your sampling plan?' You might be asked such questions immediately after assessment of your performance, or in a summative assessment check if the assessor is unclear as to whether performance and supplementary evidence meet all requirements.

If you have had the opportunity to work through similar lists of questions beforehand (for assessment techniques and for underpinning knowledge and understanding), you could include your written answers as supplementary evidence, as it may save unnecessary oral questioning. On the other hand, you may prefer to prepare the answers mentally and answer oral questions rather than put a lot down in writing. The assessor will also be determining the authenticity of your evidence – this is particularly important where candidates have been working as part of a team and where there may be some 'common' evidence. If this is the case, it is really important that candidates are clear about why the evidence demonstrates their competence, rather than that of a team itself or of another team member.

You should of course receive constructive feedback after any assessment. Most assessors will give this verbally, but usually there will be an additional written report confirming satisfaction with the evidence or detailing where competence has not been fully shown.

Assessments can vary considerably in time. The variation may be due to the *amount* of evidence presented, the *nature* of the evidence (an assessor may choose to look at the whole of an assessment recorded on video in addition to other performance evidence), the overall grasp of the assessment process shown by the candidate, and the candidate's ability to respond concisely to the details needed. New assessors frequently take longer to complete the assessment process, owing to a variety of factors, not least of which can be the lack of coordinated planning of assessment opportunities in the workplace and the impulse to encourage candidates to include additional material unnecessarily 'to be on the safe side'.

RECEIVING FEEDBACK

Chapter 3 gives lots of advice on giving and receiving feedback. It sounds rather simplistic to say that candidates who incorporate advice into their practice, and reflect on how this is changing the way they work, tend to move forward in leaps and bounds. It is very easy to miss out on this springboard. One of the most common reasons is that some candidates find it difficult to commit to their planned observations, and cancel them. Obviously there are times this cannot be avoided, but we know that often this is through bad planning or simply nerves at the thought of being observed. They then have a cluster of observations towards the end of their training time and don't really have the opportunity to act on any advice that may be given. Another reason is that your assessor may not write down the verbal feedback he or she gives you, and then you forget some of the key points. Ask the assessor to record the key points in some format (assessors should anyway) or do it yourself at the time, and check out your understanding with the assessor. If you try something that has been suggested and it doesn't work, then talk to your mentor or colleagues or your assessor and see if there are other avenues that can be explored.

SPECIFICATIONS, SOURCES AND PURPOSES OF EVIDENCE

Always select evidence of performance and knowledge that shows the consistency of your activity over time. Any evidence must meet the requirements of authenticity, validity, reliability and currency (see Chapter 3) and, of course, if you are making these selections alongside your assessor, perhaps as you negotiate your action and assessment plan for a unit, you are getting immediate feedback. Table 11.1, although by no means comprehensive, may provide you with some ideas on the variety of evidence you can use to demonstrate competence as an assessor or internal verifier both from present work roles and from previous experience or achievements.

The purpose of Table 11.1 is to prompt you as to what might be useful corroborative evidence when undertaking professional discussion in your workplace. We are not suggesting that you collect together lots of documents and put them into your portfolio. In fact, don't do this unless you absolutely have to. If you can show evidence to your assessor *in situ*, in your workplace, and the assessor can note down then and there what he or she has seen, where it is stored and what criteria have been covered, then the job is done.

PRESENTING YOUR WORK

Recording your sources and avoiding plagiarism

Most candidates for vocational awards and NVQs are practical people. They often prefer doing to reading. However, its likely that you will need to broaden your knowledge, and the most common ways of doing this are by reading (trade journals, textbooks, internet articles) or by viewing (relevant television programmes, video clips, informational DVDs). It's sensible to make a note of what you used. It's also highly likely that, especially in an L4

Table 11.1 Advantages and disadvantages of different types of evidence

Evidence	Purpose
Action plans	To show details of initial assessment and review with your own candidates.
APL documents	To show previous competence/experience and to infer current competence.
Appraisal records	To indicate activities you have undertaken or planned that meet CPD requirements and/or assessment strategy.
Assessment plans	To show you are supporting your candidates in the required way.
Assignments (marked)	To show knowledge and understanding of your specialist subject, whether you are meeting deadlines and whether you are making accurate judgements.
Audio recording	To provide a record of questioning or professional discussion between assessor and candidate.
Briefing notes to staff	To show how you communicate relevant information.
Candidate tracking documents	To show how you regularly record your assessment decisions.
Certificates (original)	To provide evidence of your relevant qualifications.
Costings (time, money)	To show you understand efficiency.
Data printouts	To provide information for verification and quality assurance.
Feedback sheets to candidates	To show how you give constructive feedback.
Forms, pro formas	To show how you input information.
Graphs	To show how you analyse quantitative data.
Individual learning plans	To show how you plan achievable targets with candidates.
Induction documents	To use, if completed, as a focus to show how you use candidate information to support their learning.

Job specifications	To give a context to your discussion.
Memos	To show how you communicate with others.
Minutes of meetings, etc	To use as a focus for discussion – only useful if they show how you have contributed in a way that meets specific criteria.
Photographs	To show artefacts/products that assessors are not able to view themselves – but you need to be able to authenticate these.
Policies and procedures	To use as a focus in professional discussion for explaining how policy impacts on own practice, but in themselves these say nothing about your knowledge, understanding or competence.
Questions, written or oral	To show the techniques you use if answers are logged and recorded.
Record sheets (completed)	To show your ability to track, eg monitoring of assessors, or candidate work.
Reports (qualitative)	To show how you have carried out and evaluated your activities.
Reports (quantitative)	To show how you have used data to analyse and summarize.
Review sheets (completed)	To show how you are monitoring assessment progress with candidates.
Sampling plans	To indicate your monitoring activities.
Staff lists	To use as a discussion focus for showing your understanding of internal communications and operations.
Verifiers' reports	To show, if they include your name, how you have performed against awarding body criteria.
Videotapes	To provide evidence of professional discussion or workplace performance.
Witness statements	To give validation of performance and product evidence not seen by your primary or observational assessor.

qualification, your assessor may wish to check your sources. There are agreed ways of recording this information. The most commonly used method is called the Harvard system. If you turn to 'Supporting Materials' at the end of this book, you will see the ways to record information. A quick click on 'Harvard referencing guide' in your search engine will take you through to lots of websites that will explain more about referencing and bibliographies. Get familiar with these before you start your course, and then you can keep a running list of what you use, which will save you lots of time in the end.

Plagiarism is a serious offence and occurs when you pass off information as your own without attributing it to the original author. Sometimes this is deliberate, and you may have read stories where candidates have been asked to leave a course/institution or been told that they cannot have their qualification awarded. In other cases, it can be due to candidates being disorganized. If you keep a list as described above, for both websites and written material, and make notes as to which pages any direct quotes are taken from, the attribution of sources will not take up too much of your time, and you will find that you have a useful reference tool that you can use later.

The paper-based portfolio

As you progress through your qualification you will use and accumulate a number of documents and products, such as assessor reports and feedback on your performance, video- or audiotapes of professional discussion, photographs or samples of your own candidates' achievements, and assessor comments that go with written assignments. This evidence of your work as a candidate-assessor or candidate-verifier is normally presented for assessment in a referenced file, folder or box, usually termed a 'portfolio'.

A familiar example of a portfolio is that of the art student, who has a varied collection of samples of work. Items that are inappropriate for folder presentation, such as sculpture or ceramics, are often represented by photographs or by written reference to their location if, for example, they have been sold. Other examples are an actor's portfolio, representing the range of roles played, and the portfolios held by Cabinet ministers, which are the range of activities and responsibilities expected of them.

Your own portfolio is likely to be a collection of mixed evidence, much of which may not be in written form. Most candidates opt to keep all the notes and supplementary information gathered as part of learning (but that is not part of the assessment) in an A4 lever arch or box file. However, please don't use A4 lever arch files to hand in work to assessors unless you are specifically told to do so! Your assessor is likely to have at least 20 candidates. Assessors who work in a college could have many more. Where are they going to put all this stuff? We have seen countless staffrooms over the years where desks and floors are covered with big files, often with very small amounts of paper in them. We also know staff physically injured trying to carry bulky portfolios to their cars or, worse still, on to public transport. Also consider this: if you are producing so much paper, are you doing the correct thing? Shouldn't you be taking a more proactive approach with your assessor and getting him or her to assess a lot of your paper-based materials at your workplace? When practical competencies or skills are being assessed, the best way to do this is to take a process-based, rather than a product-based, approach. In other words, the focus must be on assessing in the workplace, rather than the candidate producing huge files of documentation.

Many documents should never be put in the portfolio, but will be viewed *in situ* in a candidate's workplace, and be acknowledged through assessor reports of assessed activities including video and photographic evidence. Candidates commonly include irrelevant or superfluous material. Not only does this take up unnecessary space, but it alerts the assessors or verifiers to the fact that you may be unclear as to what constitutes relevant evidence. You could therefore be advising your own candidates poorly and encouraging them to think that the process is about chasing paper rather than performing jobs in an informed way to particular standards.

Look at your collected works and declutter by asking yourself the following questions:

- Does this relate to my assessment plan?
- Is this evidence relevant to the unit(s) and, if so, to which element(s)?
- Does the evidence demonstrate competent performance, have I explained the context in which the tasks are done and/or does it demonstrate underpinning knowledge or understanding?
- If so, how am I going to explain or indicate to my assessor what competencies or knowledge I am claiming?
- Is the evidence recent and authentic? In other words, does it prove that I am currently competent?
- Do I have sufficient examples of meeting performance criteria over time?
- Does this evidence need to be physically included in my portfolio, or would it be better to show it to my assessor during or following an observation, or during professional discussion?
- Has my assessor seen this already and made a decision on it? Can I replace it where it came from?
- Is my assessor asking me to put more documents into my portfolio because the assessor is not making assessment judgements when we meet? Would we be better meeting at my workplace instead of the assessor's and getting some assessment done?

If you are unsure, get advice from your assessor. The standards now give clear guidance as to the agreed evidence that you must show to your assessor, and if you follow this guidance you should have no problems with sufficiency or validity.

Remember – one of the signs of a good assessor, or candidate, is that he or she is able to identify relevant evidence that covers as many performance criteria as possible. There is no positive correlation between large paper-based portfolios and good assessor or verifier practice!

Electronic evidence and portfolios

Some centres are moving towards online systems for recording candidate achievement. The downside of this is that they can be a bit mechanistic, as well as requiring everyone to be fully familiar with the technology involved. The positive side is that necessary information can be scanned, and downloaded from videophones or PDAs, and assessments and feedback can be entered all in one virtual space.

There are electronic recording systems on the market that enable the assessor to capture all assessment activity on-screen. All necessary recording pro formas are online. Candidate work may be scanned into the system. Feedback comments can be sent online to candidates. Assessment and verification records can be entered straight into the electronic system. Internal and external verifiers can access the system at any time to verify assessment activity.

The paperless portfolio is, like any recording system, as good as those using it. Like a paper-based system, it relies on the assessor or internal verifier to enter data regularly and on the candidate to arrange appropriately timed workplace visits for observation and professional discussion.

Reducing the paperwork

Perhaps the best 'paperless portfolio' is that which is focused on well-planned workplace observations, witness testimony and professional discussion. An assessor who spends time in the candidate's workplace talking to witnesses, seeing activities and looking at the outcomes of that performance, and records what the candidate has achieved in detailed but concise statements matched to the standards, should eliminate the need for the candidate to collect any 'paper evidence'. The assessor's reports should provide a sufficient audit trail of the candidate's competence.

CHECKING YOU ARE ON TRACK FOR CERTIFICATION

The major factors influencing the time you take to get your award are likely to be:

- *The support, advice and documentation provided by the awarding body with which you register.* Make sure you have a registration number from the awarding body as soon as you have been identified as a suitable candidate for an award. Check you have a full copy of the occupational standards and any helpful materials provided by the awarding bodies. The awarding body and standards websites will be helpful here (see 'Supporting Materials'). For NVQs, you will have to wait a minimum of 10 weeks from registering for your awards before you can be entered for certification. This is known as the '10-week rule'. Some awarding bodies have regulations that require you to be registered within a certain number of weeks, say four, of the course start date. This means you may need to be sure that you can fulfil practical work-based requirements before you are able to start the course.

- *The support, advice and documentation provided by the centre with which you enrol.* Check out the amount of time your centre has allocated for your support, and plan with your assessor at the outset how it will be used. Keep appointments, and let your assessor know in good time if you need to cancel visits. If you do have to cancel visits on more than one occasion, you may be jeopardizing your ability to complete the course on time. Ask what additional support the centre can provide, such as computing or library facilities. Make sure you have access to key documents. For NVQ candidates, these will include the NVQ Code of Conduct, the JAB guidelines and the document *Access to Assessment*. For teacher candidates, these will be the scheme document and maybe the relevant awarding body guidance to centres. Reading these will help you to get an understanding of the issues around assessment and internal and external quality assurance and give you a broader perspective than that of your centre or awarding body. Ask if you have any queries.

- *Your familiarity with your vocational standards.* Discuss these with other staff or candidates at your workplace. Make sure that your mentor, if you have one, is familiar with the standards. You need to get to the point where you have a good overview of your award, as well as understanding how the assessments you have to do are linked to the criteria. If you are an A1/A2 candidate, decide which units are likely to be most quickly achievable by your own candidates, as you need to assess completed (but not necessarily satisfactory) units before you can get your own qualification.

- *Your familiarity with the assessment and/or internal verification process.* The more experience you have of this and the closeness with which you are integrated into the centre's operation, the easier it will be to undertake the process as a candidate. Almost every course offered has some internal and external quality assurance monitoring, and if you are teaching, training or assessing it is highly likely that you will be involved at several points during a typical year. For candidate-assessors/-verifiers, you will need to ensure that your own internal verifier is including you in standardization activities and that you are able to carry out all the activities required by the standards. No simulation is required. If this is a problem, you need to take advice, as the A&V awards may not be appropriate for you *or* your centre may need to review its processes if it wishes you to achieve.

- *The progress of your own candidates or your assessors.* If you have accurately assessed the learning that each of your own candidates is making, your assessments for your own candidates will be matched to the work you have set them. This will allow everyone to progress at the correct rates. You have to be in a position to assess a complete unit for at least two candidates for A1 and have those assessments built into the internal verification system. For V1, you will need to be in a position to meet with your assessors regularly and have regular contact with your supervising internal verifier. You also need to be able to participate in the centre's quality assurance process and make reports to key people, so you need to know when the centre conducts its audits and how your verifications will link with the centre's external verification process.
- *The support of your workplace colleagues as, for example, witnesses or vocational observers.* Assuming your manager has suggested that you get the award, then hopefully the staff will be fully behind you and prepared to carry out observations or verify your practice as required. Even so, staff may well need to meet with you initially so that they are clear about your expectations. If you are taking the certificate on your own initiative, you need to think carefully about whom you will need to work with in the centre, their own work commitments, and what you can do to have your award seen as useful to the centre and those you are working with.
- *Your commitments in and outside work.* However well you plan, the unexpected often happens, so it can be worth thinking through some contingency plans, for example for when your candidates leave unexpectedly or there is a home crisis. Ensure you let your assessor and others who may be affected know as soon as possible in case they are able to help.
- *Your ability to select and present evidence clearly.* If you understand the standards and can see that they represent a job broken down into its constituent parts, you will find it easier to select assessment opportunities that cover substantial parts of your required performance. The more clearly you are able to link your evidence to performance criteria/ performance indicators, range/scope and knowledge, the easier it will be for your assessor to make the necessary judgements. Your assessor should be looking to see that you have confidence in your role and that

you understand what you should be doing and how you should be working.

If things go wrong

Your trainer, teacher or assessor will support you regarding your progress towards your qualification through his or her assessment and feedback. You will no doubt have one or two tutorials that will be focused on your workplace or academic progress. Your mentor, if you have one, should support you to develop your understanding of your specialist subject and its requirements. However, you all need to be clear about the extent to which these people should support you if you encounter problems that are not directly connected with their teaching, training, support or assessment. Find out what additional support your accredited centre or workplace has, such as confidential counsellors or study staff who can support you with issues that are beyond the call of duty of your assessor or teacher.

Examples

- A candidate had relationship difficulties that were affecting her ability to get work done at home. She arranged to see a counsellor, to deal with that side of things, but also started to use the centre's study facilities to do her work.
- A candidate had inadvertently booked a holiday that clashed with her workplace assessments. She let her assessor know early enough, and a substitute assessor was found who could observe her as soon as she returned.
- A candidate fell behind with his work and had not completed by the end of the year. The centre arranged for him to pay additional fees so that he could receive additional tutorials and assessment the following year.
- An anxious candidate used a lot of his allocated tutorial time talking about his concerns rather than discussing his work. The tutor suggested he used the specialist in the study centre to help him with structuring and referencing assignments, as well as with time management.
- A candidate cancelled two workplace assessments for different work-related reasons. The assessor arranged to see the internal verifier at the candidate's workplace, who was able to work with the candidate's line manager and arrange observation dates that suited all parties.

SUMMARY

This chapter should have helped you with:

- pre-assessment activities;
- induction and self-assessment;
- being questioned and receiving feedback;
- presenting your work;
- what to do if things go wrong.

12

Assessors and Their Records

This chapter focuses on how assessors can record the progress of their candidates so that:

- there is a clear audit trail for verifiers to follow;
- candidates know what they have achieved;
- assessors are clear at all times just how much each candidate has achieved.

This chapter should be of use to both intending and qualified assessors as well as candidates for assessment.

RECORDING PROGRESS

The way that an assessor records candidate progress achievements can make all the difference to the progression of candidates. Candidates need feedback. Assessors are usually very good at giving oral feedback, but for a variety of reasons are less consistently good with written feedback.

Your centre will probably have documentation that has been approved by the awarding body on which you should keep your records. If you don't like this documentation, you should talk to your internal verifier before using something you have devised yourself, just in case there are quality reasons why you must stick to what everyone else is using.

Table 12.1 The basic written records you should refer to, generate or keep

Interview	Including details of original certificates seen, vocational background and relevant CV information.
Initial assessment	Including details of Key Skills assessments, learning styles.
Assessment plans	For individual assignments (vocational) or individual units (NVQ).
Action plans	For bridging gaps in knowledge, skills or understanding.
Formative feedback	Following the review of draft written assignments (vocational) or following individual observations and assessment activity (NVQ).
Summative feedback	Following each completed piece of work: assignments, the requisite number of observations, a full NVQ unit.
Tracking document	To show the stage that each candidate has reached at any point in time.
Mark book or file	To log the summative results of all candidates.
Standardization marking	If you are asked to mark work from candidates for whom you are not the primary or independent assessor.
Data on your classes	Numbers enrolled, numbers retained at census points, numbers achieving.

Keeping your records

Assessors need to keep their records in an easily accessible but secure location. The two ways of doing this are paper based, in locked cabinets, and with password-protected computerized records. There are now many e-portfolio systems on the market. If you are assessing candidate work, it too must be kept securely. Make sure, when candidates hand work in for assessment, that they ask for and are given a receipt and that the centre keeps copies of these. We know of candidates who have attempted to sue centres on the basis that work has been handed in and subsequently lost by the centre – records can help prove the case one way or another. If candidates' work is lost, it will be the quality of your written records that can save them from having to repeat everything. Remember our earlier advice and insist that any paper documents are presented to you in lightweight plastic files – it is very difficult to find the space to store A4 hard ring binders, particularly lever arch files. You might need to think about who might legitimately need access to your records, should you be absent when sampling is required, and what procedures need to be put in place to enable this access. Your internal verifier needs to understand how and where you are keeping your records and may need to be able to access them if you are absent. You need to give particular thought to back-up systems. We have known assessors who have had work stolen from parked cars and had no additional records to support the work that had been done by candidates. This can result in the whole assessment process having to be repeated.

RECORDING YOUR ASSESSMENT JUDGEMENTS

The assessment planning process for each NVQ unit involves assessors in discussions with candidates about how candidates will show that they meet all the relevant unit requirements. The assessors' job is to record what they see against the relevant performance criteria/performance indicators, scope/ range, and knowledge and understanding of the standards.

In the past, it has been common practice to ask candidates to cross-reference their activities and any documentary evidence to the standards, in the belief that the assessment was then 'candidate led'. In some cases, candidates were encouraged to write up their observed practice, identify the criteria they believed they had reached, sometimes after discussion with the assessor, and then give it to the assessor for signature. Whatever the reasons for these activities, current thinking is now along the lines of the 'minimum portfolio' model. The assessor can guide the candidate towards the most cost-effective and efficient activities that cover as wide a range of performance criteria as possible. However, it is the job of the assessor to note down what has been seen and what criteria the candidate has covered. This means that the assessor needs to be thoroughly familiar with the standards and be able to describe in enough detail what he or she has seen without giving a blow-by-blow account of a two-hour observation.

So it follows that, if the valid way to demonstrate competence is through workplace performance, and the valid way to assess that competence is through observation, questioning and professional discussion, then the documentation that an internal verifier (IV) needs to see is that completed by the *assessor*. This means that assessors must describe who was involved, what they have seen and where they saw it (location), explain how they made the judgement (why the evidence met the standards or not) and say when all this took place. It is not enough to tick boxes.

Giving written feedback

Candidates should be able to learn from their feedback. It needs to be written down for them, because normal human beings forget things, even things that are important.

Candidates need to know:

- what they did well;
- what needs to be worked on to bring it up to scratch;
- what they could think about to improve the breadth or depth of their understanding;
- whether the references they selected are appropriate;
- what other resources they could use.

Table 12.2 Sample assessment judgement and feedback to an A1 candidate

Evidence	Standards
Today I met with Rasika in her workplace for the first time. I observed her assessing two candidates, Joe and Lyn, who are both candidates for the NVQ L2 in Beauty Therapy. The workplace is a new, well-equipped salon in an FE college, and the session was one where the salon is run by a candidate, and there are paying clients. Afterwards, we met with Toni, the internal verifier for the Beauty NVQ. In the assessment plan (attached) we had negotiated that during this visit we would be covering criteria from all four elements from A1. R worked first with J and then with L, using exactly the same process. I have noted below any differences between the two assessments. The assessments overlapped in time, and I was able to move from one to the other as necessary. I was in the salon for 2.5 hours altogether.	
R checked through the assessment plans that she had negotiated with J and L. She asked both candidates to talk through the preparations they had made with their clients. J was doing a manicure with two clients, and L was doing a pedicure with two clients. Her approach was professional. She put the candidates at ease, but was careful not to ask leading questions or make suggestions.	A1.1
Each candidate carried out her treatments. During this time, R observed, and questioned J and L at various appropriate points during the treatments to check underpinning knowledge. She asked questions for clarification (Why did...? How are you...?).	A1.2 A1.3

R completed her checklist, making notes on the performance of each candidate.

J was doing a French manicure, but did not remember the correct names of the products, nor did she apply the varnish correctly. R asked J to go through the procedures she had used, and J realized her mistake. R and J agreed a date for a further assessment, and R revised the assessment plan. A1.1 A1.3

R judged L as being competent in this assessment. Another assessment was arranged for the following week, and L asked to be observed doing some epilating techniques.

Feedback was given in a positive way to each candidate, using the 'praise sandwich' method. R made a note of the key points she made to each candidate on their assessment plans, and went through these as she showed each candidate which criteria had been met. Both candidates signed and dated their log books to show they agreed with the assessment and the feedback.

Following these two assessments, we met with T, the IV for beauty. She showed me her sampling plan that included R, and she and R talked through the recent standardization-of-assessment exercise that had been held the previous week. R has four years of experience in working in the Beauty industry, and T confirmed that R's assessment judgements were found to be in line with those of the qualified assessors in the salon. T was working with R on the ways in which the college wanted assessor documentation to be presented. A1.4

I completed the check sheet attached to the assessment plan to show R which criteria she had met. We reviewed the assessment plan and fixed another observation for the same time next month, but for just one hour. R will have a second observation in the meantime by T, who has L&D qualifications as well as in Beauty.

I gave R a copy of the criteria and feedback sheet. R signed and dated this feedback sheet at the end of the visit to show she agreed with the assessment and the feedback. Professional discussion will be planned for at the end of this third observation, following my review of all three observations...

Note: The performance criteria still need to be recorded by the assessor into the right-hand column. The internal verifier should pick up an omission such as this in his or her sampling.

Marking other types of work

It's almost impossible to make accurate judgements unless there is some sort of scheme to which you can refer. Even with standards of competence, there is often some leeway for assessor interpretation, so this is why it's important to have standardization of assessment exercises and why it is useful to have internal verifiers carrying out observations with you so that the assessor judgement can be compared with that of the verifier.

Much of the problem for marking is solved once you are really familiar with the standards that the candidate has to achieve. This familiarity is not just the type of performance that is needed. If you know the layout of the observations sheets you will use, the task gets so much easier.

When an assignment or project has to be marked, there should be a mark scheme drawn up by you or provided by the centre or awarding body. There should also be guidance on what to look for at different levels. For example, candidate work at L3 is often descriptive, saying what is happening and giving examples. At L4, assessors will be looking for the candidate to be thinking through the topic and using that analysis to suggest different approaches.

Assessors need to share their mark schemes with candidates. Candidates should be totally clear on what they are expected to do in order to pass at different levels (eg merit/distinction).

Checking for authenticity and plagiarism

Assessors need to be sure that they are making judgements based on the competence, knowledge and understanding of the candidate. The purpose of a candidate using materials from books, journals or the internet is so that they increase their knowledge and understanding. This means that candidates need to show exactly how their thinking or practice has been changed. They will do this through written explanation or through professional discussion in most cases. Including a document with no reference as to how this links with the candidate's learning against particular standards or learning outcomes is useless.

Authenticity is usually indicated by the signature of the candidate against a statement that the work is the candidate's own. This means that all information gleaned from sources other than candidates themselves must be properly acknowledged. If quotations are used, these need to be cited as references in a footnote or in a list at the end of the work or specific chapters. In order that references can be checked by the reader/assessor, or the source used again, the source needs to be listed in a standard format. Photographic evidence, especially digital photographs, also need to be authenticated, perhaps by a line manager who witnessed the event. This is particularly important if the photograph is included to show competent work, as matters of health and safety could later depend on the correct assessment of this evidence.

Plagiarism occurs when work that is not the creation of the candidate is deliberately passed off as such. It is an extremely serious offence. The internet hosts a number of sites where assignments are 'sold' to unscrupulous candidates. Luckily, assessors are aware that this can happen, and there are sophisticated software programs that aim to detect plagiarized work.

SUBMISSION OF PORTFOLIOS/ASSIGNMENTS FOR ASSESSMENT

Accessibility and legibility

Awarding bodies rarely state the way in which work should be presented for assessment or verification other than that assessors will need to be able to link assessments to previously agreed assessment plans, and internal verifiers need to be able to find copies of assessor judgements and feedback on evidence. Your awarding body or centre may have specific pro formas, such as assessment plans or feedback sheets, that you need to complete. Ensure that any dating, signing or countersigning of assessment observations, assessments or other documentation such as witness statements is done at the time activities take place. The purpose of signing and dating is to confirm certain activities happened at that particular time and place, between those particular people.

All documents assessors complete should be legible and fit for purpose and conform to the Data Protection Act. Pro formas completed by hand while observing or interviewing candidates, or other types of working documents such as memoranda, should be kept in their handwritten state, as they are primary evidence. Retyping such evidence is not advised or necessary. However, all handwritten evidence should be legible, especially as it must be read by candidates or verifiers involved with the assessment process. Digitally recorded or taped workplace activities need an accompanying written explanation, showing what elements and performance criteria have been met. Similarly, photographs need to be verifiable, and there are plenty of cheap cameras on the market that insert the date and time on to images. The ways that assessors prepare and present their assessment plans and reviews, record assessments and feedback and complete their tracking records are likely to be the model that they give their own candidates, whatever they tell them in training!

Advising candidates on their portfolios

Sometimes centres will ask candidates to put their evidence together in a particular way. Verifiers should be checking that the national standards have been met, and not the arrangement of the portfolio, unless an awarding body lays down specific requirements for presentation of evidence for assessment. If candidates need some guidance, the following points may be helpful:

- Label your 'portfolio', whether a file, wallet or box, clearly, with your name, your awarding body registration number, the units you are claiming and your organization (if relevant).
- Include a contact number or address, with candidate name, address, awarding body registration number, and names of all assessors and witnesses.
- Include witness statement sheets with sample signatures, including those of everyone who has contributed to candidate assessment to help the assessor with his or her judgements.
- Provide a list of the evidence being used for summative assessment, with any reference numbers. This list should also include evidence that has been reviewed and logged by the workplace assessor and does not need to be included in the portfolio. Include the location of any such evidence (eg filing cabinet, display board in classroom).
- Include the assessment plans signed by candidates and the primary assessor, reviewed as necessary.
- Include record(s) of professional discussion.
- Include written formative and summative assessment decisions and feedback from all assessors.
- Include any supplementary evidence not yet seen by the assessor but that is needed in order to make a final decision.
- Ensure that everything is secure and that nothing is likely to fall out or drop off.

Candidates should be advised to leave out:

- original certificates or photocopies, as these should have been checked and noted at registration or induction;
- any materials given as part of training;
- any paperwork or documents that are not clearly related to a candidate's competence;
- any paperwork or documents not clearly related to a candidate's understanding and application of knowledge in the workplace. For example, an equal opportunities policy says nothing about how the candidate uses this in his or her everyday work. It would be much better for the candidate to use this alongside professional discussion.

WORKING WITH QUALITY ASSURANCE REQUIREMENTS

Sampling

The assessment centre's internal verifier may wish to sample your records at any point in the assessment process. The internal verifier should also be monitoring your practice by observing you, and involving you in standardization exercises, where the accuracy of your assessment decisions against the standards, your interpretation of the requirements and your feedback to candidates will be matched against those of other assessors in the team. Note that sampling your assessment records does not mean that the internal verifier will automatically want to see your candidates' own work. Your assessment records, if completed properly, should give enough detail for the internal verifier to complete the audit trail satisfactorily. The external verifier may request, as part of his or her sampling process, to see the assessments you have made. Centres normally retain completed candidates' portfolios until after the next external visit. Records of assessment decisions you make need to be kept for three years.

Standardization

You will probably be asked to a meeting and to bring with you some work that you have already assessed, the relevant standards and any other marking criteria you use. Standardization is a really good way of enabling assessors to check that they are making decisions in the same way and giving feedback in similar ways. The internal verifier will probably manage the meeting, often using the action plan he or she has received from the awarding body. You should get feedback on how your practice compares with that of the rest of the team, together with advice on where improvements can be made.

SUBMITTING FOR CERTIFICATION

Assessors must ensure that, by the time candidates have completed all their assessments, there is a clear record of assessment for each candidate. This will include written developmental feedback to candidates following summative and formative assessment. The dates on which summative assessments were handed in and the dates on which they were marked and returned are important, as these data can form part of the quality assurance process for centres and/or awarding bodies. Once this is complete, the assessor can give the candidate his or her view as to the overall outcome for that candidate, though candidates should be pretty certain of their likely outcome. Assessments of a candidate's work may have already been included in sampling or standardization activities, and assessors should check that any feedback given to them by internal verifiers has not been slipped into candidate files but is stored securely elsewhere. All necessary paperwork must be completed before making the application for certification. This should be done by giving a copy of the candidate and assessment details to your internal verifier. Usually, it is the relevant administrative staff at the centre who will submit the required documentation to the awarding body. At registration, candidates will have provided information such as date of birth and the name that they wish to have printed on the certificate, and this should have been double-checked by internal verifiers and assessors when the registration records were received from the awarding body. Clarify with the centre what happens once they receive the certificate and make sure that your candidates are aware – some centres post certificates to candidates and others prefer candidates to call in for them, for security reasons. Your centre may send out letters of congratulation to candidates or arrange presentations for them later on, and your candidates should know what to expect and whether to keep a date free in their diary.

SUMMARY

This chapter should have helped you with:

- record keeping;
- written feedback;
- quality assurance.

13

The Internal Verifier and the Quality Assurance Process

Internal verification is a critical role. Good IVs can spot areas for improvement long before they become a problem. There is a range of people who rely on the internal verifier for feedback and action regarding a range of quality issues. Some organizations are able to give more time and flexibility to internal verification than others, so, where there are limited resources, internal verifiers need to plan their audit trails and monitoring to make best use of their time. In this chapter, we take some aspects that are often cited in awarding body action plans as needing improvement.

MANAGING ASSESSMENT

Monitoring the progress of candidate assessment

Candidates invest their money and time into their programme of training and assessment. IVs can affect the quality and progress of candidates' achievement by monitoring the rate at which assessors are conducting assessments (not reviews) with their candidates and checking on a regular basis that there are clear signs of candidate progression. They will do this by regularly reviewing assessor tracking documents for groups and individuals. These should show when assessments are planned and how and which performance criteria are met as a result of each assessment.

Regular monitoring of the progress that assessors are making with candidates should show up whether individual assessors are experiencing any difficulties and alert you to the need for help. Problems could include a learner cancelling a number of planned assessments or perhaps the assessor not being available at times when a candidate is available for workplace assessment.

Sampling assessor feedback

Assessors should be trained to write up their assessment reports, both formative and summative, so that the way they have made their judgement is clear to the candidate. Not only do they need to give a grade or make a judgement on competence, but that judgement needs to be backed up by a written report. This may take the form of assessment feedback for vocational candidates or a report against the assessment plan that the candidate is following. In both cases, it is essential that assessors detail the criteria on which they have made their judgement.

Below are some comments commonly given by assessors to their candidates that are sometimes not picked up through the quality assurance process.

NVQ assessment

1. 'This work meets the criteria.'
2. 'I have assessed all your evidence for A1 as a pass. I will now give your action plan to the independent assessor to be signed off.'
3. 'You have collected all the required evidence into your portfolio. Before I can pass it to the IV to be signed off you need to put in your CV and make sure that you and your candidate have signed all the necessary documents.'

In the first case, there is no way that the internal verifier can judge how the assessment has been made. The assessment needs to be returned to the assessor. The assessor will need to indicate as a minimum what criteria have been met, what evidence was seen in order for this judgement to be made and its location, where the assessment took place and when, what was done well, and any areas where things could be done differently or better (even if criteria have been met).

In the second case, it appears that the primary assessor is exceeding his or her role. The independent assessor should be assessing one of the three agreed A1.1 action plans. The primary assessor has two other plans he or she can assess! Neither is it the independent assessor's role to 'sign off' work assessed by another assessor. The assessor should sign off each element or unit as the candidate is judged to have met the criteria, and signatures should be checked at that stage, when they are relevant to the process. Finally, candidates taking competence-based qualifications are normally judged 'competent' or 'not yet competent' rather than 'pass' or 'fail'.

The assessor in the third example seems to misunderstand his or her own role and that of the internal verifier. The evidence that an internal verifier may wish to see should be that which the assessor has already assessed against the national standards. The internal verifier is more likely to need to see the assessor's assessment records. These records should detail the documents that have been shown by the candidate to the assessor and how they are relevant to the qualification. A curriculum vitae is unlikely to give any evidence of current competence, but might be referred to in the assessment report following a professional discussion or as part of the information seen by an assessor or adviser at induction for the qualification. It is possible that the internal verifier might request a whole portfolio for sampling purposes, but it is more likely that he or she will request evidence that shows how an assessor has assessed a particular unit or element.

Vocational assessment

1. 'Well done.'
2. 'Excellent work, but you still need to add a bibliography and give another example. Pass.'
3. 'You have written your assignment within the word count, used three sources and answered the four points in the assignment brief. Good pass.'

In the first example, the candidate has no idea of what has been well done and could well draw the wrong conclusions, which could have bad consequences later. The assessor could be praising effort rather than achievement, for example. Often, an assessor wants to encourage a candidate, particularly if it is the candidate's first assignment. In this case, distinguishing between effort and achievement is vital, particularly if the candidate needs to develop his or her writing or research techniques. The candidate also needs to know why the assessor thinks aspects of the work have been well done so he or she can build on this for future assignments.

The second example cannot be a true statement. If work is excellent, the highest accolade possible, then there should be no outstanding items for inclusion. The academic work itself could be 'excellently written, with appropriate references'. However, a pass grade should not have been awarded if there are essential components outstanding. A clear assessment plan can be used by candidates as a checklist before handing in assignments.

The third example is representative of those assessor comments that seem to give the candidate some feedback but, in reality, just state back to him or her the required criteria. It tells the candidate nothing about why the work was good – was it because of the examples chosen, the sources, the fact that it was within the word count, or all three? If the assessor cited the actual examples and sources and explained why they were good, this would also provide some evidence if the assignment were to be lost or if the assessor's comments were included in a standardization exercise.

If internal verifiers find examples of written feedback such as the above (or, worse still, none!), a standardization meeting can be a useful environment for improving practice.

MANAGING STAKEHOLDERS

Centre management

The centre will be concerned that it keeps a good reputation with candidates, employers and the awarding body. Internal verifiers are the key to ensuring that internal and external processes go smoothly. The training and verification of assessors and their work, the communication of issues and the keeping of accessible, accurate and useful records are the focal point of a successful centre.

The awarding body

The awarding body will be represented by the external verifier, who is likely to make two visits a year if there are NVQ courses in the centre. A detailed study by the internal verifier (and the assessors) of the external verifier's last report will bring benefits all round. Not only will there be the action points that the centre should have been addressing (and not just in the week before the next EV visit), but the questions that the centre will need to answer are on the form. If the IV has the required data at his or her fingertips or at the click of a computer mouse, then the visit will be much swifter and the IV grading is likely to be satisfactory or higher.

Most awarding bodies have detailed guidance, which is sent to the named centre administrator. They nearly all now have well-developed websites where the answers to common queries can be found and also from which documents can be downloaded.

Employers

Employers generally want their employees to complete their training as effectively and efficiently as possible. If employers are involved in the planning process for setting up the award and are clear on the amount of time that a candidate will need to be away from work or observed in the workplace, they can organize work schedules appropriately. It is also good if employers are involved in award ceremonies or are willing to provide 'good news' copy for the local press.

Parents and dependants

Where candidates are under 16, parents or guardians will need reports of progress and results. For those candidates over 19, it may be those around them, such as partners and children, who are most aware of the demands of a learning programme. It is good to acknowledge the support that such people give to candidates, again in award ceremonies. Such people will also appreciate candidates being able to share with them the training and assessment plans, as these may affect their own arrangements.

RECORDING ACTIVITY

Effective internal verifiers keep all the information relating to a particular awarding body and its qualifications visits together, as suggested in V1.4.

Evidence checklist for V1:

- a portfolio of evidence relating to the internal verifier's relationship with the awarding body, including details of his or her internal verification strategy relating to a particular award;
- an internal verification portfolio for one external verification, relating to the signing off of candidate achievement and showing evidence of the internal verifier making satisfactory support arrangements for assessors and that his or her systems documentation and evidence have been acceptable to the external verifier;
- a record of observing assessor performance for at least two assessors on two occasions, with different candidates on each of the four occasions, to include the observation of provisional feedback to candidates and to include written records;
- a record of the IV being monitored by an external verifier or qualified second internal verifier, plus a written report by the monitor;
- a sampling framework for at least two assessors, plus external verifier reports indicating that assessor support arrangements are satisfactory.

Record keeping

Records can be paper based, or stored in a computer, or a combination of the two. Even if all the documents, records and data are available in electronic format, many people still prefer to keep their records, or some of them, in paper format. Booklets, such as *Access to Assessment*, the NVQ Code of Practice and the JAB guidelines, along with copies of standards, are often kept in paper format for ease of use. Assessor records are often photocopied or carbonized, and easier to keep in that format.

Some centres are well down the way to computerizing all their records. There are many systems available. Each awarding body will need to approve the systems used by different centres, and their external verifiers will need access to, and possibly training in how to use, the system when they visit.

One of the great benefits of electronic records for quality assurance is that internal verifiers can access assessor records whenever they like and so monitor more easily the progress that is being made with candidates.

Internal verifiers will need to maintain the following information and have systems for sharing and processing this appropriately with their centre and with the external verifier:

- centre information;
- awarding body information;
- their sampling strategy;
- standardization of assessment records;
- records of sampled assessment;
- data from the IV;
- actions resulting from internal quality assurance;
- actions resulting from external quality assurance;
- a list of their current assessors and IVs;
- CPD plans for each assessor;
- course/qualification start and finish dates;
- lists of each cohort of candidates, with the assessors linked to each cohort;
- schemes of work and timetables for taught programmes.

Using data

Centres need to know not just that they are meeting legal and funding requirements, but that the centre is operating efficiently and effectively. Analysis of easily available data can help with this. Such data and records can be:

- awarding body enrolment numbers for each candidate;
- candidates enrolled, withdrawn and continuing at various census points;
- candidates who have completed, with start and finish dates;
- average time of completion of a qualification or a particular unit;
- candidate comments – praise or problems;
- class size;
- class attendance;
- percentage of candidates getting particular grades (on non-NVQ qualifications);
- retention rate (those who remained on the programme as a percentage of those who were initially enrolled);
- achievement rate (those who achieved the qualification as a percentage of those registered for it).

Reports to centre managers and external verifiers that include these data are very useful and also give teachers and assessors feedback on their performance and where changes might need to be made. For example, if there is a low retention rate, some of the reasons could be:

- poor pre-course guidance or induction;
- poor teaching;
- poor learner support;
- inconvenient times or location for the course;
- a lack of feedback to candidates;
- slow progress with workplace assessments, causing candidates to lose motivation;
- an unusually high number of candidates with external issues that are nothing at all to do with the course (redundancy, for example).

THE EXTERNAL VERIFIER'S VISIT

This should be a smooth and enjoyable experience if you can do the following:

- Make a note of the next planned visit, so that you are ready to send accurate pre-visit data to your external verifier when it is asked for. Most external verifiers do this work on a part-time basis, sometimes in addition to full-time jobs. They have deadlines to meet for awarding bodies as to when data have to be returned, and may have only a particular day on which to complete pre-visit documentation.
- Implement your action plan as soon as it is given to you by your external verifier so that you will have communicated any successes or problems well before the next visit.

- Read your last report carefully and note all the information that the external verifier will need to get at the visit. Make sure you have all this readily available, in the order listed on the report.
- Let your external verifier get on with his or her work, which is to check your own audit trails. Your external verifier will have discussed with you what staff and candidates he or she wishes to see and at what times.
- Be prepared for timings to change. Timings can increase if the internal verifier is having difficulty accessing your records or if he or she is interrupted.
- Give the external verifier a room where he or she can be uninterrupted and talk to candidates or staff in privacy.
- Make sure the external verifier can get a drink and knows the layout of the building in case he or she needs to get a breath of fresh air, use the toilet, visit the resource centre, make a workplace observation or respond to an alarm.

A FINAL WORD

For many candidates, getting your assessor or verifier award is a bit like taking your advanced driving test. One might have been driving satisfactorily for years, but it is only by doing the ADI training that errors of performance which have crept in over the years are shown up and corrected. In the same way, and in common with many professions, you will need to show regular updating of your competence as both an assessor or verifier, and as a practitioner in your area of vocational competence.

Your certificate qualifies you to practice as an assessor or internal verifier. You are now seen as a 'guardian' of the standards and of the internal quality assurance system of your centre. Awarding bodies and ENTO provide constant support to those involved with competence-based assessment, via newsletters, websites and training.

Who knows, in time you may end up as an External Verifier, needing to take V2!

SUMMARY

This chapter should have helped you with:

- managing assessment and stakeholders;
- record keeping;
- data for report writing;
- the external verifier's visit.

Appendix 1

Frequently Asked Questions from the Employment National Training Organisation Website

ENTO is constantly responding to queries from assessors and verifiers via its online service the Learning Network. As a result of this, a regularly updated list of frequently asked questions (FAQs) is accessible to users of the site and can help minimize unnecessary contact. A selection of FAQs follows:

4. The assessment strategy requires that an assessor must have one year's experience in the past two years in the activities described in the standards. When does this one-year period commence from?

The one year's experience starts from certification of the assessor unit.

7. Does the second assessor or independent assessor need to be independent of the centre?

No, the requirement is for the second assessor to be independent of the candidate and primary assessor but not necessarily independent of the centre, although this may be the case in some instances where an organization uses peripatetic assessors.

11. Who decides on appropriate CPD [continuing professional development] for assessors and verifiers?

The requirement for CPD activity for assessors and internal verifiers must be part of the internal verification strategy and planned in advance. Evidence of the activity must be retained as proof; a certificate of attendance is not evidence of CPD. This would have to be accompanied by some form of evaluation of the activity by the assessor or verifier.

12. Who approves and monitors the planned activity?

The planned CPD activity should be agreed with the external verifier for the awards and monitored by the verifier during normal centre visits. In all cases, all CPD activity should be recorded.

21.   Can the assessor of the A&V units be 'working towards'?

No, all assessors and verifiers (internal and external) of the assessment and verification units must themselves hold the appropriate units.

25.   Can non-NVQ evidence be used to achieve the assessment and verification units?

In some cases, non-NVQ evidence may be accepted where this evidence is gathered in the workplace. However, you must seek the approval of your awarding body prior to using this type of evidence.

30.   Element A1.4 requires the assessor-candidate to contribute to internal quality assurance processes. What does this actually require the assessor-candidate to do?

In the main, this requires the assessor-candidate to comply with internal procedures relating to quality assurance. It also requires the assessor-candidate to contribute to an internal standardization meeting. An internal standardization meeting will normally involve all assessors for a particular qualification and their internal verifier. At the meeting, evidence produced by candidates and judgements made by the assessors will be compared to ensure that there is a level of consistency and that the decisions being made meet national standards across the team. Equally, there will be consideration of evidence that has been deemed not to meet the national standard. The meeting might focus on a particular unit, an assessment method or a type of evidence.

39.   Is L20 an assessment unit?

L20 is *not* an assessment unit but is suited to those individuals working with candidates in the workplace who are able to ensure that the candidate has the breadth of experience and opportunity to achieve the units of his or her chosen qualification. In addition, the unit supports the role of witness testimony, but is not required for a witness testimony to be valid.

The view of ENTO is that where possible those supporting candidates in the workplace and as a result providing vital witness testimony should achieve unit L20.

42. What must be included in an internal verifier's sampling strategy for an N/SVQ?

Over a period of time, the following must be sampled by the internal verifier:

- all candidates;
- all units including those that have been assessed by the independent assessor;
- all locations where assessment occurs;
- all assessment methods;
- all assessors responsible to the internal verifier.

Appendix 2

The NVQ Code of Practice Tariff of Sanctions

This is found as Appendix 4 in *The NVQ Code of Practice*, and all assessors and verifiers should be thoroughly familiar with it. The tariffs are applied when a centre falls out of compliance with some aspect of the approved centre criteria. There are five levels of tariff, which relate to the element of risk that non-compliance has for candidate certification and centre quality assurance.

On each visit to an NVQ centre, the external verifier will complete an action plan. The action points in the plan will normally relate to the non-compliance with centre approval criteria that will have been approved (and updated where appropriate by formal notification) by the awarding body. If action points produced on one visit have not been addressed by the required date (often, but not necessarily, the date of the next visit), the response of the awarding body will normally be to apply a response at the next level up.

In considering the tariff applications, the external verifier will consider the following points:

- combinations of non-compliance;
- the persistence with which faults fail to be rectified;
- the recurrence of non-compliance;
- malpractice.

Tariffs may be higher, depending on the centre's history.

The results of applying tariffs range from the need to comply with an action plan by a specified date through suspension of regulation and/or certification to withdrawal of approval.

Level 1

Where non-compliance is no threat to the integrity of assessment decisions, the lowest level will be applied; the centre will continue to register candidates and certificate them as they complete, without waiting for the visit of the external verifier (also known as 'direct claims status'). The centre will be expected to address the issues by the agreed date.

Level 2

If there is a possibility that some assessment decisions may be unsound, then the centre will be able to register candidates, but all claims for certification will need to be authorized by the external verifier.

Level 3

If the visit reveals areas of non-compliance that pose either a threat to candidates or a real danger of invalid claims for certification, then the centre will have either its registration or its certification (or both) suspended until the matters are resolved.

Level 4

The centre may have approval for specific NVQs withdrawn where it is found that management and quality assurance arrangements for specific NVQs have broken down.

Level 5

Centre approval for all NVQs will be withdrawn if management and quality assurance arrangements for all NVQs run by the centre have irretrievably broken down.

Appendix 3

Learning and Development Assessment Strategy

INTRODUCTION

The standards require evidence of consistent occupational competence as defined by the standards, through relevant work activities. A variety of assessment methods should be used to confirm competence as defined in the standards. Assessment of knowledge should be integrated with the assessment of performance wherever possible and appropriate.

The Employment NTO has an Awarding Body Forum, which will implement and review these assessment strategy arrangements in the light of the prevailing requirements of the regulatory authorities.

ASSESSMENT OF PERFORMANCE AND KNOWLEDGE IN THE WORKPLACE

All evidence must be derived from performance within the workplace, with certain exceptions (see Table A3.1). The standards relating to these aspects of competence have been identified and specific forms of assessment attached to them as part of the assessment guidance. Table A3.1 provides a summary of the relevant elements.

Table A3.1

Element and criterion	Preferred form of assessment
L5.1. h)	Assessor questioning using hypothetical context.
L5.2. d)	Assessor questioning using hypothetical context.
L6.1. c)	Assessor questioning as to alternatives considered.
L7.1. e) and f)	Candidate presentation of the ILT alternatives considered.
L7.2. h)	Assessor questioning of selection of materials against equality and diversity criteria.
L7.2. i)	Assessor questioning on checks conducted to ensure training facilities meet HSEP requirements.
L8.3. e)	Assessor questioning using hypothetical context.
L9.3. c), d), e) and f)	Assessor questioning using hypothetical context.
L12.2 b)	Candidate presentation of the ILT alternatives considered.
L13.1. e) and g)	Assessor questioning using hypothetical context.
L15.2 d)	Candidate presentation of the ILT alternatives considered.
L15.2. h)	Assessor questioning using hypothetical context.

Source: ENTO.

SIMULATED WORKING CONDITIONS

Performance of real work activities in the real working environment means that none of the performance criteria in the standards requires the use of simulations.

EXTERNAL QUALITY CONTROL: INDEPENDENT ASSESSMENT

Independent external assessment will require candidates to present a balance of evidence, which must include a substantive component that has been assessed by someone who is independent of the candidate. 'Substantive' is defined here as a primary piece of outcome evidence for one or more units of competence. 'Independent' is defined here as a competent job holder who is qualified as an assessor but will not act as the candidate's primary assessor.

REQUIREMENTS FOR OCCUPATIONAL COMPETENCE OF ASSESSORS AND VERIFIERS

Assessors

All assessors selected by centres must have sufficient occupational competence to ensure an up-to-date working knowledge and experience of the principles and practices specified in the standards they are assessing. 'Sufficient occupational competence' is defined as:

- having held a post for a minimum of one year within the last two years that involved performing the activities defined in the standards as an experienced practitioner;

or:

- being an experienced trainer or instructor of at least one year's standing in the competence area of the standards;

and for both of the above:

- having demonstrated updating within the last year involving at least two of the following activities:
  - work placement;
  - job shadowing;
  - technical skills update training;
  - attending courses;
  - studying for learning and development units;
  - study related to job role;
  - collaborative working with awarding bodies;
  - examining;
  - qualifications development work;
  - other appropriate occupational activity as agreed with the internal verifier.

All assessors will have a sound working knowledge of the content of the standards they are assessing and their assessment requirements. All assessors will either hold the relevant qualification for assessors of national occupational standards or have a development plan indicating progress towards that qualification.

Assessors of candidate-assessors are required to have achieved their relevant assessor unit(s) before they can start to assess candidate-assessors. Similarly, assessors of internal and external candidate-verifiers need to have achieved their own assessor and verifier units before they can start to assess candidate-verifiers.

Internal verifiers

All internal verifiers will have sufficient experience of having conducted assessment of the specific national occupational standards they are verifying or in an appropriate and related occupational area. 'Sufficient occupational competence' is defined as:

- having been an assessor for the standards being assessed, or for a set of standards in a related occupational area, for a minimum of one year within the last two years;

and:

- having demonstrated updating within the last year involving at least two of the following activities:
  - attending awarding body verification training courses;
  - studying for learning and development units;
  - study related to job role;
  - collaborative working with awarding bodies;
  - qualifications development work;
  - other appropriate occupational activity as agreed with the external verifier.

All internal verifiers will have direct responsibility and quality control of assessments of the occupational standards or the quality assurance of the assessment process within an assessment centre that has been approved by an awarding body. All internal verifiers will have a sound working knowledge of assessment and verification principles as defined in the national standards for internal quality assurance and the particular internal verification requirements. All internal verifiers will either hold the relevant qualification for internal verifiers of national occupational standards or have a development plan indicating progress towards that qualification.

Internal verifiers of candidate-assessors are required to have achieved their internal verification unit before they can start to internally verify candidate-assessors. Similarly, internal verifiers of internal and external candidate-verifiers need to have achieved their own assessor and verifier units before they can start to internally verify candidate-verifiers.

External verifiers

All external verifiers will be drawn from experienced senior practitioners in the broad occupational area of the standards they will verify. 'Experienced senior practitioner' is defined as:

- having held posts of responsibility involving the monitoring and review of the occupational competence of others;

or:

- having been responsible for internal verification and assessment of national occupational standards;

and for both of the above:

- having demonstrated updating and continuing competence within the last year involving at least two of the following activities:
  - attending at least one external verifier induction/training event run by an awarding body;
  - shadowing an experienced external verifier on centre visits;
  - collaborative working with awarding bodies such as redevelopment of external monitoring systems;
  - study related to job role.

All external verifiers will have a sound working knowledge and experience of vocational assessment. They must be familiar with internal as well as external verification procedures as defined in the national standards for external quality assurance. They must also demonstrate competence in the particular external verification procedures set down by the awarding body for the qualification (including appeals and complaints procedures).

All external verifiers will either hold the relevant qualification for external verifiers of national occupational standards or have a development plan indicating progress towards that qualification.

External verifiers of candidate-assessors are required to have achieved their external verification unit before they can start to externally verify candidate-assessors. Similarly, external verifiers of internal and external candidate-verifiers need to have achieved their own assessor and external verifier unit(s) before they can start to externally verify candidate-verifiers.

Appendix 4

Evidence requirements for A1 and A2

A1 assessor	A2 observational assessor
• A minimum of two candidates • Three assessment plans, each covering one full unit of competence, which have each been reviewed and updated • Minimum of four assessment methods to be used to assess evidence for each unit • One written or spoken explanation (recorded) explaining why the four assessment methods have been chosen, why they are valid, reliable and fair, and precisely who and how others have been involved • Three assessment decisions for a minimum of the two candidates identified in the assessment plans • One record of observation and feedback to one of the identified candidates • Two records of feedback	• A minimum of two candidates • Three assessment plans, each covering one full unit of competence, which have each been reviewed and updated· Two written progress reviews for two candidates • Evidence of having updated assessment plans and outcomes of review • Three assessment decision records relating to the three assessment plans, for the two candidates • Professional discussion (recorded) where candidate presents shows how they have: 1) used observation of performance to demonstrate achievement of particular standards; 2) evaluated the effectiveness of the assessment

A1 assessor	A2 observational assessor
provided on two other occasions, with written records of observation, or endorsement by, an experienced assessor from a registered centre	methods in the light of assessing candidates
• One record (ideally taped or video-recorded at the candidates' workplace) of professional discussion, which can cover the explanations needed for all four elements, ie	• Three assessment decision records for at least two of the three different assessment plans for A2.1
1. *developing plans*	• Record of professional discussion to show how candidate has: 1) used questioning to demonstrate the knowledge requirements; 2) evaluated the effectiveness of the assessment methods in the light of assessing candidates
2. *judging at least three different types of evidence*	
3. *the use of observation*	
4. *the implementation of assessment methods*	
5. *the evaluation of effectiveness of the method*	• Minimum of one observation by the assessor of the assessor candidate providing feedback to one candidate
6. *the demonstration of competence in relation to criteria c, d, g*	
7. *providing feedback and support relating to criteria a, d, f*	• Evidence of feedback on two other occasions – written records for endorsement by another recognized assessor
• Two assessment records, one for each of two different candidates	• Assessment methods for two different candidates which have been passed to the IV (or QA person)
• Two instances of reviewing candidate evidence (two pieces of evidence for two different candidates), which must have contributed to the internal standards procedure	• Written statement from IV to show that assessor has contributed to agreed QA procedures
• One written statement from the person responsible for internal verification and monitoring, showing how the assessor has contributed to agreed quality procedures	

Appendix 5

Principles and Practice of Assessment L3 and L4

UNIT TITLE: Principles and Practice of Assessment
LEVEL: 3
CREDIT VALUE: 3
UNIT CODE:

This unit has six learning outcomes.

Learning Outcomes	Assessment Criteria
The learner will:	The learner can:
1. Understand key concepts and principles of assessment.	1.1 Identify and define the key concepts and principles of assessment.
2. Understand and use different types of assessment.	2.1 Explain and demonstrate how different types of assessment can be used effectively to meet the individual needs of learners.
3. Understand the strengths and limitations of a range of assessment methods, including, as appropriate, those which exploit new and emerging technologies.	3.1 Identify the strengths and limitations of a range of assessment methods with reference to the needs of particular learners and key concepts and principles of assessment. 3.2 Use a range of assessment methods appropriately to ensure that learners produce assessment evidence that is valid, reliable, sufficient, authentic and current.

Learning Outcomes	Assessment Criteria
	3.3 Explain how peer and self-assessment can be used effectively to promote learner involvement and personal responsibility in the assessment of their learning.
4. Understand the role of feedback and questioning in the assessment of learning.	4.1 Explain how feedback and questioning contributes to the assessment process. 4.2 Use feedback and questioning effectively in the assessment of learning.
5. Understand how to monitor, assess, record and report learner progress and achievement to meet the requirements of the learning programme and the organization.	5.1 Specify the assessment requirements and related procedures of a particular learning programme. 5.2 Conduct and record assessments which meet the requirements of the learning programme and the organization including, where appropriate, the requirements of external bodies. 5.3 Communicate relevant assessment information to those with a legitimate interest in learner achievement.
6. Understand how to evaluate the effectiveness of own practice.	6.1 Reflect on the effectiveness of own practice taking account of the views of learners.

Values and commitments included in this unit:
AS 3; AS 4; AS 5; AS 7
BS 2;
ES 1; ES 2; ES 3; ES 4; ES 5
FS 1; FS 2; FS 4

Standards included in this unit:
AK 3.1; AP 3.1; AK 4.2; AP 4.2; AK 5.1; AP 5.1; AK 5.2; AP 5.2; AK 7.1; AP 7.1;
BK 2.6; BP 2.6
EK 1.1; EP 1.1; EK 1.2; EP 1.2; EK 1.3; EK 2.1; EP 2.1; EK 2.2; EP 2.2; EK 3.1; EP 3.1; EK 3.2; EP 3.2; EK 4.1; EP 4.1; EK 5.1; EP 5.1; EK 5.2; EP 5.2; EK 5.3; EP 5.3
FK 1.1; FP 1.1; FK 1.2; FP 1.2; FK 2.1; FP 2.1; FK 4.1; FP 4.1; FK 4.2; FP 4.2

UNIT TITLE: Principles and Practice of Assessment
LEVEL: 4
CREDIT VALUE: 3
UNIT CODE:

This unit has six learning outcomes.

Learning Outcomes	Assessment Criteria
The learner will:	The learner can:
1. Understand key concepts and principles of assessment.	1.1 Summarize the key concepts and principles of assessment.
2. Understand and use different types of assessment.	2.1 Discuss and demonstrate how different types of assessment can be used effectively to meet the individual needs of learners.
3. Understand the strengths and limitations of a range of assessment methods, including, as appropriate, those which exploit new and emerging technologies.	3.1 Evaluate a range of assessment methods with reference to the needs of particular learners and key concepts and principles of assessment.
	3.2 Use a range of assessment methods appropriately to ensure that learners produce assessment evidence that is valid, reliable, sufficient, authentic and current.
	3.3 Justify the use of peer and self-assessment to promote learner involvement and personal responsibility in the assessment of their learning.
4. Understand the role of feedback and questioning in the assessment of learning.	4.1 Analyse how feedback and questioning contributes to the assessment process.
	4.2 Use feedback and questioning effectively in the assessment of learning.
5. Understand how to monitor, assess, record and report learner progress and achievement to meet the requirements of the learning programme and the organization.	5.1 Review the assessment requirements and related procedures of a particular learning programme.
	5.2 Conduct and record assessments which meet the requirements of

Learning Outcomes	Assessment Criteria
	the learning programme and the organization including, where appropriate, the requirements of external bodies.
	5.3 Communicate relevant assessment information to those with a legitimate interest in learner achievement.
6. Understand how to evaluate the effectiveness of own practice.	6.1 Evaluate the effectiveness of own practice taking account of the views of learners.

Values and commitments included in this unit:
AS 3; AS 4; AS 5; AS 7
BS 2
ES 1; ES 2; ES 3; ES 4; ES 5
FS 1; FS 2; FS 4

Standards included in this unit:
AK 3.1; AP 3.1; AK 4.2; AP 4.2; AK 5.1; AP 5.1; AK 5.2; AP 5.2; AK 7.1; AP 7.1
BK 2.6; BP 2.6
EK 1.1; EP 1.1; EK 1.2; EP 1.2; EK 1.3; EK 2.1; EP 2.1; EK 2.2; EP 2.2; EK 3.1; EP 3.1; EK 3.2; EP 3.2; EK 4.1; EP 4.1; EK 5.1; EP 5.1; EK 5.2; EP 5.2; EK 5.3; EP 5.3
FK 1.1; FP 1.1; FK 1.2; FP 1.2; FK 2.1; FP 2.2; FK 4.1; FP 4.1; FK 4.2; FP 4.2

Glossary

All terms are commonly used in training; there is an emphasis on terms related to assessment.

access (to assessment)   Making sure that candidates can be assessed in the most appropriate ways; ensuring that barriers to assessment are minimized; enabling candidates to have some control over the assessment process.

accreditation   The formal recognition of a candidate's work against pre-scribed criteria; candidates can be accredited for all or part of a unit, or in all or part of an award.

accreditation centre *see* **centre**

accreditation of prior learning (APL)   The formal recognition of work done previously that is eligible to count towards an award; this work can be from both certificated sources, eg qualifications, and uncertificated sources, eg previous experience (also: accreditation of prior experimental learning – APEL; accreditation of prior achievement – APA).

achievement   The amount of skill, knowledge or understanding that an individual is able to demonstrate.

action plan   The tasks an individual needs to undertake to reach particular goals. Plans usually include target and review dates, may cover any time period, include one or more goals, and may be recorded on formal documentation or be in note form; usually agreed with a supervisor or mentor after review against required standards for an award.

Apprenticeships   These are for 16- to 24-year-olds who want to work and train on the job.

assessment (competence-based)   Judging the degree to which a candidate has met predetermined criteria; candidates must show that they can do certain tasks in a prescribed way and that they know the context of the task and why it must be performed in certain ways.

assessment centre *see* **centre**

assessment criteria The standards against which assessments are judged. They must be explicit before the assessment is agreed and undertaken; they determine the minimum of what must be taught, if part of a programme of learning.

assessment instruments Not some medieval torture device, but the range of questionnaires, tests, checklists and other materials used to assess specific skills, knowledge, qualities or understanding. For example, there are tests designed to pick out weaknesses in grammar, or count the number of facts remembered, or tell us how confident we are; languages can be tested through the use of specially designed audiotapes, and skills by using real or simulated work tasks.

assessment opportunities The range of options to candidate and assessor to determine competence or achievement. These may be either work-based or training centre-/college-based; they may be formally planned, occur during normal work, and be based on a whole range of sources of evidence. Candidates and assessors need to be aware that there may be alternative opportunities for assessment, other than those normally used.

assessment plan An agreed detailed, written statement between candidate and assessor(s) of how the candidate will demonstrate competence. NVQ assessors should negotiate with their candidates one plan for each unit to be assessed. Plans need to specify as a minimum what will be assessed, the methods to be used, the criteria for assessment, how the assessment will be undertaken and by whom, the timescale and people involved and any special arrangements that need to be made. Assessment plans can be for individuals or for groups.

assessment record A document produced by an assessor, an organization or an awarding body that records the assessed progress of a candidate against outcomes. It should give sufficient detail for the assessor to know what, how and when the outcomes have been reached.

assessor-devised questions Questions composed by the assessor as opposed to being drawn from a bank of prepared questions produced by, for example, an awarding body.

assignment A practical or written task given to a candidate that tests skills, knowledge or understanding, or combinations of all three. Tasks should be explicit, and candidates should be clear about what is required of them.

authentic Refers to evidence that can be established as relating to the candidate rather than another, or a group. If group work is used as evidence, the candidate's contribution should be clearly identifiable.

award A certificate or record of achievement issued by an awarding body that confirms accreditation. In the case of the assessor and verifier awards and mini-awards, the awarding bodies have identified one or more units from the

Learning and Development standards and offered them as a 'package'. Some of the awards consist of units that form part of a full NVQ.

awarding body A body (organization) that gives awards, eg Edexcel, the Royal Society of Arts, the Construction Industry Training Board. All awarding bodies that give NVQs (including the assessor and verifier awards) must first be approved by the national regulatory body, eg in England this is the QCA.

barrier (to access) Anything (physical or mental) that prevents a candidate from taking up opportunities for training or assessment.

candidate A person who is preparing to be assessed for an award. In this book the term is used to indicate anyone who is presenting him- or herself for assessment, eg someone being assessed for NVQs within the workplace or someone being assessed for vocational GCSEs in a school. Depending on the context, the candidate can be an employee, client, trainee, student or pupil.

candidate- (student-)centred Refers to any approach in training and assessment that considers the needs of the candidate and that involves the candidate in making choices about the processes to be used.

candidate report A term used in range statements to indicate oral or written reports from the candidate that involve descriptions of activities and processes and some self-assessment, eg a work diary.

centre An organization approved by an awarding body to assess and accredit on its behalf; its advisers, assessors and the awarding body should also approve all internal verifiers.

certification The process of registration, assessment, recording results, completing documentation and applying for and receiving certificates.

competence The ability to perform within a work-related function or occupational area to national standards expected in employment.

contingency An unexpected occurrence that can happen at work, which a candidate will need to show he or she can deal with. A candidate's competence in dealing with contingencies is often explored through use of questioning, eg 'What if...?' questions. Simulations may be another means by which the candidate can be assessed.

continuous assessment Making judgements on a candidate's performance or ability over a period of time.

Core Skills *see* **Key Skills**

credit accumulation An arrangement that enables candidates to collect individual units or elements of competence over a period of time; these can then be matched and accredited against appropriate awards or qualifications. Reassessment does not have to take place should a credit be used for credit transfer; many credit accumulation and transfer schemes (CATS) already exist in higher education and in future will be used in further education as well.

credit transfer   Using credits (units, qualifications) from one award to count towards another different (but usually related) award.

criterion-referenced judgement   A judgement made against agreed criteria.

currency   Refers to evidence that shows that the candidate can perform competently at the time of the assessment. Currency often depends on the subject: for example, computing changes quickly, bricklaying techniques less swiftly. Evidence less than two years old is usually required, but all cases need to be individually negotiated.

curriculum   All the aspects of learning, including methods, resources and syllabus content, that make up a programme of study.

differing sources of evidence *see* **diverse evidence**

direct assessment   Assessing a product or process, eg a cake, a completed stock sheet, a training session.

direct evidence   Evidence that candidates have produced themselves.

direct support   Help that is offered directly to the candidate, eg an offer of advice.

diverse evidence   Evidence drawn from a number of different sources, including natural performance.

element (of an award)   A description of a set of assessable outcomes. A number of elements make up each NVQ unit; all elements of a unit must have been satisfactorily assessed before a unit award is given, an element being an identifiable or complete task within a unit.

endorsed assessment plan   An assessment plan countersigned by a recognized assessor; the endorsement could relate to the original plan, or subsequent modifications after review with a candidate.

e-portfolio   A collection of evidence put together electronically by the candidate using a software package approved by the appropriate awarding body.

evaluation   A process of determining the value of something as judged through gathering data from a variety of sources (eg interviews, questionnaires, informal discussions, results) and analysing this feedback.

evidence   Information from a variety of sources that proves a candidate's competence.

experiential learning   Learning that has happened through and from experience, as opposed to formal programmes of education or training. Much adult learning occurs in this way, and the learner often needs help to recognize skills, knowledge and understanding gained in non-formal ways.

external assessment   Assessment by an assessor who is not part of (is external to) the assessment or accreditation centre.

external auditing and sampling   Auditing and sampling normally carried out to the specifications of an awarding body by an external verifier or moderator. It will follow a process agreed with the external auditor and will normally involve sampling a range of assessment and internal verification/moderation practice and procedures.

external verifier   A person appointed by the awarding body who approves assessment centres and then regularly monitors their operation to national standards. This person acts as a quality assurance link between the approved centre and the awarding body.

fairness   Refers to the ensuring of just and equitable conditions in the assessment process for all candidates, eg by providing for candidates with special assessment needs and by following the national standards for assessment.

feedback reviewing   A process of giving constructive oral or written comment to candidates so that they understand the strengths and weaknesses of their performance/evidence and understand what to do as a consequence.

formative assessment   Assessment made to help determine future actions and development or to confirm progress.

functional analysis   The process of breaking down a whole job or task into its component pieces according to the different tasks performed in that job. NVQ competences have been determined through the process of functional analysis.

generic competence   A competence that occurs across many occupational areas, eg competence in maintaining standards of safety or competence in working with people. Competence in assessment is a generic competence, as individuals have to be able to assess as part of their job role within every occupational area.

indirect support   Help for a candidate that is organized from another source, eg by putting the candidate in touch with someone who could train him or her in certain techniques.

internal assessment   Assessment by an assessor who is a member of staff of the assessment or accreditation centre with which the candidate is registered.

internal verifier   A person approved by the external verifier to coordinate the assessment processes and practices within a centre, and who liaises with the external verifier and the awarding bodies.

Key Skills   A set of generic skills transferable across all occupational areas, developed in response to employer demands. Key Skills are incorporated into the majority of vocational programmes, with mandatory units on communications, application of number and information technology, and optional units on personal skills (working with others, and improving own learning and performance) and problem solving. They can also be used as free-standing units or in conjunction with NVQs.

knowledge evidence A means of showing that candidates know and understand both what they are doing and the context in which they are working. Knowledge evidence is also a means of showing that candidates know what to do in a range of different situations.

Learning and Skills Council (LSC) Responsible for funding and planning training for those over 16 years old in England. There is a national office and nine regional offices.

level (of qualification) NVQs have five levels, from basic competence (level 1) to strategic management (level 5). The levels are determined by job role and are defined on the basis of the skill, knowledge and understanding required, together with the degree of responsibility and supervision involved in performing the related work roles.

log book A document issued by many awarding bodies to candidates in which detailed tasks and tests are set out, together with the required units and elements of competence. Both assessor and candidate are required to sign in the book as competence is confirmed.

moderation A process whereby the results of assessments from more than one source are compared together and against an agreed, accepted standard. Moderation can be internally or externally conducted.

moderator A person approved (by an awarding body, if an external moderator) to conduct moderation, usually with considerable experience in the curriculum area. A moderator often helps with training and with interpretation of the curriculum.

module A self-contained unit of learning that can build towards a qualification. A BTEC leisure studies course might include modules in organizing sporting events and obtaining sponsorship for sport.

national occupational standards Originally set by National Training Organisations, but now developments are overseen by the standards and qualifications unit of the Sector Skills Development Agency working in conjunction with Sector Skills Councils. The standards have usually been derived by a process of functional analysis. The standards are set for each element of a task within a complete job, and cover the performance, context of operation and underpinning knowledge and understanding required.

National Vocational Qualification (NVQ) A qualification related to employment, recognized by the NVQ, and part of an approved framework of levels. An NVQ *is not* a course in itself; NVQs are awarded when a candidate has successfully demonstrated competence in a required number of units of competence related to job role. They can be taken without giving up work, and are assessed primarily by a portfolio of work-based evidence and by observation.

natural performance Refers to the way in which a candidate normally undertakes tasks in the course of his or her employment.

naturally occurring evidence Evidence that occurs as a normal part of an individual's work, ie forms part of his or her job or part of a programme of study.

norm-referenced assessment Assessment that is judged against the achievements of others undertaking the same assessment. Grades awarded depend on the ability not only of the candidate/student but also of the whole group under consideration.

open access Refers to systems of learning, training, education or assessment that are open to as many people as possible, as a result of the removal of as many barriers to participation as possible.

open learning Refers to methods of acquiring skills, knowledge and understanding that do not involve traditional attendance at classes and do not even require contact with a tutor. They often involve the use of interactive learning packages (written or video), supplemented by appropriate tutor support.

peer group A group of people equal in status to each other or from the same or a similar group.

peer report An oral or written description of activities or processes from the candidate's peer group, providing information about the candidate's performance that can be used for assessment purposes.

performance criteria Statements that indicate the standards of performance required for each element of competence. All performance criteria need to be met before an element can be accredited.

performance evidence Evidence from an activity carried out by the candidate, or something produced as a result of that activity.

portfolio A collection of evidence, usually produced over an extended period of time, and from various sources, that is presented together as a demonstration of achievement. The term is sometimes used to indicate the receptacle in which the evidence is contained, eg a ring binder.

pre-set test Any oral or written test prepared in advance by an assessor or by an awarding body. Pre-set tests often form an integral part of assessment for all candidates at particular levels. They are often set out in candidates' log books or are provided separately by the awarding body.

prior experience Experience acquired by the candidate before registering for an assessment that may provide evidence against units or elements.

prior learning Learning acquired by the candidate before registering for an assessment or training programme. This learning may or may not be certificated.

pro forma A template document devised to record a particular stage of a process or procedure.

professional discussion A recorded dialogue held between candidate and assessor. The assessor will plan for the areas that need to be covered, but this is *not* a question-and-answer session, and ideally will be candidate-centred. The discussion should allow the candidate to discuss the understanding behind his or her practice and, if held in the candidate's workplace, can also enable the candidate to, say, present additional documentary evidence or introduce others involved in the assessment to the assessor where evidence has been judged insufficient to meet the standards.

progress review A meeting between assessor and candidate for the purpose of identifying the candidate's progress against action plans. Action plans updated following a review will identify areas for development and areas of success.

project An extended piece of practical and/or written work involving planning and research and often presented as a report.

qualification A certificate legally provided that indicates that the holder has reached a necessary standard, eg a driving test certificate, an A level.

quality assurance Refers to methods by which standards are regularly checked and monitored; systems that ensure that procedures are done in certain ways.

questioning A range of techniques involving written or oral questions designed to elicit knowledge and understanding from candidates.

range statement A description of the context(s) and circumstances in which performance criteria described in the element should be able to be performed by someone competent in the activity.

record of achievement A composite record of a person's varied achievements and learning experiences over a period of time. It typically contains records of formal and informal learning experiences, credits gained, modules studied, reflections on achievements, agreed learning plans and evaluations.

regulatory bodies Official organizations that are responsible for policy. The QCA and its Welsh, Northern Ireland and Scottish equivalents are responsible for the way in which qualifications and the curriculum for education and skills are developed. Key work is modernizing the examinations system, developing the National Curriculum and building better qualifications for the workforce.

reliability The degree to which an assessment can be administered with the same results to others; the consistent ability of the assessment or the assessor to distinguish accurately between competent and non-competent performance.

review The formal or informal process of reflecting on performance, often conducted between an adviser/assessor and a candidate, usually on a one-to-one basis. Used as a basis for planning future activity.

sampling plan   Document showing what or who will be sampled, when and by whom; will relate to the sampling strategy devised by an internal verifier.

sampling strategy   The basis on which sampling is taking place. It needs to meet awarding bodies' requirements, and it must show the rationale for sampling so that all candidates, assessors, methods of assessment, evidence, locations and assessment judgements are sampled over time. It could also include details of standardization events devised by an internal verifier.

satellite centre   An organization that conducts its own assessments under the supervision of a larger approved centre; staff follow the same practices and procedures as those of the approved centre.

Scottish Vocational Qualification (SVQ)   The Scottish equivalent of an NVQ.

Sector Skills Councils (SSCs)   Employer-led independent organizations covering 25 occupational sectors across the UK with a major role in promoting learning and accreditation through Apprenticeships, higher education and national occupational standards.

Sector Skills Development Agency   Responsible for funding, supporting and monitoring SSCs.

simulation   A realistic exercise set up specifically to assess knowledge, skills or understanding. It should replicate a real work situation and should be used in circumstances in which it would be difficult or costly to assess within the work context (eg fire-fighting procedure or dealing with an emergency first-aid situation). The internal verifier should be able to advise on the acceptable use of simulation in consultation with the external verifier. Some awards do not allow simulation as evidence.

skill   The ability to carry out a task or perform an activity.

special assessment needs *see* **special assessment requirements**

special assessment requirements   NVQs and vocational qualifications in general emphasize the importance of access to fair and reliable assessment. According to candidates' circumstances, this may involve special arrangements being made, eg in relation to physical access.

standardization of assessment activities   Activities designed to check that assessors would make similar judgements on the same evidence.

systems documentation   Documentation produced by the awarding body or centre, to record all aspects of the assessment process, including internal verification and quality assurance.

training needs analysis   The identification of individual or organizational training needs through a systematic analysis of current skills against future performance requirements.

transferability   The ability to relate learning or performance in one area or context to another. For example, a candidate who can measure in metric in a training environment should be able to do so in the workplace using different materials and equipment.

underpinning knowledge/understanding Knowledge or understanding that ensures that tasks are not performed unthinkingly. Rather, it shows that candidates know why things are done in a particular way and that they have a general and/or specific knowledge about the task overall.

unit (of competence) A group of elements of competence that together constitute a particular work role and that form the smallest grouping of competence able to be recognized separately for certification towards an award.

unit credit Units within NVQs can be accredited separately; a unit is the smallest amount of achievement or competence that can be submitted to an awarding body for accreditation.

validity An assessment process has validity if it measures what it is supposed to measure.

verification The process of checking that the correct and agreed procedures and systems have been used.

verifier *see* **external verifier** and **internal verifier**

vocational qualifications Usually taken in a college or with a training provider, they are courses that are good for starting off in a particular subject. They have a greater knowledge and skills training content than NVQs. There is varied assessment, eg assignments, written exams, multiple choice tests.

witness testimony A third-party statement confirming competence against specific units/elements.

work-based assessment An assessment conducted in the candidate's workplace or made on evidence produced from or at the workplace.

work-based learning Learning that occurs at the place of work rather than, for example, through attendance on a formal programme of study based in an institution. Some programmes of study do, however, include work-based training as part of the course, eg work experience or sandwich courses.

work-based training Training that takes place within the work environment as opposed to being conducted elsewhere.

Supporting Materials

FURTHER READING

Ainley, P and Corney, M (1990) *Training for the Future: The rise and fall of the MSC*, Cassell, London

Armitage, A *et al* (2003) *Teaching and Training in Post-Compulsory Education*, Open University Press, Buckingham

Black, P (1997) *Testing, Friend or Foe? The Theory and the Practice of Assessment and Testing*, London, Falmer Press

Confederation of British Industry (CBI) (1989) *Towards a Skills Revolution: Report of the vocational education and training taskforce*, CBI, London

Cotton, J (1995) *The Theory of Assessment*, Kogan Page, London

Department for Education and Employment (DfEE) (1996) *Review of 14–19 Curriculum*, final report (chaired by Sir Ronald Dearing), DfEE, Sheffield

DfEE (1999) *Improving Literacy and Numeracy*, DfEE ref: CMBS (known as The Moser Report), DfEE, Sheffield

Department for Education and Skills (DfES) (2002) *Success for All*, Strategy Paper, DfES, London

Ecclestone, K (2005) *Understanding Assessment and Qualifications in Post-Compulsory Education, 2nd edition*, NIACE, Leicester

Edexcel (2003) *Continuous Professional Development*, a conversion pack for assessors and verifiers, Edexcel, London

Further Education Unit (FEU) (1992) *TDLB Standards in Further Education*, FEU, London

FEU (1993) *Standards in Action*, FEU, London

Haines, C (2004) *Assessing Students' Written Work: Marking Essays and Reports*, Routledge Falmer, London

Hyland, T (1999) *Vocational Studies, Lifelong Learning and Social Values: Investigating education, training and NVQs under the New Deal*, Monitoring Change in Education Series, Ashgate, Aldershot

Jessup, G (1991) *NVQs and the Emergency Model of Education and Training*, Falmer Press, London

MSC and National Economic Development Council (1986) *Review of Vocational Qualifications in England and Wales*, HMSO, London

Mullin, R (1992) *Decisions and Judgements in NVQ-Based Assessment*, NCVQ, London

National Council for Vocational Qualifications (NCVQ) (1993) *Awarding Bodies Common Accord*, NCVQ, London

NCVQ and SCOTVEC (1996) *Review of Top 100 NVQs* (chaired by Gordon Beaumont), NCVQ, London

Qualifications and Curriculum Authority (QCA) (1999) *Developing and Assessment Strategy for NVQs and SVQs*, QCA Publications, London

Race, P, Brown, S and Smith, B (2004) *500 Tips on Assessment*, Routledge Falmer, London

Read, Hilary (2006) *Excellence in Assessing: Putting it into practice*, Read On Publications, ENTO, Leicester

Read, H and Herniman, B (2004) *Excellence in Assessment and Verification: Putting it into practice*, Read On Publications, ENTO, Leicester

Rees, I and Walker, S (2006) *Teaching, Training and Learning 6th Edition*, Business Education Publishers, Sunderland

Rowntree, D (1987) *Assessing Students: How shall we know them?*, Kogan Page, London

Training and Development Lead Body (1992, rev 1994) *National Standards for Training and Development*, HMSO, London

Tummons, J (2005) *Assessing Learning in Further Education: Meeting the National Occupational Standards*, Learning Matters, Exeter

Wolf, A (1995) *Competence-Based Assessment*, Open University Press, Buckingham

USEFUL WEBSITES

Adult Learning Inspectorate: www.ali.gov.uk/htm/index.htm

All public services in one place: www.direct.gov.uk/en/EducationAnd Learning/QualificationsExplained

Assessment and Qualifications Alliance: www.aqa.org.uk

Association of External Verifiers: www.ava.org.uk

City and Guilds: www.city-and-guilds.co.uk

Department for Education and Skills: www.dfes.gov.uk

Department for Education and Skills Lifelong Learning: www.lifelonglearning. co.uk

Department for Work and Pensions: www.dwp.gov.uk

Edexcel: www.edexcel.org.uk/qualifications

ENTO: www.ento.co.uk

Federation of Awarding Bodies: www.awarding.org.uk

Learning and Skills Council: www.lsc.gov.uk

Learning and Skills Development Agency: www.lsda.org.uk

Learning Network: www.thelearningnetworkonline.com

Lifelong Learning UK: www.lifelonglearninguk.org

Local authority site with publications from six government departments: www.info4local.gov.uk

Modern Apprenticeships: https://www.realworkrealpay.info/lsc

National Assessment Agency: www.naa.org.uk

National Database of Accredited Qualifications: www.accredited qualifications.org.uk

New Deal: www.newdeal.co.uk

NVQ website: www.dfes.gov.uk/nvq

Qualifications and Curriculum Authority (QCA): www.qca.org.uk

QCA assessment for learning resources: www.qca.org.uk/294.html

QCA regulatory principles for e-assessment: www.qca.org.uk/18578.html

QCA reports on awarding bodies: www.qca.org/UK/regulation

QCA revised qualifications framework January 2007: http://aoa.ico3.com/resources/files/Dickinson%20and%20Roodhouse%20Diagram.doc

Quality Improvement Agency: www.qia.org/pursuingexcellence/aims/employers/html

Sector Skills Development Agency: www.ssda.org.uk

Teachernet: www.teachernet.gov.uk

Index